COASTING

JONATHAN RABAN

Simon and Schuster

New York

Copyright © 1987 by Foreign Land Ltd.
All rights reserved
including the right of reproduction
in whole or in part in any form
Published by Simon and Schuster
A Division of Simon & Schuster, Inc.
Simon & Schuster Building
Rockefeller Center
1230 Avenue of the Americas
New York, New York 10020
SIMON AND SCHUSTER and colophon are registered trademarks of
Simon & Schuster, Inc.
Designed by Levavi and Levavi
Manufactured in the United States of America
10 9 8 7 6 5 4 3 2 1

Library of Congress Cataloging in Publication Data

Raban, Jonathan.
  Coasting.

  1. Great Britain—Description and travel—1971–
2. Coasts—Great Britain. 3. National characteristics, British. 4. Raban,
Jonathan. 5. Authors, English—20th century—Biography. I. Title.
DA632.R33 1987   914.1′04858   86-17845
ISBN: 0-671-45480-3

The author gratefully acknowledges permission to reprint the following:

Lyrics from "It Doesn't Matter Any More" by Paul Anka. Copyright © 1958,
1974 by Spanka Music Corp./Management Agency and Music Publishing, Inc.
International copyright secured. Used by permission.

Excerpt from "The Old Fools" from *High Windows* by Philip Larkin. Copyright ©
1974 by Philip Larkin. Reprinted by permission of Farrar, Straus and Giroux, Inc.

Excerpts from "Dockery and Son" and "For Sidney Bechet" from *The Whitsun
Weddings* by Philip Larkin, copyright © 1964. Reprinted by permission of Faber
and Faber Limited.

To Caroline
and another, shared, voyage

Contents

1. Coasting 15

2. In the Archipelago 53

3. An Insular War 96

4. Hunting for Fossils 146

5. The Merrying of England 191

6. Voyage to the Far North 247

7. Envoi: A Peculiar People 292

There is in this aspect of land from the sea I know not what of continual discovery and adventure, and therefore of youth, or, if you prefer a more mystical term, of resurrection. That which you thought you knew so well is quite transformed, and as you gaze you begin to think of the people inhabiting the firm earth beyond that line of sand as some unknown and happy people; or, if you remember their arrangements of wealth and poverty and their ambitious follies, they seem not tragic but comic to you, thus isolated as you are on the waters and free from it all. You think of landsmen as on a stage. And, again, the majesty of the Land itself takes its true place and properly lessens the mere interest in one's fellows. Nowhere does England take on personality so strongly as from the sea.

—Hilaire Belloc, "Off Exmouth"

Coasting the British Isles on
GOSFIELD MAID

0   25   50   75   100
MILES

Moray Firth
Loch Ness
Inverness
Aberdeen
Caledonian Canal
Stonehaven
Ft.William
L.Linnhe
Oban

SCOTLAND

NORTH SEA

Leith
Edinburgh
Clyde
Firth of Clyde
Holy I
Farne Islands

Galloway Mts
Stranraer
Blyth

ULSTER
Mull of Galloway
Scafell Pike
Whitby
Flamborough Head

IRELAND

ISLE OF MAN
Ramsey
Douglas

ENGLAND

Bridlington
YORK
Kingston upon Hull

IRISH SEA

Doncaster
Grimsby
Sheffield
Humber

LINCOLN

Dublin
Holyhead
Mt Snowden
Wicklow Hills
Wicklow
Pwllheli
Bardsey I

WALES

NORFOLK
Yarmouth
Lowestoft

SUFFOLK
Felixstowe
Harwich

ST.GEORGES CHANNEL

Fishguard

ESSEX
Tilbury
London
Greenwich
Dover
North Foreland

BRISTOL CHANNEL

Thames

DEVON
Lyme Regis
Chichester
SUSSEX
Rye
Dungeness

DORSET
Portsmouth
Brighton
Newhaven

CORNWALL
Fowey
Looe
Plymouth
Torquay
Dartmouth
Start Pt.
Portland Bill
ISLE OF WIGHT

Land's End
Falmouth

ENGLISH CHANNEL

CHAPTER 1

COASTING

The Marriner having left the vast Ocean, and brought his Ship into Soundings near the Land, amongst Tides or Streams, his Art now must be laid aside, and Pilottage taken in hand, the nearer the Land the greater the Danger, therefore your care ought to be the more.

Being in Tides-ways, narrow Channels, Rocks and Sands, I hope the ingenious Mariner will not take it amiss in recommending this to your care, your Tides, Courses, Soundings, and the goodness of your Compasses.

Captain Greenville Collins, *Great Britain's Coasting Pilot*,
1693

All morning the sea has been gray with rain under a sky so low that the masts of the boat have seemed to puncture the soft banks of cloud overhead. The water is listless, with just enough wind to make the wavelets peak and dribble dully down their fronts. Sails hang in loose bundles from their spars as the boat trudges on under engine, dragging its wake behind it like a long skirt.

The engine, the engine. Its thump and clatter, all mixed up with the smell of diesel oil and the continuous slight motion of the sea, is so regular and monotonous that you keep on hearing voices in it. Sometimes, when the revs are low, there's a man under the boards reciting poems that you vaguely remember in a resonant bass. Sometimes the noise rises to the bright nonsense of a cocktail party in the flat downstairs. At present, though, you're stuck with your usual cruising companion at sixteen hundred revs, an indignant old fool grumbling in the cellar.

Where'd I put it? Can't remember. Gerroff, you, blast and damn you. Where'd I put it? Can't remember. Sodding thingummy. Where'd I put it? Can't remember.

Way out in front, England shows as a dark smear between the sea and the sky like the track of a grubby finger across a windowpane—a distant, northern land. We're crossing into the cold fifties of latitude, as far from the warm middle of the world as Labrador at one end of it and the Falklands at the other. The light is frugal, watery, and it always falls aslant, even in high summer. The sun, when it manages to find a break in the cloud, fills the land with shadows. It's no wonder that England, seen from the sea, looks so withdrawn, preoccupied and inward—a gloomy house, all its shutters drawn, its eaves dripping, its fringe of garden posted against trespassers.

All the pilot books warn one of the dangers of an English landfall. The *Admiralty Pilot* cautions all those who sail up from the south: "Fogs, bad weather and the long nights of winter frequently render it impossible to obtain a position . . . under such circumstances the course steered, the log, lead and nature of bottom are the seaman's only guides." The first signs of England aren't very encouraging either:

> The edge of soundings may generally be recognised
> in fine weather by the numerous ripplings in its
> vicinity; and in boisterous weather by a turbulent sea

and by the sudden alteration in the colour of the
water from dark blue to a disturbed green.

The sea is never still. Even when it's calm, the tides sweep
at speed along the English coast, racing round headlands
and throwing up acres of churning white water—water so
violent and unnavigable that even big cargo boats have been
lost in these rapids and overfalls.

There are ledges of submerged rock designed to rip your
floor out from under you, hidden shoals of gluey mud, and
such a lacework of sandbars and narrow channels that even
Her Majesty's chartmakers get into a helpless tangle about
what is properly England and what is properly Ocean. This
serpentine and tricky coast is ringed around with devices to
scare ships off, back into the deep water where they're safe.
Bell buoys clang, lights flash. On console screens in wheel-
houses and on ships' bridges, radar beacons paint their
warnings like fat white exclamation marks, glowing and
fading, glowing and fading. When the fog comes down
(and it's never long before the fog *does* come down) the
diaphones in all the lighthouses along the shore begin to
moo, making a noise so bottomless and sinister that you'd
think it could be heard only in a nightmare. England's message to every ship that gets near to her coast could hardly
be clearer: DANGER—KEEP OUT.

The navigator, now anxiously busy with his 4B pencil
and parallel rules, will know a bit about the reputation of
the natives of this place, which is not good. The Roman
poet Virgil, one of the earliest foreign observers, wrote that
"Britons are wholly sundered from all the world." They're
famous for their insular arrogance and condescension. They
love fine social distinctions and divisions and are snobbishly
wedded to an antique system of caste and class. Yet the
upper lips of this superior race are so notoriously stiff that
they can barely bring themselves to speak, preferring to
communicate in monosyllables interleaved with gruff si-
lences. They are aggressively practical and philistine, with
a loud contempt for anything that smells abstract or theoretical. They are a nation of moneygrubbers and bargain

hunters, treasuring pennies for treasuring's sake. When the English reach for a superlative to praise someone for his general moral excellence, they say he has a "sterling character," meaning that he has some of the same quality as the coins which they like to chink noisily in their pockets.

When it comes to sex, they are furtive and hypocritical —and their erotic tastes are known to be extremely peculiar. Many Englishmen will pay a woman money to take their trousers down and spank them. Others cultivate a neoclassical passion for small boys—preferably boys of a lower caste or another color. For the most part, though, the English, both men and women, are afflicted by such a morbid decay of the libido that it has always puzzled the rest of the world how the English manage to reproduce themselves at all.

They are casually rude—a vice which they claim as a virtue by labeling it forthrightness. They are also violent; feared in all the neighboring countries of Europe for the marauding hooligans who accompany their football teams and sometimes murder spectators who have come to cheer a rival side. In compensation, however, they are softhearted about animals, for which they have an arsenal of sentimental nicknames, like "pooches," "bunnies," "pussies" and "feathered friends." Yet they enjoy dressing up in ceremonial outfits to go round the country on horseback setting packs of dogs on foxes. When the fox has been dismembered, it is the English custom to smear the faces of little girls with its blood. This sport is a favorite subject with the artists who design English Christmas cards. The English are addicted to cheese. But they detest garlic, a vegetable associated with "foreigners," who are held in more or less universal contempt and are the main butts of the jokes which the English like telling to each other. These jokes are bartered in public places, and they increase in value as they grow older and more familiar. For the English are very famous—at least among themselves—for their sense of humor and pronounce it an essential component of a sterling character.

The pilot books, the folklore and the weather ("Cloud amounts are everywhere high at all seasons; depressions

may occur in long series at any time of the year") don't
exactly make one's heart leap at the prospect of England.
But all that's forgotten in the high excitement of making a
landfall as the coastline across the water slowly thickens and
takes shape. It is a wonderful conjuring trick. The land
surfaces lazily out of the sea, first gray and indistinct, then
flecked with hazy color, then decorated with a sudden scatter of sharpening details—a broad scoop of chalky cliff, a
striped beacon like a stick of seaside candy, a continuous
waterfall of slate roofs down the slope of a valley. There is
something satisfyingly eerie about a landfall—any landfall.
The growing coast ahead, no matter how exhaustively
charted it is, or how old and familiar its history and internal
topography, looks so imaginary from this sea distance.
Watching it come slowly alive, inseparable from its broken
reflection in the water, you feel that you're making it up as
you go along. It's not *real*. On a green hill above the town
you see a fine, bran-new medieval castle—turrets, towers,
keeps, drawbridges, the lot. Like a novelist toying with an
invented landscape on the page, you think, *That won't wash;*
and, obedient to the thought, the handsome castle rubs
itself out and in its place there comes up a stolid clump of
gas-storage tanks or the cooling towers of a power station.

Downstairs, the engine is talking to itself. *Pease-porridge
hot, pease-porridge cold, Pease-porridge in the pot, nine days old.* The
floor rolls a little in the swell and the land sinks under the
sea again. When it reappears, it rises from the water
changed. There are people out there now. A lone wind
surfer, clinging to a sail painted in the brilliant acrylic colors
of a tropical butterfly, skims and flits through the surviving
trelliswork of a burned-out pier and the sunless beach is
dotted about with matchstick men. A little espionage with
the binoculars and you can catch their swollen images,
swimming and jerking in the lenses. Anglers, spaced at wide
intervals along the pebbly shore, squat under their golf
umbrellas with thermos flasks. A man is throwing a stick for
a giant poodle—the only creature in sight which looks
properly dressed for the weather. Families huddle in small
self-absorbed groups in the shelter of seaweedy groins.

Some people are laid out, entirely alone, on towels, as in the aftermath of an accident. On the wet promenade, a psychedelic ice cream van betrays the improbable fact that this is summer.

As a first glimpse of the natives of the place, the scene will do nicely. "The English take their pleasures sadly after the custom of their country," said Maximilien de Béthune in 1630, a remark for which the *Admiralty Pilot* might usefully find room, just as it might point out that English bell buoys manage to strike a much lower, clangier and more dismal note than their tinkling French counterparts on the south side of the Channel.

With the soundings getting shallower every minute, this is too close for comfort. Bearing in mind the shoals that lie inshore, you turn the wheel and haul the rudder round, leaving England to sidle slowly past on the beam, a mile and a half, a world, away.

I took to coasting early on in life. To begin with, the word was used to stain my character.

"Raban has coasted through yet another term, and I can hold out little hope for his prospects in the forthcoming Examinations."

My father was reading my housemaster's report aloud over the after-breakfast litter in the parsonage dining room. The Easter sunlight was blue with pipe smoke and thick with dust.

"*Coasted?* Through yet *another* term?"

For days I had been dreading the arrival of the brown envelope with the Worcester postmark. Now it had come, there was something soothing in its dreary litany of undistinguished sins. The boy described in it was lazy. He showed no house spirit, no team spirit, no application and precious little intelligence. On the page headed GEOGRAPHY, there was just one word—"Slack," followed by an irritable squiggle of a signature. My father read on, in the same voice that he used to say weekday Evensongs in a church empty except for three devout old ladies. The recitation was making me feel sleepy.

The cassock that my father wore had belonged to my grandfather before him, and before that it had been my Great-uncle Cyril's. Generations of clerical wear had given its black threads a lizardy sheen. It looked as old as the Church of England.

At thirteen I was easily fooled by clothes, and this aged cassock made my father himself seem like a very old man to me, a tall and shaggy Abraham whose presence in a room was enough to make any child shiver a little in awe at a famous patriarch. He was thirty-six. Sitting now in another dusty room, its air thickened with pipe smoke of the same brand, I find myself staring back, puzzledly, at a man much younger than myself—a man with a pained boy's face, his own hurt showing, as if it were he and not his son who was being dressed down by the schoolmasters. His hair is black and thick, his skin unlined. His preposterously old clothes only serve to underline his youth as he returns my gaze— astonished to find himself the father to this bulky, balding fellow, in his forties.

It was my father's uniforms that I saw—never my father in person. When he came home from The War (there was only one war then), he was in battledress, and at three I embarked on a dangerous romantic affair with his rough army khaki. I was a secret transvestite. Finding his tunic, impregnated with manly sweat and St. Bruno Flake, sprawled on a chair back, I pulled it round my own shoulders and felt the tickle of its doormat bristles against my bare arms and neck. It weighed me down; its giant waist and mighty sleeves trailed behind me on the floor. A major's embroidered crown was sewn onto each epaulette, and the colored strip of campaign ribbons on its left breast was decorated with a miniature bronze oak leaf to show that my father had been mentioned in dispatches.

I was found, and shamed, by indulgent grown-up laughter. Later, though, when the night-light guttered in the draft on the table beside my cot, I lay dreaming furiously of the soldierly imprint of the coarse cloth on my skin. I fell asleep putting Germans to the sword, in a rainbow of ribbons and oak leaves.

It was five years later that I learned to chant *amo, amas,*

amat and parse *pater* and *patria*, father and fatherland. It was
one of the few things in Latin that I ever understood, the
intimate connection between those two words. For England
really was my father's land, not mine. It was the country
where the uniformed warrior-priest, returned hero and man
of God, was at home. Blue-chinned, six-foot-two, robed in
antique black and puffing smoke like a storybook dragon,
my father was a true Englishman—and I knew that I was
always going to be far too puny, too weak-spirited, ever to
wear his clothes except in make-believe.

"Wouldn't you say, old boy . . ." he said, tamping his
pipe with his forefinger, "that it was about time that you put
a pretty abrupt end to this . . . coasting?"

Beyond the leaded windowpanes, the uncut lawn was
spattered with early dandelions like so many teaspoonfuls
of scrambled egg.

"Yes."

"Yes *what?*"

"Yes, Daddy."

The truculence on my part was a bold affectation. Every
time I looked my father in the eye, I felt the depth of my
own failure. He represented all the things that I knew that
I was doomed to flunk. In an austere time, when people still
carried ration books and everyone's clothes were darned and
patched, my father was Austerity itself. Once a week he
bathed in two and a quarter inches of lukewarm water.
Carving a Sunday joint, he peeled off the meat in slivers as
fine as microscopic slides; you could see shafts of gray daylight through the lean. With razor blades, he performed
miracles of honing, wiping, drying, and gave them something close to everlasting life. There was nothing mean in
his approach to domestic economy—he was just keeping
perfectly in step with the times. His thrift and self-denial,
his willingness to tighten his belt when the call came made
him a pedigreed specimen of Winston Churchill's bulldog
breed.

What I saw across the breakfast table—and saw with the
pitiless egotism of the thwarted child—was not my father,
it was England. Towering over the stoved-in shells of the

pullets' eggs in their floral ceramic cups, there sat the Conservative Party in person, the Army in person, the Church in person, the Public School system in person, the Dunkirk Spirit in person, Manliness, Discipline, Duty, Self-sacrifice and all the rest. His threadbare cassock clothed the whole galaxy of terrible abstractions.

Seeing him now through different eyes, I find myself watching a sorrowful lean and angular young man, hopelessly lost for words. He coughs. He reaches for a brass ashtray made from the base of an old artillery shell and knocks out his dottle in it. He makes a busy show of burying my school report under a bill from the gas company and an overdraft notice from Lloyds Bank. He searches the face of his child for a clue as to how to go on, and finds there only a vacant, resentful, supercilious gaze—a mask more impenetrable than the mask he presents to his son.

The child is blind to all this. He's putting the finishing touches to his Bored Aristocrat face. His eyeballs are rolled so high that he can't see anything much except his own eyelashes. He is levitating. Inch by inch he rises Above This World, leaving his father down at the breakfast table with the smashed eggs. He is afloat over England. Airborne.

The young man pretends to study the columns of advertisements on the front page of *The Times*. Eventually he says: "D'you think—old boy—that there's any way we can do something about this business of—Geography?"

The astral child replies (in a fine and withering phrase that he's filched from the lips of his housemaster, Major MacTurk): "I don't know and I couldn't care less."

This was very barefaced stuff. I cared. Had I seen any way of worming my way into my father's exacting version of England, I'd have leaped at it. Give me only the legs for the job and I'd score the winning try in the house match and bring home the family bacon. I'd furnish the parsonage with prizes—the Latin prize, the Greek prize, the Colonel's Efficiency Shield and the leather-bound set of Macaulay awarded annually for Outstanding Contribution To The Life Of The School.

Every morning in chapel I stood singing manly hymns:

"I bind unto myself today the strong name of the Trin-i-tee—"

Overhead were the richly scrolled and varnished pine boards emblazoned with the names of boys from the school who had attained the ultimate in English citizenship. DULCE ET DECORUM EST PRO PATRIA MORI. There were hundreds of them, every name picked out in scarlet edged with gold, with their houses and the dates at which they'd attended the school. In the 1914–18 war, the Old Boys had done the school proud, dying in whole dormitoryfuls; in 1939–45 there were enough to man a platoon-and-a-bit or put on a Shakespeare play.

For a would-be Englishman, there was clearly some sort of opening here. Some of these certificated heroes had probably been as dim as I was, yet they had still managed to go over the top, buy it, or meet a bullet with their name on it—expressions which, in 1955, didn't yet sound dated in the least. But did LAYCOCK, R. W. P. (SCHOOL HOUSE 1938–1943) have asthma, hay fever and flat feet too? I bet he didn't. The chances were that the Army wouldn't want my services at all—and if it did, I'd probably land up as a lance-corporal in the Pioneer Corps, digging latrines in Wales.

So I looked at my father with his campaign ribbons, his priestly vocation, his pipe, his English reticence, and knew I'd never make the grade. Maybe there was some run-down South American republic where I might have passed myself off as an averagely respectable type, but it wouldn't wash in England—at least, not in the dutiful, constrained, genteel 1950s England that I knew. The schoolmasters were unarguably right when they dismissed me as a hopeless coaster.

The dictionary does the word proud. To coast is to proceed without great effort, to move by momentum or force of gravity, to march on the flank of, to skirt, to sail from port to port of the same country, to explore or scour, to bicycle downhill without pedaling, and to slide down a slope on a sled. The coaster—as my school report pointed out in no uncertain terms—is someone who uses the minimum of effort to go down a slippery slope on the margin of things.

The coaster never stays in one berth longer than he can help. He'll take on any cargo for a short distance—coal, scrap iron, timber, day-old chicks. He doesn't quite belong either to the land or to the ocean. He is a betwixt-and-between man, neither exactly a citizen nor exactly a foreigner. Choosing to live on the shifting frontier where the land meets the water and the water shades into the land, he has to make himself the master of a specialized kind of knowledge not taught in English public schools. Admiral Smyth's *The Sailor's Word Book* of 1867 puts it nicely:

> COASTING, or To Coast Along. The act of making a progress along the sea-coast of any country, for which purpose it is necessary to observe the time and direction of the tide, to know the reigning winds, the roads and havens, the different depths of water, and the qualities of the ground.

It makes a happy metaphor for a life on the fringe. For years I coasted, from job to job, place to place, person to person. At the first hint of adverse weather I hauled up my anchor and moved on with the tide, letting the reigning winds take care of the direction of the voyage. In writing I found a good coaster's occupation, unloading my mixed cargoes at one port after another. The writer, sitting alone in a room, watching society go past his window and trying to re-create it by playing with words on a page, has his own kind of sea distance . . . a sense of pushing up-Channel on a lumpy swell while the men and women on the shore go comfortably about their business, caring nothing about the pitch and roll and flap of the solitary small vessel on the horizon.

It was only a matter of time before the metaphor insisted on making itself actual. I was nearly forty, a little older than my father, when I bought a real boat, fitted it up as a floating house and set out to sail alone around the British Isles. It was rather late in the day to run away to sea (thirteen is supposed to be the standard age for that chronically English escapade) but I wasn't going to let ordinary caution or common sense get in the way of this imperious compulsion. I was besotted by the idea. Britain still seemed to be somehow more my father's land than my own—and home is always the hardest place to get into sharp focus. If only it could be *encompassed* . . . by a slow, stopping, circular voyage . . . if only one could go back to all the stages and places of one's own life, as a stranger, out of the blue . . . couldn't one emerge at the end as a domestic Columbus, the true discoverer of a doorstep empire? With all the ardent solemnity of a thirteen-year-old, at thirty-nine I saw my trip as a test, a reckoning, a voyage of territorial conquest, a homecoming.

I was not alone. I was bringing up the rear of a long queue of certifiable obsessives. This notion of taking to a boat and grandly coming to terms with one's native land is one that regularly presents itself to a certain dubious brand of Englishman, and I should have felt more disturbed than I was by the company I found myself keeping.

John MacGregor stood at the head of the line; and MacGregor's book, *The Voyage Alone in the Yawl "Rob Roy,"* started a national craze for solitary coastal voyaging when it came out in 1867. MacGregor had a lot to live up to and a lot to prove: his father was a famous general, and when the infant John was plucked safely from a shipwreck in the Bay of Biscay at the age of five weeks, the incident was held by the MacGregor family to be a clear case of Divine Intervention, in the same category, if not quite of the same rank, as the Virgin Birth.

MacGregor grew up to be a crashingly hearty Victorian bachelor. In an age untainted by suspicions fed on Freud and Krafft-Ebbing, he was able, as an evangelical philanthropist, to devote his life to Boys. His mission was to rescue street arabs from the London slums for Christ and the open-air life. He worked for the Ragged Schools, to which all his fees as a lecturer and royalties as an author were donated. He set up the Shoeblack Brigade (whose battalions of small boys, each equipped with brushes and polish, used to assemble every morning in the Strand at

seven, to sing hymns and say prayers under MacGregor's
enthusiastic conductorship), and was a co-founder of the
Boy's Own Paper.

His adventures at sea started with the *Rob Roy* canoe, a
craft he designed himself so that his boys could paddle their
way to piety at weekends. He held Sunday rallies on the
Thames, half regattas and half prayer meetings, in which
every time a canoe capsized another boy was simultaneously
cleansed of his London dirt and washed in the blood of the
Lamb.

After a series of canoeing adventures in the Holy Land
and Scandinavia, MacGregor built himself a new boat, a
21-foot yawl planked in Honduras mahogany, with a cabin,
a galley and a half-decked cockpit that looked as it if were
closely modeled on a preacher's pulpit. He took on a cargo
of "several boxes of Testaments, books, pictures, and interesting papers, in different tongues," and set sail for Paris by
way of the Thames Estuary, the South coast of England and
the Seine. "Truly," he wrote, "there is a sea-mission yet to
be worked. Good news was told on the water long ago, and
by the Great Preacher from a boat." Wherever he docked
he handed out Bibles and "interesting papers" to passing
tourists, fishermen, bargees and longshoremen. "The distri-
bution of these was a constant pleasure to me. Permanent
and positive good may have been done by the reading of
their contents."

He supplied his own illustrations, and on page 18 of *The
Voyage Alone* he treated his readers to a flattering portrait of
the Author At Home, in which MacGregor reclines majestically against a bolster in his pulpit-cockpit, his mustaches
waxed to icicle-like points, his eyes hard and bright as a
pair of chipped flints as he gazes out to sea. His finely
sculpted head is turbaned against the sun, and he appears
to be tippling from a mug, but the prominent teapot on the
deck beside him is there to reassure you that MacGregor's
liquor is definitely nontoxic. Investigation of the crosshatching with a magnifying glass reveals an open bible
propped against the gunwale.

Here is exactly the sort of Englishman that Thomas Ar-

nold's Rugby was created to manufacture. You could trust
the colonization of Africa, or the management of the Sheffield steel industry, to this sturdy open-necked figure who
exudes the Victorian virtues of Temperance, Probity, Resolution and Independence. Setting himself up as the very
type of the hero of the age, MacGregor shows a well-built
athlete sailing westward in the service of God and Queen.

Out at sea, MacGregor meditated on the condition of
England:

> In all our great towns there is a mass of human beings
> whose want, misery, and filth are more patent to the
> eye, and blatant to the ear, and pungent to the
> nostrils than in almost any other towns in the world.
> Their personal liberty is greater, too, than anywhere
> else. Are these two facts related to each other? Is the
> positive piggery of the lowest stratum of our fellows
> part of the price we have to pay for glorious freedom
> as guaranteed by our "British Constitution"? and do we
> not pay very dearly then? Must the masses be frowsy
> to be free?

From the long-distance perspective afforded by *Rob Roy*
running before the wind off Southsea, the answers to the
nation's problems came pat: what was needed was "strong
Tory government" and a great Christian crusade.

The Voyage Alone became a Victorian best-seller, not for
its religious or political content but because it managed to
glorify yachting as much more than a mere sport. Mac-
Gregor turned sailing a small boat into a species of high
moral endeavor. He wrote infectiously of the pleasures of
the business. *Rob Roy* was, he said, "my floating freehold,"
and the water was "my road, my home, my very world." His
somewhat embroidered adventures at sea were conveyed in
the elementary heroic prose which was to become the standard note of the *Boy's Own Paper*. Yet simple adventure and
simple pleasure weren't enough in themselves. What was
needed was a sense of uplift; and when MacGregor saw
yachts, he didn't see a collection of rich men's toys, about

which they ought to feel a stab of Christian guilt as they left the office on Friday for a long weekend's messing about on the water, but rather—

> That noble fleet of roaming craft which renew the nerve and energy of so many Englishmen by a manly and healthful enterprise, opening a whole new element of nature, and nursing a host of loyal seamen to defend our shores.

If MacGregor was an ace at flattering himself, he was also very clever at buttering up his readers. It was from Mac-Gregor that the amateur sailor learned that he wasn't just indulging himself in a hobby, he was sailing for Victoria, England and Saint George.

One contemporary reader of the book was Empson Edward Middleton, a disgruntled ex–officer in the Indian army, a man whose head was peppered with stings from the swarm of bees that he kept in his bonnet. He was the first man to sail singlehanded round the British Isles, and in *The Cruise of The Kate* he explained how his own voyage started:

> My wearied thoughts were wandering down the High Street of Southampton, during the Christmas week of 1868, and conducted tired limbs to the excellent circulating library of Messrs. Gutch, where faded eyesight fell upon a work bearing the title of *The Voyage Alone in the Yawl Rob Roy*. An instant sympathy with its contents created an exchange of matter; five shillings causing a deficiency of ballast in one pocket, while extracted essence of old clothes created a bulge in my starboard coat, correcting my proper trim, and allowing me to cruise to my usual station without more rolling than was actually necessary, in proportion to the paved or muddied depressions on the way. All hail *The Voyage Alone*.

He commissioned an enlarged replica of *Rob Roy*, and had his boat personally inspected by MacGregor before he put to sea. *The Kate*, also a yawl, was 25 feet long (according to *Lloyd's Register*) or 23 feet (according to Middleton, who was probably foreshortening it for heroism's sake). The big difference between the two boats—and the two voyages they made—was in their cargoes.

Middleton loaded *The Kate* with his own discontents. He was a misunderstood genius whose inner nobility had gone unrecognized. He had proved conclusively that the earth was—not quite flat, exactly, but bowl- or saucer-shaped. This important discovery had not been taken up by the Royal Geographical Society or the British Academy with anything like the excitement it deserved. He had also worked out that Heaven was located in the Sun whose rays were emitted by the combined souls of the blessed—another theory in which no one seemed to be at all interested. At the time of his voyage he was "engaged in the production of an arduous literary labour," the verse translation to end all verse translations of Virgil's *Aeneid*, of which several samples were smuggled into *The Cruise of The Kate*:

A sylvan scene adorns the dizzy height;
A gloomy grove refracts a softened light
On grots, and cooling springs within a cave
Where nymphs resort to dabble in the wave.

No eager publisher came forward with a contract, and Middleton smelled the London literary conspiracy at work. One surefire best-seller—a translation of Aristotle's *Ethics*, "in large print, for the poor to read"—had already been rejected. Middleton was making the unoriginal discovery that publishers are astonishingly stupid and shortsighted and are in the business only of promoting their friends.

So he went to a vanity press and had privately printed a fat pamphlet called *The World of Wonders*—a digest of his Latin translations, his scientific theories, his quarrels with various authorities, his cures for rheumatism and gout. The after-locker of *The Kate* was packed solid with copies, which he proposed to distribute round Britain on the model of MacGregor and his tracts and bibles. Like MacGregor's,

Middleton's voyage was a sea mission, a crusade of enlightenment. Brave, cranky and in deadly earnest, he taught himself to sail in a week on the Solent, and set out to conquer his native land.

The Cruise of The Kate is a solemn chronicle. Wherever he stepped ashore, Middleton came face to face with the insolence and cupidity of his fellowmen. The builders were lazy and failed to finish his boat on schedule. Pilots overcharged him. Navigational aids, like buoys and lighthouses, were deliberately put in the wrong places, in order to tempt Middleton to shipwreck. Hoteliers refused to cash his checks. He saw himself as a stoned martyr in a naughty world, and stubbornly went on telling the good news. "The World of Wonders Magazine made me numberless friends."

The dominant tone of the book is pained and blustery. Middleton's voice is that of the well-spoken bore with a gigantic chip on his shoulder:

> I can assure the world at large that I am about the last man to care about publicity; I do not care one straw for praise; I would not care one straw if praise were purposely withheld, where there could be no doubt that it was my due. What do I want of my fellows? I want their esteem, their goodwill, but not their praise. What am I driving at? You will see. I have stated that I do not care about publicity; but I have wished before today to be a voice in my own nation, to be able to speak when I like, to hold my tongue when I like. Such is my idea of society, and I would associate with the nation; nothing less than the nation will please me.

Middleton's habit of continually asking himself questions and immediately answering them makes it miserably clear that no one else ever asked him the questions whose answers he was burning to expound. His aggrieved loneliness stares so vividly through his writing that The Cruise of The Kate deserves a place among the classic psychiatric case histories.

He wasn't built for society. Yet as long as he remained

offshore, his mortally bruised ego did find some measure of comfort. The sea—huge, empty, frightening and unpredictable—provided a kind of objective correlative for Middleton's gross inner solitude, and he found himself more at home at sea than he had ever been on land. The sea never ridiculed him. Alone in *The Kate*, like a cross baby adrift in a cradle, he was secure for the first time in his adult life. When passing fishermen threw him a few herrings to cook on the hob of his dangerous coal fire, or shouted helpful directions to him across the water, he even found a kind of human companionship that had evaded him on shore.

Middleton was, perhaps, not quite so alone as he believed himself to be. Among his contemporaries there was at least one other subscriber to his theory that Heaven was situated in the sun—the London stockbroker and yachtsman R. T. McMullen, whose book *Down Channel* is still read by amateur sailors as the best-known personal account of coasting in British waters. McMullen's continuing appeal certainly can't be explained by his talent as a writer, which was rudimentary. His surly record of courses sailed, weather encountered and ports entered would set no one's imagination alight—unless there was something in the character of the man himself that found an answering chime in the character of his seagoing readers.

McMullen was above all else a tidy man. He hated messiness and excess. Catholicism, with its ripe symbolism and its unseemly pandering to the sensations with candles, vestments, incense and the rest, revolted him. He was the author of a choleric pamphlet called "Priestly Pretensions and God's Work," in which he detected Romans under the beds of half the vicarages and rectories of the Church of England. In social matters, too, he abhorred the least hint of disorder. Trades unionists were members of The Idler's Union; and those passages of *Down Channel* which are most nearly vivid are the bits where he is abominating the smell, laziness and general scurrility of the lower classes. Paid hands, fishermen, harbor employees are treated by McMullen with testy condescension.

His book is governed by a single sentence: "In language

too mild to express my real sentiments, I dislike a sloven; a slovenly reef, a slovenly furl and a dirty mast look disgraceful on a yacht of any pretensions." The Church was a slack ship—Gladstone's England was a slack ship—but McMullen ran a succession of tight ships; ships offered as exemplary models of the social order as it might be in an ideal world, every line coiled just so, every shroud taut, every paid hand set firmly in his proper place in the fo'c's'le. At sea, McMullen put England to shame.

This cold stockbroker's utopia found a large and approving audience. His Protestant authoritarianism has gone down very well with the men's men who prop up yacht club bars. He is himself the model of a certain kind of Englishman, with his contempt for clutter and show, his philistine certainties about how things should be run and his chauvinist attitude toward women. At the beginning of *Down Channel* he does tersely vouchsafe the existence of a "Mrs McMullen"—that, indeed, she shared some of his voyages, or was, at least, to be found in the galley during the course of them. She is never mentioned thereafter.

The most memorable thing about McMullen, and his outstanding qualification as a sterling English hero, was the way he died. On June 14, 1891, he was sailing alone in his 27-foot yawl, *Perseus*, somewhere in the English Channel, when a heart attack killed him. Two days later, *Perseus* was spotted by a fishing boat off Cherbourg. It was maintaining a steady westward course, its sails tight and filled with wind. The dead man, his limbs locked in *rigor mortis*, was keeping a firm grip on the tiller. If a member of the French lower orders (a category which had given McMullen no end of trouble during his life) had not unsportingly intervened, he might well be still sailing today.

McMullen, prematurely conducted to his paradise in the sun, must have blazed with pure rage when he saw Hilaire Belloc, a generation later, out in the *Nona*. Belloc was a Catholic, and ran his boat in a state of happy catholic disorder. In *The Cruise of the Nona* he exhorted his readers, McMullen fashion, to *Get everything shipshape and, so far as you can, keep everything shipshape*. Then he confessed.

My own boat has usually come into port more like the
disturbed nest of a dormouse than like the spick and
span arrangement which I advise. Half the blocks will
be jammed, the anchor will be caught under the
bows, and as like as not, the fluke of it hooked over
one of the whiskers. The falls will be all tangled up
together. The warping ropes will be mixed up with
the anchor chain in the fo'c's'le, so that there is no
getting at the one, or paying out the other. She will
perhaps be coming in under three reefs with hardly
enough wind to move her, because it has been
blowing a few hours ago, and I have been too lazy to
shake them out. Her jib will be slack, her cabin light
broken where I have put my heel through it . . .

But the amiable sloppiness which reigned on Belloc's boat
did not—unfortunately—correspond to his vision of how
things should be managed in society. Of all the lone sailors
who have coasted round Britain and used the sea as a place
of meditative exile, Belloc is much the most frightening.

He took to the *Nona* in pessimism and bereavement. His
young wife had died (Belloc wore black for the rest of his
life); his brief political career, as Liberal member for Sal-
ford, was over. The *Nona*, of which he writes with a tender-
ness more suited to a lover than to a boat, was his chief
remaining refuge. Lying at anchor on the water in the domestic snuggery of the *Nona*'s lamplit cabin, Belloc was able
to come close to re-creating the whispered confidences of
the marriage bed. *The Cruise of the Nona* reads like pillow talk,
with Belloc telling secrets about himself—and more disturb-
ing secrets about England.

Half of the book is entrancing. Belloc loved, feared and
respected the sea, and he wrote about it with more accuracy
and conviction than anyone else in English bar Melville and
Conrad. The sea brought out the best in the essentially
theological tenor of his mind:

Sailing the sea, we play every part of life: control,
direction, effort, fate; and there we can test ourselves

and know our state. All that which concerns the sea is profound and final. The sea provides visions, darknesses, revelations—

Or (in a passage which I later pinned up in the cabin of my own boat and saw as the defining motto for this voyage, this book):

> The cruising of a boat here and there is very much what happens to the soul of a man in a larger way. . . . We are granted great visions, we suffer intolerable tediums, we come to no end of the business, we are lonely out of sight of England, we make astonishing landfalls—and the whole rigmarole leads us along no whither, and yet is alive with discovery, emotion, adventure, peril and repose.

In Belloc, too, the sea is a place—or rather, a huge and rich assortment of particular places—as solid, real and recognizable as the individual landscapes of a continent. When he writes about the neck of sea between Bardsey Island and the Lleyn Peninsula in a high gale, or about the great tide races of Portland Bill and St. Albans Head, or the luminous, mirrorlike entry to Port Madoc on a still summer evening, he does for water what landscape painters do for trees and rocks and architecture; he gives it unforgettable body and life.

For every page about the sea there is another about the land, and when Belloc looks back at the shore from which he has sailed, his pillow talk takes a dirty turn. The freedom of the sea, the lapse of a few nautical miles between himself and the British coast, released in Belloc a flood of confidences which were better not told.

All his embitterment came tumbling out as he looked back at England. Belloc had failed as a parliamentarian, and so he despised parliaments, despised democracy itself. He talked of "the vomit" of parliamentary rule. The House of Commons he characterized as "the slime of the Lobbies."

There is no form of parliamentary activity which is
not deplorable, save in aristocracies.

For, in aristocracies, which are, of their nature,
governments of a clique, a Parliament—which is a
clique—can be normal and natural. In communities
based on the idea of equality, and of action by the
public will, they are cancers, under which such
nations always sicken and may die.

For Belloc, England's treason was her return to the rule of
Parliament at the end of the First World War, instead of
"continuing the rule of soldiers as [she] should have done."

It is like listening to the rambling unconscious mind of a
profoundly disappointed man whose sense of hurt has
turned to poisonous spite. Belloc, with his copious fluency
of language, makes the bluff irritations of plainer men like
Middleton and McMullen seem trifling and beside the
point. When Belloc hates, he hates with spine-chilling ar-
ticulacy. At Clovelly, he sees some tourists, innocently de-
bouching from a line of sightseeing coaches for a day at the
seaside.

We heard a murmur like that of bees swarming. As we
came nearer it was a confused clamour of human
beings, and as we came nearer still we saw the
dreadful thing in its entirety.

The day-trippers are "black ants"—"lost souls"—"dark
clothed mortality"—"an immense mass"—"this mob"—"like
black pressed German caviare, the acid stuff which is sold
for the destruction of the race." Tourists, politicians, Jews,
("Eh, Rosenheim? Eh, Guildenstern?"), pacifists, atheists,
journalists are all lumped together in the same nightmare
ball. They are the horrible Modern England from which the
Nona is sailing away under as much linguistic canvas as she
can carry.

Belloc sees one glimmer of hope on the European horizon
—Mussolini, who had risen to power in Italy in 1922, three
years before The Cruise of the Nona was published.

> What a strong critical sense Italy has shown! What
> intelligence in rejection of sophistry, and what virility
> in execution! May it last!

The word "virility" crops up again and again in Belloc's
book. To be out in the open air, sailing a small boat on a
rough sea, was a "virile" thing to do—unlike the indoor,
pallid, unmanly occupations of people in coach parties, or
Jews or Members of Parliament. In Mussolini, Belloc met a
man of his own stamp—exactly the right sort of hearty,
Catholic fellow with whom he could comfortably quaff ale
in the cockpit of the *Nona*.

> What a contrast with the sly and shifty talk of your
> parliamentarian! What a sense of decision, of
> sincerity, of serving the nation, and of serving it
> towards a known end with a definite will! Meeting
> [Mussolini] after talking with the parliamentarians in
> other countries was like meeting with some athletic
> friend of one's boyhood after an afternoon with racing
> touts; or it was like coming upon good wine in a
> Pyrenean village after compulsory draughts of marsh
> water in the mosses of the moors above, during some
> long day's travel over the range.

Belloc manages to insinuate that if you fall for the virile
maritime romance of *Yachting Monthly*, you may be guided
by divine providence to the politics of *Mein Kampf*. The
strangest thing of all about his strange book was the way it
was received in England. The London *Observer* said that
Belloc "has never perhaps written better"; the *London Mercury*
came purring up to Belloc, saying *"The Cruise of the Nona* is
certainly the most companionable, possibly the most beautiful, of his books."

This, then, is the band of men which I was about to join as
a raw recruit. They are a desperate bunch. Despair, or
something very close to it, shows through their aggressive,

bottle-nosed politics and aggressive, bottle-nosed religion. Even in ripe middle age, they are still neurotically anxious to prove their manliness, and the rigid authoritarian streak which fissures all their personalities looks like the symptom of some serious inner weakness. They are all lonely men— stiff and out of kilter with their times; and, as lonely men do, they see themselves as heroic prophetic outcasts. For each of them the sea is the prophet's necessary wilderness in which he must spend his ritual forty days and forty nights before coming home and enlightening the world with his awful news.

The *Rob Roy,* *The Kate,* *Perseus* and the *Nona* are a lot more than mere yachts. Loaded down on their marks with testa- ments, theories, dogmas and solutions, they are like arks of the Covenant; holy vessels bearing sacred texts. Jesus Christ . . . Aristotle . . . Malthus . . . Mussolini . . . each of the lone sailors puts to sea with a ghostly first mate. And the boats themselves are miniature ships of state, their trim style of domestic economy set side by side with the ramshackle and disordered house of England across the water.

Reading the books, I can feel their authors bristling irrit- ably at me from behind their black masks of print. I'm not their sort of man at all: my politics are soft and wet, my tastes indulgently urban, my home a dishevelment of un- opened bills and untidied clothes. I am not shipshape. I am irreligious and a physical coward. Fear of getting hurt has kept me clear of dentists for a decade. The tips of my fingers go white at the first nip of cold. Among the objects gen- erally thought to be desirable on voyages, I fall clearly into the same category as umbrellas and wheelbarrows.

I would no more try to stow away with MacGregor, Middleton, McMullen, Belloc, or the rest of the hearty gang, than I would have volunteered for service in the Ton- tons Macoute. Yet here we are, assembled at the same dock- side, our boats jostling together in the water as we load up with provisions and brush against each other at the counter of the ship chandler's. We're much of an age. Well past the point where life still seems unrationed, we are all beginning to run short of teeth, hair, wind and options. What unites us more deeply is a compulsive itch for the escape valve of a wilderness, an open frontier, and our common discovery that even now Britain does have a last frontier, in the sea.

For there's an obvious reason why this sudden craze for solitary coasting should have started when it did, in the 1860s. It is not so long since Britain had its own internal wildernesses—places into which people in search of solitude and some danger could literally disappear. In 1726, Defoe wrote of a visit to the Lake District in his *Tour Through the Whole Island of Great Britain*. He was much shaken by what he saw.

> Here, among the mountains, our curiosity was frequently moved to enquire what high hill this was, or that. Indeed, they were, in my thoughts, monstrous high; but in a country all mountainous and full of innumerable high hills, it was not easy for a traveller to judge which was highest.
>
> Nor were these hills high and formidable only, but they had a kind of an unhospitable terror in them. Here were no rich pleasant valleys between them, as among the Alps; no lead mines and veins of rich ore, as in the Peaks; no coal pits, as in the hills about Halifax, much less gold, as in the Andes, but all barren and wild, of no use or advantage either to man or beast . . .
>
> Here we entered Westmoreland, a country eminent only for being the wildest, most barren and frightful of any that I have passed over in England, or even in Wales itself. . . .

The "unpassable hills", the "frightful appearances to the right and left," made Defoe beat a fast retreat to civilization. In Westmoreland he had seen a landscape just as savage as anything to be found on the American Frontier. It's not hard to imagine a Donner Party, or an Alferd Packer (the man

who is reputed to have eaten five of the seven Democrats in
Hinsdale County, Colorado), in Defoe's aghast vision of
the English Lakes.

Within a very few years no one could possibly have
seen Cumberland and Westmoreland in Defoe's terms. The
eighteenth-century vogue for the paintings of Claude Lor-
raine, and the importation, late in the century, of German
romanticism, turned wild savagery into the merely picturesque. When Wordsworth (in 1799) wrote of "a huge peak,
black and huge," striding after him in his "little boat" on
Lake Windermere, he was fairly promptly ridiculed by
Byron (in 1819) for—among a multitude of other things—
the overblown grandeur of his conception of his own solitude in Nature.

> We learn from Horace, Homer sometimes sleeps;
>   We feel without him Wordsworth sometimes
>   wakes,
> To show with what complacency he creeps
>   With his dear *Waggoners* around his lakes.
> He wishes for 'a boat' to sail the deeps.
>   Of Ocean? No, of air. And then he makes
> Another outcry for 'a little boat'
> And drivels seas to set it well afloat . . .

By 1850, when Wordsworth died, the craggy English wilderness of leech gatherers and terrified small boys in little
boats had become (largely by Wordsworth's own agency) a
tourist resort. The mighty mountains were dotted with hik-
ers. Horse-drawn carriages were transporting more sedentary holidaymakers to see Wordsworth's houses at Rydal
Mount and Dove Cottage. Easels and sketchbooks were
pitched on every convenient rock, so that Sunday painters
could catch the prettiness of Defoe's "frightful appearances."
The Lake District had turned into Britain's first theme park.

In 1867, when John MacGregor cast off to sea in the *Rob
Roy*, there was no domestic wilderness left. There were the
colonies, of course. There were keepered grouse moors,
whose appearance of desolation hid the fact they they were

in reality artfully husbanded for the pleasure of the sporting gentry. In 1862, George Borrow had just managed to find some remaining wilderness in *Wild Wales*, whose chapter headings ("Wild Scenery—Awful Chasm—The Robbers' Cavern—An Adventure—The Gloomy Valley—A Native of Aberystwyth") nicely give the frontier flavor of the book. But the railways were rapidly taking care of that. Aberystwyth itself, the capital of wildest, deepest mid-Wales, was being transformed into Birmingham's main holiday resort, with a pier, a promenade and a stucco quarter-moon of boardinghouses and hotels. In the 1860s England (if not quite Scotland and not quite Wales) was so thickly peopled, so intensively farmed, so industrialized, so citified, that there was nowhere to go to be truly alone or to have Borrow-style Adventures, except to sea.

The ports of departure from which the four coasting voyagers set sail tell a good deal about the nature of the voyages themselves. MacGregor's book starts in the slums of the East End; Middleton's in Southampton; McMullen's in Greenhithe, a thirty-minute railway journey from London Bridge and the Stock Exchange; Belloc's in the tame teashop country of half-timbered Sussex. These lonely saltwater romances are all products of suburbia and the city; they are postindustrial dreams at heart, as urban in their own way as the glass-and-steel romances of St. Pancras Station and the Crystal Palace. In part, at least, they belong to the literature of national pathology. They express the simple claustrophobia of living in a country that has suddenly grown too small, too smoky, too intimate, too manmade and civilized for comfort. They show England as an overloaded, sinking ship, and they propose the obvious solution—to take to the lifeboats.

For however thoroughly you may brick up the land, there's nothing much that you can do to the sea except humbly chart it. You can fiddle about on its edge building groins and floodwalls and breakwaters, but the sea will not be civilized. Even the most household corridor of sea is a very wild place indeed. On the map of Europe the Dover Straits appear as a piddling canal bisecting industrial England and industrial France. But from a boat . . . Build in a warm wet wind from the southwest—not a full gale, just a stiffish, hang-on-to-your-hat sort of breeze. Add an incoming spring tide, sluicing into the straits from the North Sea at a speed no faster than that of a jogger in a park. The water bunches and crumples as it hits the wind head on. The breakers all around you are as angular and gray as boulders of granite. Where the sea collides with the submerged whalebacks of the Goodwin Sands, it explodes in forty-foot plumes of powdered white. Racing shallowly over the sands, it raises quills of spray as if a herd of aquatic porcupines was on the run. The boat rolls and plunges; the sky tips on its end. Heart in mouth, shaken about like dice in a cup, you hang on to the wheel for dear life. Here really are frightful appearances to the right and left, wild scenery, awful chasms, monstrous high hills with a kind of inhospitable terror in them. This is wilderness, and I cannot imagine a solitude more absolute than that of being in a small boat on a rough sea out of sight of land—or even in sight of it, for that matter. You are genuinely alone in nature, a creature of the weather and the tides, thrown back on fundamental skills like navigation and seamanship.

It once used to puzzle me that in every corner newsagent's in every English big city I visited, there would be a stack of yachting magazines. The man at the counter had never heard of the *Times Literary Supplement*, and didn't think it worth his while ("There's no demand") to stock *The Times* itself. But between the garters, tits and bums, the custom cars and *True Romances*, there they invariably were—*Yachting*-this and *Yachting*-that, the touched-up pornography of the wide-open spaces. No one in the shop looked remotely like a yachtsman to me. Who bought these things? And why, if the man was prepared to cater to such eccentric tastes, could he not keep on hand a few copies of a paper with obvious mass appeal like the *T. L. S.*?

There is no puzzle in it. In high-rise flats on Inkerman Streets everywhere, where the plane trees below are choked with blue exhaust fumes, where people live tight-packed as football crowds, someone is dreaming himself to sleep over

stories of hurricanes, wet sleeping bags and sunsets in an-
chorages of idyllic, empty calm. His main halyard has gone.
He's under jury rig. An iceberg looms on the starboard
beam like a gigantic nightmare wedding cake. With frozen
fingers he thrusts the tiller to the lee. When people for
whom no other wilderness remains dream of a ritual self-
purification in heroic solitude, they dream of what John
MacGregor called "the wholesome sea."

There's no history in a wilderness. It just *is*. And because it
has always been this way, a wilderness serves as an elemental point of continuity from which it's possible to measure
the pace of the civilization on its outer rim.

A few weeks before I took to my own lifeboat, I came
across a great, foxed, yellowed, torn and salt-stained book
of charts in an antiquarian bookseller's. Holding the heavy
pages at an angle to the light, I saw that they were spotted
with tiny punctures, where an eighteenth-century ship's
captain had been marking off his course with a pair of sharp
compasses. Some of the charts had faded pencil lines ruled
in along the deepwater channels. Pleased by this vivid,
accidental connection with the anonymous dead sailor who
had once gone exactly where I planned to go, I bought the
book and lugged its deadweight home.

Great Britain's Coasting Pilot by Captain Greenville Collins
was first published in 1693. Until that time British naviga-
tors had had to rely on Dutch charts of their own waters—
charts which, after the outbreak of the Dutch Wars, were
designed to wreck ships rather than lead them safely home.
Charles II appointed Collins as Hydrographer to the King,
equipped him with a yacht and sent him off on a seven-year
survey of the British coast. His *Pilot* was used as a guidebook
by professional coasters for more than a century.

It is still usable now. Imagine trying to find one's way
about the landmass of Britain, or anywhere else, with a map
three hundred years old—but this is a map of a perennial
wilderness, and it works. Collins' tide tables, based on the
phases of the moon at "Full" and "Change," are as reliable as

they ever were, and you can still steer to his sailing directions.

> Directions for failing into *Fowey* or *Foy*.
>
>   FOY lieth 4 Leagues NE from the *Deadman*, and two miles to the Weftward of a great Bay called *St Blazey Bay*, *Predmouth Point* being the weft-fide of the Bay. There lieth a Ledge of Rocks SE, about half a mile from the faid Point, called the *Canneys*, and fhew themfelves above water at half-Tide; there is but 7 and 8 foot Water within them at low water. From thefe Rocks to the going in to *Foy* the Shoar is bold. Keep the *Deadman* within the *Winehead Rock*, and it will carry you clear of the *Canneys*.
>
> Foy
>
> *Foy* may be very eafily known, lying in between two high-lands; on the weft-fide the going in, is an old Church and Caftle, and on the eaft-fide the Ruins of an old Church, as you may fee by the making of it in the Draught of *Foy*, N° 17. The going in is a Cable's length over from fide to fide, and no danger; when you are in you may anchor before the Town, or run up above the Town. And whereas it hath been reported to be a Bar-Harbour, and that you cannot enter till half Tide, I do affure you that there is no lefs than 3 Fathoms at low-water at a Spring-tide: Here you may lie afloat to Wafh, Tallow, ftop Leeks . . .

It is all exactly as described, and I have myself ftopped Leeks at *Foy*. Collins' churches and castles are the same churches and castles that serve as landmarks on the latest Admiralty charts; his silhouettes of the major headlands are larger, more detailed and easier to decode than the diminished and foggy photographs used in modern Admiralty pilots; his soundings are mostly still sound, and so is his advice about negotiating the main tide races and overfalls. Some things have changed. Sandbars have shifted, but sandbars shift from gale to gale anyway. Buoys have been moved, removed and multiplied, though the majority of them have kept their names. A few new artificial harbors have been built; but otherwise the sailor's view of Britain from the sea is just the same.

Sailing around with Collins' *Pilot* in the wheelhouse induces a kind of historical vertigo. On one hand the book is bang up to date. It is so accurate on the watery front that all subsequent additions to the landscape, from Georgian country houses and Martello towers to radio masts and nuclear power stations, look equally raw. If it's not in Collins it must be new, and probably still only in its experimental phase. Yet here is a complete city, trailing a ragged crew of suburbs behind it over the hills, where not even a hamlet is shown on the chart. The smooth top of a Collins headland has sprouted towers and chimneys like the teeth of a broken comb. Staring, with some annoyance, at these upstart intrusions, you'd think they could be erased as easily as I could push a button and lift off this line of type.

Possessed by the idea of making my own escape into this wilderness, I joined the moon-faced gang whose members loaf, hands in pockets, on every English quayside, gazing innocently at water, floating fish crates, dead jellyfish and old boats, dreaming themselves away to sea. Working my way around the coast from the Wash to Cornwall, I spent all summer searching for a boat. I clambered awkwardly over decks full of meaningless rope and rusty pieces of marine ironmongery whose function appeared to be to bark a landsman's shins. Economic recession meant that half the boats in England were up for sale. They lay unattended, their paintwork scabbed, their coach roofs marbled with gull shit, in picture-postcard fishing ports, in dull marinas, in seaside resorts where chip-papers swirled in the streets and the promenades buzzed with the chatter of electronic war games. These depressing trips were not entirely wasted. I learned what scantlings were, and rubbing strakes and stemposts. I bought a penknife, and pretended that I knew what I was doing when I shyly jabbed its point into the oak frames of the latest stranded hulk.

I kept on meeting my double. He was living alone aboard his boat, which was posted for sale with a broker although the owner himself appeared to have no serious expectation of ever finding a buyer for it. He lived in jeans and torn jerseys. He rolled his own cigarettes and kept his tobacco in an Old Holborn tin which had worn down to the bare metal. He gave off the faint old-dog smell of the man who can't quite put a date on his last bath.

Wherever I met him—in Wells in Norfolk, in Maldon in Essex, in Newhaven in Sussex, in Falmouth in Cornwall—his story was very nearly the same. He'd been divorced—last year, or the year before, or the year before that. He'd been made redundant when the factory where he'd had a quiet desk job had closed down. Prematurely retired from the world at forty or thereabouts, he'd sold up his semidetached in the suburbs, settled the mortgage and put what was left into this ramshackle ark which he was now listlessly trying to sell to me.

If we stood together in a salty puddle where the floor should have been it was: "You always expect to see a bit of water in the bilges in a boat like this. It's a good sign. It means she's able to breathe."

In just a year to two, my double had turned himself into a Robinson Crusoe of the foreshore. He gathered samphire and knew how to fry seaweed. At low tide he set crab pots; at high tide he fished from the veranda of his back room. Once a week he collected his dole money. His postal address was care of John, or Eric or Hattie, whoever was landlord of the Old Ship, the Fisherman's Rest or the Anchor on the quay.

"But what will you do when you sell the boat?"

"Oh . . . friends, you know. I'll have to look around. I was thinking of getting a catamaran. A catamaran's a very stable boat at sea."

For now, my double tinkered his days away. He caulked the leaks in his home, not often to much visible effect. He sat with the *Ashley Book of Knots* open in front of him on the saloon table, plaiting the frayed ends of a piece of rope into a monkey's fist. He laid in driftwood for the winter. He made plans.

All my doubles had plans. Lodged like hippos in their mud berths, they lived on dreams. Aboard every boat I was shown charts—as if the charts themselves were voyages as good as made. Charts of the Azores, of the Caicos Islands, of the Baltic, of the Turkish coast, of the French canal route to Marseilles . . . Every one was marked out with compass courses, distances, the likely landmarks ringed in soft pencil, the ports of refuge carefully arrowed in.

"If only this bloody weather would change. Suppose that Azores High drifts north a bit, into Shannon, say, I'd go next week."

"I'm just waiting for an alternator. It was meant to be here Tuesday."

"When my girlfriend stops working—"

"My only trouble is the dog—"

In the meantime they scraped at the layers of old varnish on their spars, messed with paintpots and reread their way through their soggy paperback libraries of adventures at sea. When September came and equinoctial gales tore chimney pots off houses and made boats groan and shiver on their moorings, and the holidaymakers all went home, the doubles were still there waiting for their breaks.

The margins of England are lined with these men and their rotting boats. Redundant in many more senses than one, they have crossed the seawall that defines the outer limit of society and live in a tidal no-man's-land—Huck Finns going to gray, all talking in the accent of the same minor public school. The men from the Income Tax department have long ago lost touch with them. They are beyond support orders, electricity bills, door-knocking clergy on their rounds, colored circulars, credit cards and all the other privileges and interferences of civilized life. Visiting them —by dinghy, or in gum boots over a hundred yards or so of soft and smelly mud—I listened to them all telling me solemnly that they were "free." But it was a freedom which they had all, with whatever little enthusiam or real hope, put up for sale.

In Fowey I found a boat. It wasn't a romantic discovery. The tide had gone out, leaving the flats of the estuary gleaming dully and riddled with wormcasts. The boat was stranded, propped up between baulks of timber and secured to the ground with a dripping cat's cradle of ropes and chains. With its masts gone elsewhere, its wheelhouse sticking up at the back and its high, bulbous front end, it looked in silhouette like a cracked army boot.

Its owner had emigrated to Hong Kong, and for three years the boat had lain here untenanted and uncared-for. The local yard had given me keys and a warrant to view; and I slithered across the mud in city clothes, pushing past bait diggers forking worms into buckets. Each new footstep released another bubble of bad-egg air. The trees on the foreshore were speckled a dirty white with china-clay dust from the docks downriver and looked as if they had contracted a bad case of dandruff.

There's always something absurd and disproportionate about any boat seen out of the water. The most graceful craft go dowdy and frumpish when you see them in the nude. This one looked gross—a huge and flabby Amazon. Her bottom had come out in an eczematic rash of limpets. The blue paint on her superior parts was bleached and peeling. Scabby, trussed, leaning heavily on her crutches, she looked incapable of ever putting to sea again.

My shadow scared a sunbathing family of fiddler crabs in the muddy pool which the boat had dug for herself as she grounded with the tide. They shuffled away across the pool floor and hid in the dark under her flounced bilges.

I found a boarding ladder under a dusty tree and climbed ten feet up onto the deck, which was the usual jumble of anchors, buckets, boathooks, ropes and things. A herring gull was taking the usual leisurely crap on the wheelhouse roof, and the neat deck planking had gone a furry green with guano and disuse.

Inside, the trapped air had a pleasant bruised-apple smell. The antique binnacle compass in the wheelhouse was locked on a course of 045°, northeast, bound for Devon, Somerset and the glum Midlands. The wheel itself was a proper ship's wheel, brass-banded with varnished spokes of a size that demanded horny, capable seaman's hands as big as dinner plates. I tried swinging it myself and heard heavy chains rumbling in the cellarage as the rudder ground on mud, stones and dead crabs.

When I got below decks, I knew I'd found the right boat to run away to sea in. Brass oil lamps hung tilted in their gimbals. The dusty paneling of mahogany and teak, the red leather cushions on the settees, stuffed with odorous horsehair, the smoky overhead beams, the brass-bound charcoal stove, the rows of fiddled bookshelves (Hammond Innes next to *Admiralty Sight Reduction Tables, Volume 3*), made the place warm and clubbish. It was the Reform and the Travellers' reduced to matchbox scale: a fine setting to go gaga in, to mutter reactionary nonsense over the port or snooze away the afternoon like a blubbery dugong in an easy chair. Secure behind its bolted portholes, one could remove one's hearing aid, tell one's old stories, live on one's memories and be a ripe old bean.

I bought it that afternoon, and all winter the boatyard men chiseled and painted it to rights: scraping off the barnacles until the bare wood showed as pink as ripening plums; hacking out unwanted bunks from the fo'c's'le; doing oily, indescribable things down in the engine room. I didn't want a yacht; I wanted a one-man floating house, with a study-bedsitter up in the front, complete with library and writing table, a comfortable paneled drawing room in the middle, a kitchen, a shade cramped but sufficient for my elementary cuisine, and a proper flush toilet and washroom.

The boatyard took much the same attitude to my plans as R. T. McMullen might have done himself, had the sun's rays ever shone on Polruan that winter. I put a long-haired sheepskin rug, bought years before in the Aleppo souk, down in the saloon.

"*He'll* stink, when he gets the saltwater in he."

"He won't, because there's not going to be any saltwater down there. I'm going to be a fair weather sailor."

An Olivetti typewriter was set up on the writing table.

"*He'll* go to rust."

A portable television set was screwed down among the bookshelves in the saloon.

"He's going to be off Land's End, sick as a pig, watching *Dallas.*"

But I wanted to coast, not to sever myself completely from the land. I wanted to keep up with whatever gossip was going. A television set was just as necessary as a suit of sails.

I put pictures up on the walls: a Rowlandson cartoon called "Pleasures of Bath," a nineteenth-century View of Damascus, a precious watercolor of Conway Castle by moonlight, framed photographs of friends and family, and another photograph, cut from a newspaper, of Margaret Thatcher in full and furious flood. With her clenched fist, her three strings of pearls, her chin thrust forward, her face cast in an expression of theatrical resoluteness under its wiry halo of swept-back hair, her eyes blazing with what might ambiguously be construed as either compassion or plain scorn, she was there as a reminder that this voyage wasn't going to be a holiday from life. She glowered down from the paneling, England's latest painted figurehead.

Books went aboard in boxfuls, and my predecessors began to look increasingly ill at ease in the company they were keeping. Hilaire Belloc was bunked up with Saul Bellow. R. T. McMullen found himself next to the poems of Louis MacNeice, and John MacGregor was squashed between Ian MacEwan's short stories and Machiavelli's *The Prince.* Everything by Evelyn Waugh, even his unreadable life of Saint Helena, was signed on for the voyage, and so were the complete works of Laurence Sterne, in the ten-volume calf-bound 1780 edition. Novels by Trollope, Thackeray and Dickens . . . poems in fat, broken-backed anthologies . . . The arrival one morning of *Valmouth* and *Prancing Nigger* by Ronald Firbank drew identical scowls from the mariners.

But it was an explorer's, not an exile's library; with books on British history, British geology, British birds, British flora, books on the making of the English countryside and on the sociology of modern Britain. I wanted to find out what, on earth or sea, made my peculiar country tick: Cobbett might yield a clue, so might Defoe—and G. M. Tre-

velyan, and Nikolaus Pevsner, and Arthur Mee, and a whole
rack of books with oppressive titles like *The Development of the
British Economy, 1914–1950, Rural Depopulation in England and
Wales, 1851–1951* and *The Labour Government's Economic Record,
1964–1970.* Even if one couldn't read them, at least they'd
serve as ballast and keep the boat sailing squarely on its
waterline.

The boat was ready on February 24. It was Ash Wednesday,
the first day of Lent—just the right moment for even a
disbeliever to take to the wilderness. High tide was at seven
in the morning and it was still almost dark when the tubby
hull was cranked down the slip into the water. It looked less
like the launching of a boat than the eccentric submersion
of a thatched tudor cottage. There was no champagne
about. The wit from the boatyard yawned, shrinking himself as far as possible into his furry parka. "Give her five
minutes, and all you'll see will be the bubbles."
    She floated. By lunchtime she was fully rigged as a work-
ing ketch, with two stocky masts, her heavy sails sagging
on their booms. Shackled to a mooring buoy in the middle
of the estuary, she turned to face the incoming tide with a
broad-beamed dowager's stateliness. It was not that she
waddled, exactly; rather that her age and bulk took auto-
matic precedence over the younger, slimmer boats on the
water.
    I rowed away from her feeling house-proud as I'd never
felt house-proud before. She looked like home. Up till now,
home had always been a rented or a mortgaged box in
someone else's freehold, an unstable affair, floating adrift
high in London plane trees. This big white boat, with her
trimmings of (as yet) unscuffed white and blue, her books
and pictures, her oak beams which had been approvingly
described by the surveyor as "massive," looked so much
more solid and steady than any of the flats in which I'd
recently capsized.
    No flag wagged at the back of her. Whatever the rules
said, I didn't intend to sail under the British ensign. When I

crossed over the border from territorial to international waters, I was going to go there as a private person—in the Greek word, an *idiot*.

The boat had one visible defect: her name. The Gosfield brewer who had originally registered her as a British ship of 10.39 Gross Tons had called her the *Gosfield Maid*. This would be a fine title for a frowsty aunt who keeps cats and smells of camphor balls, but as the name of my boat I would have been happier if the brewer had chosen *Mon Repos*, *Laburnams*, or *Dunroamin*.

It is famously unlucky to change a boat's name: you are pretty well guaranteed an early death by drowning. But it is permissible, as far as I know, to switch the letters about. Chuck GOSFIELD MAID into the air, let the pieces fall where they will, and they come out as DIE, DISMAL FOG. As mottoes for British voyages go, *Die, Dismal Fog* will do well.

CHAPTER 2

IN THE
ARCHIPELAGO

For four years now, *Gosfield Maid* has been slowly circling round the British Isles. When she first rumbled down the slipway into the Fowey Estuary, I had never taken charge of a boat at sea in my life. A retired naval commander let me play the role of an elderly midshipman, and in a fortnight taught me how to raise sails, drop anchor, steer a compass course and bleed a diesel engine. In the evenings I taught myself navigation out of books, with the watery yellow lamplight dodging all over the cabin as the boat wallowed in the wakes of passing china-clay coasters. On April Fools' Day I left Fowey alone and nervously picked my way out into the English Channel. I had hardly set my course and made my first penciled cross on the chart before the land faded into the haze. First there was Captain Mitchell's Californian ranch-style house on the hill, and the Coastguard lookout, and the striped beacon on Gribben Head; then an indecipherable gray scribble across the horizon; then just the intimidating whiteness of the blank page.

The voyage turned into the usual epical-pastoral-tragical-comical-historical-amorous and lonely story—of innocence lost, ritual tests and trials, the holy terrors, funny interludes, romances caught on the wing, lightning strikes of wisdom and dim *longueurs*. It yielded calms, storms, sunsets, fogs, mirrored landscapes, welcoming ports glistering in the twilight under auroras of blown gulls, enormous skies, waves green as jade: all the set pieces in the marine painter's repertoire.

In an unscheduled gale off the coast of Sussex, the collected works of Laurence Sterne took flight in the saloon and flapped about like doves escaping from a magician's hat: hellfire sermons colliding in midair with three panic-stricken volumes of *Tristram Shandy*, and *A Sentimental Journey* making a break for it through the galley and up into the wheelhouse. Clinging on to the wheel, too busy trying to angle the bow of the boat into the next wave to be frightened, I thought coldly that death looked as if it was definitely in the cards. There were other times when the sea was as dull and gray as an infinity of lukewarm porridge, with ports extending a welcome no friendlier than the litter of bills which always lies in wait for one behind the front door.

The difficulty with a circular voyage is that once you have gone on past your original point of departure (as *Gosfield Maid* did, a little more than a year after setting out), it has no destination and no ending—at least not until it's too late to tell the tale. It would be handy to contrive a McMullen-like finale, the helmsman a bag of bleached bones held together by a rotting pea jacket and the boat surviving to sail off into the blue. But this voyage goes on. For as long as the book continues to be written, the helmsman's still alive. However, for those who insist on traveling in a more orderly sequence and demand a strict and conventional economy of literary means, here goes—

I got drunk in Torquay, had a fit of memoirs in Portsmouth, turned lyrical in Brighton and philosophical off Beachy Head, was affronted in Dover, ill in Harwich, happy in Grimsby, maudlin in Bridlington, was pleased with myself on Holy Island, got drunk again in Leith, was superior in Inverness, fell in love in Oban and out of love by Stranraer, was at my wits' end in Dublin, said some very clever things in Fishguard, lost my temper off Land's End and summed things up pretty neatly in Falmouth. THE END.

53°47' North. 4°45' West. The spot is marked by a circled cross—our last ascertained position. Nothing could be less parochial than this navigator's way of saying where he is. He sites himself in global terms, even universal ones, measuring the angles between his ship and the equator, the sun, the stars and the hypothetical meridian which stretches north and south from Greenwich to the poles.

On that particular afternoon at that particular point on the earth's surface, the water was as calm and full of mercurial color as a pool of motor oil. Earlier on there had been a wind—a steady draught from the northeast which plumped up the sails and pushed *Gosfield Maid* south with the tide. For the sea was going my way, for once. The Irish Sea is like a shallow pudding basin: twice a day it empties and fills up, the water streaming through the narrow channels at its northern and southern ends. That afternoon it was emptying out, and the sea on which I was moving was itself moving invisibly at a comfortable two and a half knots. Riding the tide is exactly like being on a moving walkway: you have only to amble for the world to whistle past.

So when the wind died I let the sails hang in useless creases from the masts, reluctant to start the engine for fear of spoiling the afternoon. The sea was empty of shipping. I went below and made coffee in the galley. I sat out in the cockpit listening to the chuckle of the wavelets against the hull and feeling something of that pride of possession which a great landowner must feel when he looks out from his window, proprietor of everything he can see.

For the moment, at least, this sea was legally mine. In territorial waters, the most one has is a meager concession called "the right of innocent passage"; but at 53°47' N, 4°45' W, you enjoy "the freedom of high-seas navigation"—a freedom with a happy multitude of entailments. You are free-floating in your own freehold. Weather permitting (the one major snag in this otherwise ideal bargain), you have absolute freedom. Out at sea, no one can prosecute you for sedition, blasphemy, or being a public nuisance. Seeing what you like, saying what you like, sailing along on any damn-fool course you choose, you are—weather permitting —as liberated a spirit as any human being on the face of the globe, with the full weight of international maritime law to back your amazing license.

That afternoon the weather did permit. My sky was wide open, and my miles of colored water were coasting companionably alongside. Two and a half knots may not sound very fast—an old lady on a sit-up-and-beg bike could easily double that speed without running short of breath. But it is a good pace for an observant free spirit; and at two and a half knots you could encircle the earth in a year, with five days to spare.

Contentedly out of reach of any of their local laws and customs, I was floating through an archipelago of distant islands, watching their indefinite dark shapes change configuration on the horizon, and taking bearings on them each half-hour to keep a check on where I was. They wobbled, fading and sharpening, over the enlarged, reflected numbers in the compass lens. One small pointed atoll showed clearly at 158°; another, lumpier one at 232°, or maybe 234°; there was a definite smoky pimple in the sea at 046° and a smudge at about 012°. Much the biggest of the islands lay almost dead astern at 358°; a commanding mass of black alps with a shallow coastal basin littered with still-just-visible towns and cities.

For almost as long as I've been able to speak, I must have been using the phrase "The British Isles" as a careless political abstraction. I had never actually seen the British isles in life until that clear-skied afternoon in September when they arranged themselves around the boat in just as tangible and diminutive an archipelago as the Cyclades. The pointed atoll on the port beam was Mount Snowdon in Wales; the irregular lump to starboard was the Sugar Loaf Mountain in the Wicklow Hills, south of Dublin in Ireland; the pimple on the port quarter was the English Lake District topped by Scafell Pike; and the smudge (I almost swear to this) was the mountains of Galloway in Scotland. The great island astern, the continental center of things, with its magnificent bulk and all the signs of a thriving civilization, was the Isle of Man, from where I'd sailed five hours before.

The coffee had gone cold in the mug, and the motion of the boat was so slight that the surface of the coffee had crazed into a milky skin. Nothing moved except the sea itself, running like a deep river down to the ocean. I loved the breadth and stillness of it—the painted islands, the flawless wash of the sky, the winking, rainbow water. The stillness was so complete that the structural tensions of the boat itself were making themselves audible. Plank on beam; larch on oak. The woods were straining, each against the other, their acids bleeding and mingling as the sea pressed in. Not many people ever know quite such a magical solitude as this.

Then I saw that I had company. It was many miles away, as small as a gnat or a dust speck; an aircraft of some sort, flying fast and low over the water to the far south.

The weather was breaking when I came to the Isle of Man. I'd sailed down from the Clyde through the straits between Ulster and the Mull of Galloway, to find every wave in the Irish Sea snarling and baring its teeth. A thin rain was falling and there was no land to be seen anywhere. *Gosfield Maid* slammed and jolted like a country bus on a bad road. I sailed it up to where the Isle of Man should have been, and found just rain and lumpy sea and untidy rags of foam. The island was not where it was marked on the chart. Either that, or I wasn't where *I* was marked on the chart. I checked and rechecked my last bearings. Nothing seemed wrong. I hunted with binoculars for a lighthouse or a cliff or the white water of a coastal shoal, and drew a monotonous greeny-gray blank.

As islands nearly always do, the Isle of Man came up unexpectedly, in the wrong place. It was steaming straight past my bows like a rusty ship, and I half expected it to disappear again into the murk, flying a disreputable flag of convenience from its stern. I slid along its side where the water was calmer, grateful for the shelter it offered but not much impressed by the vessel itself. Only a very tired sea gull would have brightened at the sight of its dank green-stone cliffs, the dripping ledges of bare rock, the heather looking like a black fungus in the rain. A castle came and went—but after Scotland I was tired of castles. Then a dismal holiday place with an empty beach and a line of boardinghouses on a promenade.

At the southern end of the island there was an islet which looked even sadder and rainier than its parent; and between Man and the Calf of Man there was a narrrow channel, no wider than a city street, through which the tide was stream-ing like a millrace, the water humped and broken, piling against boulders, creaming white as it thundered through the Sound. What was oddest about this place, though, was that I could see the sea beyond and it was definitely *lower* than the sea on which I was afloat. Calf Sound was a hill of water, a chute through which one half of the Irish Sea was doing its damnedest to fill up the other.

I had been bored before; the life of Man had struck me as being solitary, poor, nasty, brutish and mercifully, after only fifteen miles of it, short. But this was one of the most unboring performances that I'd ever seen the sea put up. I called the Manx coastguard over the radio and described Calf Sound to him in all its glory.

"And it's safe to go *through* there?"

"Stick to the middle of the channel. Keep the beacon to starboard and Thousla Rock to port."

"It's all white water."

"You've got about twenty meters under you all the way through."

Half a mile off, I poured myself a slug of whisky. Two hundreds yards from the beacon I needed another. I fed the boat into the race with the engine growling underfoot.

Bloody maniac. What you doing? Cocksure bastard. Trying to kill us? Proving something? Watch it, boyo. Bloody watch it.

The current wrenched at the rudder and the short steep waves did their best to climb on board over the bows. The beacon shot past the wheelhouse like a lamppost on a motorway, no sooner seen than overtaken. The boat was being poured down the gradient of the Sound; all I had to do was keep it pointed roughly in the right direction while the sea gathered us up and tossed us out at the other end.

The whole dizzying business took a minute at the most; and the water beyond the Sound was almost as impressively mysterious as the water in it. Shielded by steep headlands on either side, it was as still and black as a monastery fishpond. It deserved lily pads and dragonflies and the occasional bursting bubble released by a rootling carp. Its broodily calm surface was gritted with raindrops. On a ledge of rock on the Calf of Man side, five gray seals squatted on their hunkers. Sleek, big-eyed, lugubriously mustached, they had the air of a cabinet of Edwardian politicians as drawn by Max Beerbohm. When I shut off the engine, I could hear them making rude parliamentary noises.

I had meant to skip the Isle of Man and head straight on for Wales. It was getting late in the year, and I was running out of time and weather. But Calf Sound and the pool under Spanish Head made me stop, just long enough to take stock of the pleasure I'd had in that queer place. I nursed the boat through an easy sea round to the fishing harbor of port St. Mary on the southeast of the island, where I tied up to the quay and grounded with the tide. Next morning a gale was blowing and even the fishing fleet was weatherbound, huddled together in the lee of the outer breakwater as the sea feathered and plumed over the esplanade. For two weeks, whenever there was a lull in the wind the fog came down, and whenever the fog lifted the wind blew up. Stranded (if not quite like Crusoe) on the island, I had to make the most of the little world of Man.

Once, twice, three times. The aircraft was quartering the entire sea. Every twenty minutes or so I saw it flying west to Ireland, then east back to Wales, and coming nearer all the time. On this run it was heading straight for *Gosfield Maid*, its black shadow racing across the sea like the track of a submerged whale. It was a big RAF Nimrod, with a kind of glass conservatory up in the front. As it came over, its engines drummed in my back teeth and made the water crackle. It banked and encircled me with a stockade of solid noise, flying so low that I could see faces in its windows, but couldn't make out their expressions. I stood in the cockpit and waved as cheerily as I could. *I'm innocent. I'm just enjoying the freedom of high-seas navigation.* No one waved back. The huge gray wings tilted again and the plane went on toward Ireland; but the self-contained peace of the boat on the water had been shattered like an expensive vase, and I mourned its loss.

The castellated stone hotel on the hill above Port St. Mary smelled of empty rooms, of stale vegetables and disinfectant, like a boarding school closed for the holidays with only Matron and a couple of bachelor masters in residence. The tourist season had gone badly. The people from the industrial cities of northern England who had used to come to the Isle of Man in swarming boatloads every year were now going to places with a more reliable ration of sunshine, like Ibiza and Majorca and the Costa del Sol; and the locals had the hotel bar more or less to themselves. There were the local butcher, the local dentist, in a threadbare crested blazer, a smallholder and a lobster-and-scallop fisherman, freshly tanned from his own holiday in the Canary Islands. These men all appeared to be somehow related to each other, and they all spoke in the same accent. It wasn't Welsh, although it had a distinct Welsh lilt; it wasn't Lancashire, although it had Lancashire's nasality and flat vowels; and it wasn't Irish, although it had the thickness of a brogue and the Irish way of saying *d* for *th*.

"Auntie went to Douglas on the train," the butcher said, breaking a long silence with an interesting fact.

Anti wint ta Dooglus on di treen.

It was delivered in a series of tom-tom beats or sixteenth notes, as if the butcher were reciting the last line of a chorus of a popular song.

Ań-tĭ-wĭnt-tă-Dóo-glŭs-ŏn-dĭ-tréen.

Or, set to music:

Indeed, to my ears the whole conversation seemed to be all tune and no content. The men might just as well have been birds in a wood; and I had no idea whether these pleasant bursts of sound were alarm signals, mating calls, or what.

The proprietor was an exiled Englishman: florid, friendly and slow-moving, he had the unsettled-down face of an adolescent boy. He'd been a wartime naval officer, which explained the brass ship's bell behind the bar and the big tidal clock whose needle pointed at High Tide when it was in fact just coming up past Low Water. After the war he'd had a job in Essex, then run a pub in Wales; in the Isle of Man he had at last found a happy niche for himself—a place where a Lieutenant RNVR, vintage 1921, could come decently home to roost.

"We're thirty years behind the times here," he said, putting a superfluous sparkle into the glass he was drying. "And we mean to keep it that way."

The thrushes were singing at the far end of the bar. *Dooglus. Frocks. Ida. Spoods. Queenies.* The picture window looked out over a gully of pines and tamarisk leading down to a deserted cove where the sea was foaming over rocks. The proprietor assured me that what I was seeing was a New Eden. There was no crime and little income tax. Your daughter could walk alone at night without fear of molestation. There was the Youth Orchestra for culture, and the Gulf Stream for warm winters. There were Manx Shearwaters, if I liked birds. There were—oh, a hundred and one things that made the Island the best place on earth. The proprietor was himself standing for elective office, as a town councillor or village selectman, in this paradise.

"On what platform?"

"As an Independent. We don't need a Conservative Party here. Everyone's more conservative than the Conservatives. If Mrs. Thatcher came to the Island, she'd be thought too ruddy left-wing by half."

Gazing down at the empty cove, the overgrown cliff walk, the ruined jetty in the rocks, I could see one conspicuous serpent in the proprietor's garden.

"You've lost your tourist trade, though."

"Oh, it's been a bit off this year. Goes up and down, you know. There's a guest here now."

To substantiate the proprietor's veracity, the hotel's solitary guest came out to the dining room and sat at my end of the bar, where he ordered a Bacardi-and-Coke. His crushed gray suit looked as if it were in the habit of making flights, in Executive Class, all on its own; although the evening was hardly even warm, the knot of his Playboy Club tie had been wrenched down from his neck, like the ties of reporters in American movies.

"Here on business?" he said.

"Sort of," I said.

"Super place," he said wanly. "Smashing," and sipped his Bacardi-and-Coke. "Wish I could spend longer here." Saying the words prompted him to consult his watch. It was the sort of watch that one was meant to notice: people who care about Rolex Oysters and Patek Philippes would have acknowledged it with a nod. I knew the names, but couldn't fit them to their faces.

He was staying on the Island overnight to see an accountant and launder some money. He had a company here—"a useful dodge," he said. He had rented a car at the airport and was planning to drive to Douglas and spend the rest of the evening at the casino there. "Come along for the jolly, if you like."

"Sure," I said. "Thanks." I had always enjoyed the mixture of adrenaline and despair which goes with trying to Pelmanize your number to come up; it had been years since I had sat up till dawn at Monte Carlo or the Venice Lido listening to the rattlesnake *tick-tickety-tick* of an ivory ball bouncing from compartment to compartment of a roulette wheel. The prospect of doing so in Douglas, Isle of Man, made the gale warnings on the wireless easier to bear.

We took to the road, where I was intrigued by the sparse traffic. Elderly Ford Populars, like black sedan chairs, were still going here, at a breakneck twenty-five miles an hour. There were Morris Minors, their paintwork waxed and polished down almost to bare metal, of the model that I remembered district nurses driving in England in my childhood. Every so often a new gray Daimler or Mercedes, far too big for these narrow lanes, came stalking through the greenery. As we squeezed past, window to window with the gleaming fatties, our nearside wheels deep in a hedge, my companion remarked on the obvious.

"Tax exile," he said, in a voice that was oddly censorious for a man who went in for useful dodges of his own.

"What's your company called?" I asked.

"My company? Oh . . . Stepma Securities Offshore (I.O.M.) Ltd.," he said, trying to throw the name away fast. But it wasn't a name that took kindly to being thrown away.

"Whose stepmother? Yours?"

"*Stepmar.* With an *r.*" Rabbits scarpered away from us up the lane ahead in cowardly contrast to the impudent bunny ears of Stepmar's Playboy Club tie. "Stephen and Margaret. My ex. Had to buy her out, of course, after the divorce. Cost a bomb. You married?"

"I was once."

We stopped at a level crossing and waited for a bright green train to go by on the miniature railway, its heavy rolls of steam flattened by the building wind.

"Anyone can land an idea on the beach," said the offshore company. "The problem is to get it off."

"What?"

"Sorry. Just thinking."

The landscape was full of things that I couldn't remember

seeing since my childhood—steam trains, old cars, squads of butterflies, deep tangled hedgerows full of wildflowers. Beatrix Potter rabbits. We turned a corner into a darkening woody dell and crossed a small stone bridge.

"Hello, Fairies!" Stepmar said, then looked considerably embarrassed. "Fairy Bridge. You're supposed to—ah—always say hello to the fairies. They're all superstitious as hell round here. By the way. Important tip. Never mention r-a-t-s. That can cause real trouble. Always call them "long-tails" if you have to."

"Are there a lot of ra—"

"Shh!" He accelerated away from the spot where I'd said the word. "Rented cars. They've always got their systems clogged. You've got to give them a good blow-through with the gas. Yes, actually. Place is swarming with long-tails. They're bigger than the cats."

The country we were passing through was doing something funny to my sense of time and space. Each village was separated from the next by wild tracts of moorland and mountains; but a whole Dartmoor or Peak District would come and go within sixty seconds or so, and the mountains, impressively rocky and barren, were just a few hundred feet high, no more than hummocks, really. They made the sheep that grazed on them look as big as shire horses, and modest, private peat diggings at the sides of the road had the air of major industrial excavations. The villages themselves had the same stunted and foreshortened quality: cinder-block bungalows mucked in with squat stone cottages roofed in slate. Little houses, little gardens, little farms, little mountains, little towns . . . everything looked squashed and Lilliputian. Then, just occasionally, something genuinely huge would happen: a transplanted Tuscan villa with shabby palms showing over its high walls and electronic eyes guarding its wrought-iron gates; a giant slice of Mexican adobe, with twin Mercedeses left askew in the driveway; a bungalow, monstrously swollen to the size of a Texan ranch, its bilious green floodlights beating the sunset at its own game. These excessive Brobdignagians towered over the surrounding countryside, making the mountains shrink and the moorlands pucker into poorly kept suburban lawns.

One by one, Stepmar ticked the giants off his list. "Tax exile . . . tax exile . . . tax exile . . . tax exile . . . I bet the buggers are bored out of their skulls."

"I thought you liked the Island."

"Oh, it's all right. For the odd overnight, you know. But you wouldn't catch me living here, hell's bells. You been to L.A.?"

"Yes."

"Great place. Fantastic. Beverly Wilshire. Sunset Boulevard. Hollywood Bowl. Rodeo Drive. I played a hole in L.A. back in June. It was a steal."

It was nearly dark when we reached Douglas, twenty minutes away from Port St. Mary, but a twenty minutes in which we appeared to have covered several hundred miles. The casino was not quite like the ones at Venice and Monte Carlo. Instead of champagne and anisette there were mugs of draft beer. Instead of a palm-court orchestra, there was a rather faded tape of Sandy MacPherson at the Blackpool Theatre Organ on the Muzak system. There were no contessas, no gigolos, no Saudi princelings, no fidgety Dostoevskian neurotics marking cards and working out their beat-the-bank combinations. There were some fat ladies in Bri-Nylon prints, with churning laughs like concrete mixers'; some bored traveling salesmen; a few holidaying dads, out on the lam for the night away from their boardinghouse-bound wives and kids. Much the most exciting thing about the roulette table was the way one's money was changed into chips, in yet another vertiginous loop-back in time. For the Douglas casino was still using currency that had gone out of date twenty years ago: for twelve and a half pence you bought a chip marked 2/6d, for fifty pence you got one marked 10/− . These scratched and grubby wafers of old plastic had survived decimalization, inflation, deflation, revaluation, incomes policies, sterling crises, the one-dollar pound, Hayek, Keynes, Friedman and the Gnomes of Zurich. The Douglas casino was sticking to the Gold Standard.

I bet on the numbers in my birthday and the hours and minutes of High Water, Liverpool, and lost £7/2/6d. Stepmar Securities Offshore (I.O.M.) Ltd. cannily staked out the table in blocks of four, and, judging by the height of his stack of chips, it looked as if he were well past the hundred-guinea mark. Scooping up his winnings, he went off to invest them at the blackjack table. I kept my place, drinking warm beer and listening to Sandy MacPherson playing something that should have been sung by Vera Lynn.

We left at eleven, far into the small hours, Douglas-time. Stepmar's face was shining like a ripe cheese. "It was straight down the fairway for me," he said. "How did you do?"

"I got into the rough," I said.

"Oh, well," he said, "win some, lose some," as if the phrase were his own mint coinage.

On the outskirts of Douglas, a couple of hundred yards from its center, the car headlights picked out a flapping *Examiner* poster: *Fire Brigade in Peel Cat Rescue Drama.*

With its miniature railways, its miniature roads, its miniature landscape and its miniature news, it was clear that the Isle of Man was not so much itself as a scale model of something bigger.

Ten minutes later, after we'd passed a few mountains in the dark, Stepmar said hello to the fairies again, and I croaked "Hello, Fairies" too. If you can't beat 'em, join 'em, I thought, in Stepmar's voice, as we scared hell out of the rabbits, racing through Toyland.

The Nimrod aircraft was out of sight somewhere off the coast of Ireland when I heard the radio in the wheelhouse talking to me.

"*Gosforth Maid, Gosforth Maid, Gosforth Maid,* this is Holyhead Coastguard, over—"

"*Field,*" I said. "*Gosfield.* Golf Oscar Sierra Foxtrot India Echo Lima Delta."

The aircraft had reported my position to the Coastguard. Serious news followed. A fishing boat, the *South*

Stack, had gone missing after failing to return to Holyhead Harbour the previous day. I was to look out for evidence of a vessel 42 feet long, with a wheelhouse forward, red hull, white upper parts and gantry mast. Three men were on board. A close watch should be kept on the water for fragments of wreckage, lifebuoys, a diesel slick, or any other sad clue as to what might have happened. All other craft in the area were being similarly contacted.

The Irish Sea is, as Seas go, small, shallow and parochial. It responds, as parochial places do, to any news or change with the rapidity of a village. When a gale blows up, the Irish Sea turns instantly to whipped cream; when the wind dies, it goes flat in an hour. Its capacity for springing violence on one without warning is notorious, and charts of the Irish Sea are thick with the double daggers that mark lost ships. It is a dangerous, quirky, fast and malignant piece of water.

Yet on today of all days . . . On this oily sea, which was now collecting the crimsons and golds of sunset . . . The idea of the *South Stack* being "lost" in this still, idyllic lake was difficult to grasp. There must be a mistake somewhere. No doubt the crew, enjoying themselves on the water much as I was doing myself, had lost track of time and were quietly trawling, and knocking back cans of lager, in some pretty, un-Nimroded part of the pool.

I kept a close lookout. I saw a fleet of purple jellyfish sail past like tasseled lampshades. I saw some seaweed. I saw a bit of granulated polystyrene packing bob past my stern. But no lifebuoys, no wreckage, no trace of the *South Stack.*

There was plenty of wreckage in the dusty antiques shop in Peel—cracked china souvenirs from Blackpool and Southport, floral chamber pots, dreadfully oxidized daubs of boats at sea, a vintage spin-dryer, fishing rods, Brownie box cameras, cardboard boxes full of old copies of *Woman's Own* and *Picture Post,* two hat racks, a crate of tarnished silverware, a ship in a bottle, a Utility dining table plus three chairs to match, and a lot of shelves of disowned books. I

was browsing in the Poetry section, through ink-stained
school editions of Tennyson and Shelley and sepia-
inscribed, morocco-bound editions of Elizabeth Barrett
Browning's *Sonnets from the Portuguese*. The owner of the shop,
looking himself like a premature antique, was watching me
from behind his littered desk.

"You know T. E. Brown?"

"No, I don't," I said, thinking that he must be mistaking
me for someone else.

"You see—we're a roughish set of chaps," he said. I
looked at him with interest. I would have said that he was
long-boned, molting, bespectacled, shabby-suited, but
hardly "roughish" by any standards.

"That's brought up rough on our mammies' laps—" He
was, I realized, quoting, and not apologizing at all.

"And we grow, and we run about shoutin' and foolin' till
we gets to be lumps and fit for the schoolin'. Then we gets
to know the marks and the signs, and we leaves the school,
and we sticks to the lines, baitin' and settin' and haulin' and
that, till we know every fish from a whale to a sprat. And
we gets big and strong, for it do make you stronger to row
a big boat, and pull at a conger. Then what with a cobblin'
up of the yawl, and a patchin' and mendin' the nets for the
trawl, and a risin' early and a goin' to bed late, and a dramin'
of scollops as big as a plate, and the hooks and the creels
and the oars and the gut, you'd say there's no room for a
little slut. But howsomever it's not the case, and a pretty
face is a pretty face; and through the whole coil, as bright
as a star, a gel slips in, and there you are!"

"Wow—."

"T. E. Brown," he said. "The Laureate of Man. Great
Writer. There's a 'Collected' there you can have for two
pounds. It says two pounds fifty in the front, but I'll let you
have it for two pounds, seeing it's Friday. Well, that was
just the way with me and the gel I'm speaking of—Betsy
Lee."

Dazzled by the man's salesmanship, I bought the "Collected" Brown along with a 1785 Church of Ireland Prayer
Book and took them back by bus to the boat. I read Brown's

Fo'c's'le Yarns—immense dialect poems, as long as novels—
in the fo'c's'le, with the oil lamps winking and the tide lifting
the boat slowly up the quay wall. The same quick, tinny,
musical Manx voice which I kept on hearing in snatches
through the open porthole came ringing off the page.

> What was I sayin' aw yes! *the fire;*
> And what could he do? and he *wasn' wire,*
> *Nor nails,* he said: and how he'd kep'
> Out of her road; and the hold and the grip
> There was at him reglar: and allis out
> After the lines, and knockin' about
> With the gun, and tryin' to clear his head
> And studdy hisself . . .

Was I reading this, or was this just Mrs. Quillin talking to
Terry Kelly beyond the window? It was hard to tell.

Brown's poems are obsessively insular. Douglas Pier rep-
resents the limit of the known world. Saturated in the names
of local people (Quillins, Cains, Kerruishes, Kermodes,
Skillicorns and Christians) and local places (Bradda, Bal-
laugh, Thousla, Ballacraine, Calf and Ayre), they insist on
the global self-sufficiency of Man. If an experience lies outside the range of the scallop fisherman, the parson, the
draper, the miller's daughter, then it isn't an experience
worth having. "For mine own people do I sing," Brown
wrote, "And use the old familiar speech"—a speech that by
definition excluded all formal culture, all politics except
those of the parish pump, all ideas. In his address to "The
Future Manx Poet," Brown hopefully instructed his heir:

> Be nervous, soaked
> In dialect colloquial, retaining
> The native accent pure, unchoked
> With cockney balderdash.

In Brown's narrow world, anything English, let alone intel-
lectual or speculative, was cockney balderdash, to be despised long before it be understood.

The poems didn't plod. Brown had a wonderful ear for the rhythms of the local talk, and he wrote with absolute conviction about what it felt like to be out in a gale in a scallop boat or crouched in a stone cottage in front of a smoky peat fire. Yet reading them, I felt suffocated—and attacked. The dialect served as much to keep outsiders out as to include the insiders in its cozy circle; it told the foreign reader that he was an ignorant trespasser. There was a great deal of aggression in Brown's sweet-sounding home-liness, a sense of grievance and affront at the larger world for the way it treated Man as small.

Brown told his Future Manx Poet:

> Come, some soon, or else we slide
> To lawlessness, or deep-sea English soundings,
> Absorbent, final, in the tide
> Of Empire lost, from homely old surroundings,
> Familiar, swept . . .

In another poem, he saw "the coming age/Lost in the em-pire's mass." England was Man's mortal enemy, an imperial monster in whose maw everything that was Manx would be crushed and consumed; in this respect, Brown was standing shoulder to shoulder with all the Scots, Welsh, Irish, In-dian, American and African writers who have struggled against England's stifling colonial weight.

Yet there was a false note somewhere in Brown's protes-tations. For one thing, he wasn't himself a "roughish" sort of chap: he took a degree at Oxford, then spent a lifetime teaching at an English public school, Clifton College, where my own grandfather must have been one of his pupils in the early 1890s. I felt cheated at finding this out. Who was this comfortably off, expensively educated man, living in a very handsome Georgian quarter of Bristol, to shove my Englishness in my face and make me feel guilty for not being a weasel-browed Manx fisherman?

The Manx themselves loved Brown, though. He was still quoted, and not just by secondhand booksellers. Whenever I mentioned his name and said I'd been reading him, I was met by another torrent of dialect lines. I heard everyone's favorite bits—of "Betsy Lee," "Tommy Big-Eyes," "The Doctor," "The Manx Witch," "Kitty of the Sherragh Vane," "Mary Quayle" and "Job the White." People could recite whole pages at a time. They stood in pubs and in their front rooms, and even in the heartily philistine setting of the Isle of Man Yacht Club: they put their hands in their pockets if they were men, or clasped them in front of their waists if they were women, they stuck their chests out, and then they started. They produced swathes and reams and yards and bolts of Brown, with his hop-hoppity-hop meter and the rhymes chiming like a concatenation of two-tone door-bells.

> Thursday—that's yesterday—Nicky Freel
> Brings the captain's yacht from Peel,
> And anchors her inside the bay;
> And there she was lyin' the whole of the day.
> At six o'clock this evenin'
> This young pesson isn' in—
> Nither's the Captain—can't be found—
> And then, wherever she was bound,
> This yacht they're callin' the *Waterwitch*
> Is off to sea with every stitch—
> And a woman aboord. —Well, it's nathral rather,
> And, puttin' two and two together,
> It isn' cuttin' it very fine
> To think this woman is Ellen Quine—

I had T. E. Brown coming out of my ears. He was a national institution. The Bristol schoolmaster had managed to find a voice which embodied all of Man's insular pride and all its insular sense of grievance and slight. Listening to his verse, with its nostalgia for old days and folk ways, its foursquare localness, its constant undercurrent of xenopho-bia, I thought that T. E. Brown, who had won the hearts of the Isle of Man in the 1880s, might be just the poet for Britain at large in the late twentieth century.

The sea was black, shiny, creased, like the bombazine of a Victorian mourning frock. There was no further news of the *South Stack*. At least, there was no further news of the lost boat, but I was being continually reminded of it by the single flash, every ten seconds, of the South Stack lighthouse, ten miles away to the east. At this distance it was tricky to pick out—no more vivid than the flaring of a match seen across a valley on a clear night. I was trying to take regular compass bearings on it, and kept on losing it in the crowd of starlights on the water.

There were other lights too. At night the sea always seems more populous than it does by day. As your eyes get used to the darkness, you see that you're not nearly so alone as you thought. Trawlers, hard at work under the horizon, show as a sparky *ignis fatuus* of reds and greens. Trinity House puts on its great free firework show of lightships, buoys and lighthouses, every one chattering in the dark in its own code. Counting off the seconds—*a-hundred-and-one; a-hundred-and-two; a-hundred-and-three*—you figure out who they are. The quick double wink every ten seconds is the Skerries; the lazy brushstroke of light painting itself on the water every ten seconds is Point Lynas; the quintuple blip-blip-blip-blip-blip, fast as morse, every fifteen seconds, is Bardsey Island. When you're alone at sea in the nightmare hours, these marvels are as profoundly comforting as the nursery rushlight burning on the table beside the child's cot.

At eleven o'clock I watched the Holyhead–Dublin ferry pass astern of me; a complete floating city, eerily sweeping across the horizon at twenty knots, making the sea around it blaze. I thought I could hear jazz bands playing, corks popping, the late-night crowd whooping it up; but that must have been a sea delusion, since the ship was at least seven miles off.

My own navigation lamps were all cunningly shielded from me, to avoid blinding the helmsman, and the only visible thing on *Gosfield Maid* was a weak pinprick of light shining on the compass heading. Numbers were sluggishly

stirring in their bowl of paraffin: 185 . . . 190 . . . 180
. . . 185. As long as the boat was kept pointing in a roughly
southerly direction, the course was fine by me. I left it in
the charge of the autopilot and went downstairs to make a
supper of tinned soup, cheap claret and a loaf of fresh Manx
bread.

I lit the oil lamps in the saloon and stood blinking in the
sudden flood of light, the momentary oddity of finding
one's old books and pictures, the unanswered letters from
the Inland Revenue, yesterday's paper with its half-done
crossword down here, literally *in* the sea. Up on deck, or in
the wheelhouse, a boat seems a perfectly reasonable sort of
vehicle for moving around the world in; it is when you go
below that you feel its improbable frailty—a whole household and economy sustained, high over the seabed, on a
skin of water. As foundations for homes go, inch-thick
planks of larch, held on by nails, with hanks of oakum
hammered into the cracks between them, have little reassuring solidity about them. And the sea is so noisily close-
to. Even in a dead calm, it mutters into the wood at one's
ear, like an anonymous caller on a telephone.

*You awake? What are you wearing? Let me guess, now, if you've
got a nightie on.*

But everything's in place: the books on their shelves, the
pictures on the walls, the sheepskin rug on the floor. The
floating room smells of potpourri, tobacco smoke and lav-
ender furniture polish. It's all right.

I turned on the radio. It was the cocoa-and-biscuits hour
on the BBC, an actor reading *A Book at Bedtime*—something
about an Indian guru in suburban Sussex sometime in the
1920s. . . . I didn't listen very closely, but the actor's
plummy bedtime voice was soothing. On the early-evening
news there had been a mention, fairly low down in the
bulletin, of an "air and sea search for a trawler reported
missing in the Irish Sea"; but by the midnight news the item
had been dropped. London journalists evidently didn't think
missing trawlers worth mentioning more than once.

The chief business of Man had always been smuggling. An offshore island with a lot of rock, a few small plots of fertile soil, some thin veins of lead and tin in the hills and a modest annual harvest of shellfish and herrings has one resource left to exploit—its own insularity. The tax differentials between the island and the mainland were infinitely more profitable to the islanders than lobster potting or digging holes in the ground. The Manx fishing boats ferried illicit cargoes of tea and brandy and every other dutiable luxury over the forty sea miles to England.

The economy of the Island still worked on exactly the same principle, even if the means was less romantic than the one-gun luggers on moonlit nights, with cloaked men on the beach guiding them in with storm lanterns. Income tax on the Island was a flat 20 percent; income tax on the mainland was—I cannot bear to spell out the figures of income tax on the mainland. So the Manx were busy making money out of the difference, just as they had used to make money out of the two-and-sixpenny English duty on tea.

They trawled for English millionaires. They also fished, more easily and profitably, for Englishmen with company pensions and tidy nest eggs who wanted to hang on to as much as they could of their ten and fifteen thousands a year. Athol Street in Douglas—a hundred yards or so of seaside stucco and a bad place in a wind—was a smugglers' cove of tin-pot banks, off-the-peg companies, avoidance schemes and useful dodges. It was Stepmar country: the source of innumerable good wheezes . . . loans, investments, savings and pension plans, all done on the cheap, all, in the smugglers' favorite smooth phrase, "tax-advantageous."

The smugglers themselves looked the way chartered accountants do everywhere: they wore colored golf socks and thick spectacles, they went to the barbers' once a fortnight, and were shyly boastful about their handicaps after hours in the bar of the Admiral House on the promenade. Athol Street was the Douglas version of Wall Street and the City, though its brevity, its louche offshore tackiness, its cracked plaster and its pervading smell of cotton candy and fish and chips, gave it a more amiable air than the forbidding financial centers of London and New York.

Athol Street was the economic base on which a gimcrack cultural superstructure had been erected. The trouble was that for the exiles there was not a great deal to actually do on the Isle of Man. Having husbanded their precious money, they were faced with the question of what on earth to spend the stuff on. They went in for house extensions and kept a more or less permanent retinue of Manx builders, as their Edwardian villas sprouted glass gazebos, indoor swimming pools, solar panels, covered patios, brick courtyards, ornamental arches and empty guest quarters. They went to see the Grumbleweeds at the Gaiety Theatre, followed by dinner at Boncompte's (which was pronounced, with insular distrust of foreign ways, "Buncumpty's"). They wrote letters (such long letters!), they phoned long distance, they trained roses and they made Wills.

At the Isle of Man Yacht Club at Sunday lunchtime I met a desolate architect who had made his killing on the mainland and come to the Island five years before.

"It's not worth the candle," he said. "I tell you this . . ." He took a long preparatory swill from his double-Scotch-and-a-splash; a determined monologuist fueling up for a good story. "You should be here in the winter. You can count yourself lucky if you ever see daylight, then. It's the foggiest, windiest, rainiest place in the universe. No social life. Nothing. In the week, the only person I ever get to talk to is the wife, and she stopped listening long ago. You know what she does? She spends half her life writing off for catalogues of kitchenware . . . mixers and whiskers and food processors and stuff like that . . . then she spends the other half reading the bloody things. Reading catalogues! She's probably doing it now. They come by every post. The kitchen's jammed solid with machinery. She never uses it. And she goes on sending away for these catalogues; reads them aloud, too, right down to the voltage specifications. If you ever want the *Which* guide to food processors, I'm your man. What's in that glass?"

He sucked over his miseries like a man chewing green olives and spitting out the stones.

"Don't talk to me about the locals. They're as tight as clams. In five years I've never been inside a Manxman's house except to settle a bill."

"Why don't you go back to England?"

"What's the point? Sooner of later the Socialists will get in, and then where will you be? Out of the frying pan, into the fire."

Finally he played his trump. "You know the best thing about this island? What I look forward to most every week?" He waited, staring me down.

"No."

"*This*," he said with an elated glower. He took in the yachtsmen and their wives, the comfortable jokes from which he was excluded, the burgees pinned up around the bar, the cups and ship models, the antique chart of the Irish Sea. "It's a twenty-mile drive. Takes an hour—more if there's a fog, and you're lucky if you don't run over a sheep on the way. High spot of the week. Sunday drinks at the Yacht Club. And I don't even sail. What do you make of that? Not much, and nor do I."

It seemed needless to point out that he appeared to be perfectly content in his misery. He was beaming with the pleasure of it. I could imagine the sort of buildings he designed—gloomy towers in which he stacked people in their cells like bees.

"Look at that fog," he said happily. "By this evening you won't be able to see your hand in front of your face. You'll probably be here for the winter. You'll hate it. But just think of the tax you'll save. What's in that glass?"

Life in exile revolved around the island charities. There were funds for blindness, heart disease, leukemia, cancer, cystic fibrosis, arthritis, muscular dystrophy, mental handicap, physical handicap, and several afflictions that were quite new to me. Every fund produced its own dinners, dances and concerts—a dizzy Season, which ran from September to March and whirled gaily from disease to disease. I was given a ticket for a dinner and fashion show at the Castle Mona Hotel in aid of cirrhosis, or piles, or manic depression, or emphysema—even at the time I was unclear about what it was that we had all come to support in our dinner jackets and ball gowns, with the hotel driveway packed solid with smart cars.

We ate prawn cocktails, then limp chicken croquettes and frozen peas. Our voices were English, with not a Manx accent in the room except for the waitresses who were going round saying "French-fries or sauté?". We talked about house prices, and how it was a bad time to sell up; about plumbers, and how good ones were in terribly short supply; about the spread of osmosis in the hulls of fiberglass yachts.

Here I saw my chance. I suggested that a new charity be established called the Osmosis Fund. Every year there could be an Osmosis Day, with collecting boxes on every corner . . . vast amounts of money could be raised . . . huge dinners could be had . . . Hardly anyone would know what Osmosis was, but everyone hearing the name would be sure that it was contagious and fatal. It would be the ideal island charity.

One woman did laugh, but she stopped when she realized that her encouraging giggle was turning her into an object of severe attention by her neighbors. I concentrated on the remains of my potatoes, having failed to make my mark on Society.

After dinner everyone trailed through into the Ballroom for the fashion show. There were balloon glasses of brandy for the men and sweet liqueurs for the ladies. The Governor of the Island, a retired admiral, passed through us, nodding, as if he were still on his flagship at a Sunday parade. There was a long hiccup in the fashion arrangements; we were deep into our second brandies, and the conversation was taking some desperate turns, before at last a few women began to walk round the room in a ring, wearing cashmere, frozen smiles and crêpe de Chine. After each solitary circuit of the floor, there was a burst of clapping. The applause was not so much for the dresses as for the audacity of someone's wife or someone's daughter as she braved the public eye. The amateur models were being jolly good sports.

"Doesn't Cynthia look *marvelous*."

"Yes, and she's got such nice *feet*."

"Oh, now, *that* I do like."

"Of course, Margot has the shoulders for it."

I was out of my depth at the charity dinner and fashion show. Picking my way barefoot, my socks stuck into the pockets of my dinner jacket, my shoes tied round my neck, down a quayside ladder slippery with seaweed to the boat, I hoped that no real Manxmen were around to witness this ignominious descent from exiledom.

Between the exiles and the islanders there was a line which was only a little more indefinite and less exclusive than a color bar, and the islanders kept this line vigilantly guarded and patrolled. The ideal way of sustaining the line would have been by speaking in Manx, a Celtic language which had died early in the nineteenth century. Condemned to speaking in English, like the exiles, the islanders had to make do with their curious and impossible-to-imitate accent, together with a handful of phrases designed to underscore the ineradicable difference between themselves and their English houseguests. They called the exiles "comeovers." The place from which the comeovers had come was never named directly: England was "Across," while the Isle of Man was always spoken of simply as "The Island," as if there were no other.

In insular eyes, there was no more vicious trait than to "get above yourself"; and the comeovers had all got above themselves with a vengeance. The Manx saw it as their moral duty to cut the comeovers down to size. Their fancy architecture was ridiculed by the Manxmen who were even now putting it up for them.

" 'I want a pergola,' he says. I says, 'Well, you can have your purr-goal-ah, then, but don't blame me when bloody thing comes crashing down in first wee gale of wind.' "

On a famous racehorse owner:

"He likes his self—I'll say that for him."

On a famous novelist:

"He's got a fair bit of cheek to him."

On a self-made industrialist:

"He's an uppity little bugger and all."

Comeovers. Comeuppances. The Manx attitude toward the English, on whom they unwillingly depended as a client state, was neatly put in T. E. Brown's "Job the White," where Job, speaking of English women, might just as well have been talking about men too:

> Aw, drat the lot! these English swells,
> Women they're not, nor nither gels,
> But stuck-up Madams, and their airs and their cranks—
> Women! Women! Give me the Manx!

All grasp of hard reality, all common sense, all serious knowledge worth the knowing (about winds and weather, the migratory patterns of the scallop and who was related to whom and how) resided with the Manx. When they came to define their own national identity, though, they did so in entirely negative terms. What was so wonderful about being Manx? The Manx did not get above themselves.

In a fortnight of knocking about bars on the Island, I heard the same story three times. Each time it was told slightly differently and set in a different location, but in essence it was the same—a cogent, and depressing, statement of what it means to be an islander.

The scene is the quay at Peel, or Port Erin, or Laxey. A fisherman has just unloaded from his boat a shallow bucket full of crabs. All round the edge of the bucket the crabs are showing their claws and trying to scramble out. A comeover approaches the fisherman and tells him that he ought to get a bigger, taller bucket or he'll lose half his crabs.

"Nay," the fisherman says. "Them's all right. Them's Manx crabs. As soon as one gets his leg cocked over the edge of bucket, t'others all gang together and drag him down again."

The story always ended in a wheezy burst of self-congratulatory laughter. To tell it at all was to demonstrate that you were a cynical Manx realist. It was a fine and flexible story. You could use it indiscriminately against Manxmen who talked about leaving the Island and going

Across, against comeovers, against anyone who got ideas
above his station, against anyone vain and ambitious
enough to pursue an ideal of excellence which wasn't recognized by the Island. The story in itself constituted a first-
class argument for staying put and saying nowt. Either that,
or be thought pretentious by the gang and get dragged back
into the bucket. The tellers of the story always happily
identified themselves with the gang.

It was a comeover who told me that she disliked the
Manx because they were so "provincial." She was quite
wrong. The Manx were not in the least provincial; they
were profoundly insular—and the distinction is essential.
Provincial is Flaubert's rancorous little market towns aping
last year's Paris manner and last year's Paris fashion; it is
Chekhov's rusticated sisters sighing for Moscow. The Manx
aped no one else and they sighed for nowhere. Because
visibility on the Irish Sea is usually rather poor, on nine
days out of ten the Manx could see no other land except
their own, and they managed to behave as if the outside
world were an intermittent mirage, no more than the hallucination of Mount Skiddaw on a clear day.

Propped up against the quay wall at Port St. Mary in my
boat, with the tide out and another night falling, it was easy
to become infected by the air of resentfulness, belittlement
and claustrophobia that clung to the Island like its fogs. The
floor yawned at a treacherous angle under my feet. T. E.
Brown and Canon Stenning ("The pre-history of the Island
may be summarised in brief . . . .") kept on sliding away
across the saloon table. The oil lamps, tilting in their gimbals, were starting to blacken the ceiling of my tipsy room.
Every sixty seconds the siren of Langness Lighthouse let off
two long farts in the mist. I felt trapped like a crab in a
bucket.

It was difficult to keep awake in the darkened wheelhouse
with the pinpoint of light monotonously picking out the
same old numbers. I catnapped for minutes at a time, then
snapped awake in panic, expecting to see the rusty plates

and rivets of a cargo ship looming intimately overhead. But the sea stayed empty except for its charted ration of distant flashing lights. The mountainous coast of Wales showed faintly to the east—a ragged, blacker stain on a black satin sky.

The wind started at about 2 A.M. First it was a friendly wind, blowing from behind me out of the northwest. It felt like a Force 3 on Admiral Beaufort's scale:

> Large wavelets. Crests begin to break. Foam of glassy appearance. Perhaps scattered white horses.

Yawning, I pottered out on deck to pull up sails. An hour later, I was pulling them down again because the boat was lurching, surging, corkscrewing before the wind. Clipped into a safety harness, I crouched in the bow with stray ropes flailing round my ears, trying to gather in the recalcitrant, banging mass of polyester. Fighting off a flock of angry swans is no fun at the best of times, and the bow of a small boat in a gathering sea is a horrible place to have to do it. It plummets under you, ten or fifteen feet at a time; you go down with it, but your stomach stays up somewhere over your head, and the swans keep on coming.

It was too dark to see the shape of the sea; all that was visible were the streaks of phosphorescent white, arrowing away from the boat like lightning forks. The wind, I reckoned, must be close to a Force 7 now:

> Sea heaps up and white foam from breaking waves begins to be blown in streaks along the direction of the wind.

The only sail I left up was the little triangular mizzen over the wheelhouse. Working like a rigid keel stuck up into the wind, it helped to steady the swoops and rolls as I plugged on under engine.

Though the wind was blowing from behind, the tide was coming from in front, and the boat was making dismally slow progress over the ground. For an hour I watched the light on Bardsey Island, which seemed to have got stuck in the port shrouds, as the waves grew steadily bigger and more tightly packed. Inch by inch, the light shifted until it passed the shrouds and drew level with the wheelhouse.

The dawn was gray and rainy. The sea was steep and fiercely corrugated, although the waves were not nearly so high as I had imagined them to be in the dark. When the boat struck them, one could feel its oak frame jar and recoil as if it had hit a ridge of concrete. Two miles off, the plump and rain-swept figure of Bardsey Island was wearing an un-seasonable white skirt of spray.

At dawn, Holyhead Coastguard came back over the VHF radio. The search for the *South Stack* was being resumed. The tone of the coastguard's voice was different now, though. It had the routine flatness of no hope in it. It was the beginning of a no-hope day: miserably sunless, rough, with a full gale warning out for the Irish Sea and the sea itself looking like a place in which people were more likely to be found dead than alive.

I was scared on my own account by this time. I didn't want an RAF Nimrod flying low for me. Sleeplessness, and the constant bash and tumble of the water, was making me hallucinate, as people alone on small boats nearly always do. Robin Knox-Johnston, rounding Cape Horn, found himself engaged in a long conversation with his father-in-law, who was up in the crosstrees; Joshua Slocum had a ghostly pilot aboard; Naomi James came across an old friend who had stowed away in the chain locker. I was saddled with Commander King, the man who had taught me to handle the boat in Fowey. He kept on slamming the wheelhouse door behind me, and standing at my back. Every so often he coughed—a constrained, gentlemanly, naval cough that meant I was doing badly. Once, he pushed past me and went below.

"Just checking the bilges," he said. "Something you should have been doing at least every hour in a sea like this. Never mind."

I apologized out loud and kept on steering, leaving the bilges to the care of the Commander. Trying to rid myself of the hallucination, I set to wondering if I felt seasick. I had never yet been seasick, because of some defect of sensitivity in my inner ear, but always half-expected to be. I ticked off my symptoms: fright, shiveriness, dry mouth, lack of sleep, an anxiety that seemed rooted in the bowels, but hardly amounted to a real case of seasickness. This playing at doctors-and-nurses seemed to work. I was no longer being harassed by the spick-and-span Commander King.

At seven o'clock I managed to coax the boat round the south side of Bardsey Island into Cardigan Bay. Shielded from the wind, the water here was like a ruffled lake in a civic park. I was able to set the autopilot, put on the kettle for morning coffee, smoke a pipe and sit at the chart table in fair comfort, reading the instructions for getting into the harbor at Pwllheli, while the radio over my head repeated the words *South Stack, South Stack*. It was clear that everyone thought the men on board must have been drowned long ago.

I'd sailed two thousand miles to reach the Isle of Man. Fowey was still four hundred miles off, down the Irish Sea and round Land's End. Yet I felt that I'd arrived at the place where the voyage really began—this insular, enclosed world with its 1950s cars and 1930s trains, where you could still spend half-crowns and seven-and-sixpences, where the long days dragged, where butterflies flopped about the country lanes in droves, where the men went about in their old trousers, where strangers were watched from behind curtains, and the eggs were fresh and the boredom stifling. I was indignant when I was mistaken for a comeover, because this, surely, was exactly where I'd spent my childhood: the Island was Home with a capital *H*—the home I'd always been running away from.

The parsonage was our island. The house was surrounded by a high wild hedge of privet, nettle, holly and blackthorn. No one ever thought of trying to tutor it with shears, and the hedge grew as tall as the trees; every year it encroached farther into the garden, swallowing old herbaceous borders as it came. On windy days, the tumultuous hedge rolled and broke like the sea.

The invisible world beyond this hedge kept on changing: one year, there was a pallid brick council estate on the fringe of a city out there; the next, a Hampshire village with rustic thatch, an Oldest Inhabitant, and a Common of gorse and primroses, where you could find adders sinisterly coiled in the grass. But the hedge was the same hedge. It changed only with the weather. Sometimes there were whitecaps of honeysuckle on it; sometimes combers of bare twigs crackled in it like winter surf.

Although the architecture of the house had a protean habit of sprouting an extra bedroom or two, then suddenly contracting again, the house itself remained as fundamentally unvarying as the hedge. It had been furnished not by my parents but by some dreadful personages whom we called The Ancestors. The Ancestors were our board of guardians. They provided the books on our shelves—Baker's *Sport in Bengal*, the *Royal Kalendar* for 1832, *Sermons* by The Revd. W. Dunsleigh, the 1908 edition of the *Encyclopaedia Britannica*, and a faded black platoon of *Crockford's Clerical Directories*. The Ancestors had left us the krisses, kukris, dress swords and elephant bells which hung as ornaments on our walls. We had General Sir Edward's medals nestling in rosy velvet in their glass case, the colored coat of arms which had been granted to some Ancestor or other for a bold piece of commercial sharp practice in the early nineteenth century, along with the Ancestors' carriage clocks, games tables, antimacassars, aspidistra bowls, barometers, walking sticks, pincushions, samplers, crested silver and old shoes. The Ancestors themselves were there too—in miniature, on ovals of ivory, in cutout silhouette, in great slablike oil portraits framed with tousled gilt. Cousin Emma sat at her writing desk. The Recorder of Bombay wore his wig. The Suffragan Bishop of some other Asian outpost looked like an overdressed doll in his clerical furbelows and frills. Colonel William . . . George Caspar . . . Tom Priaulx . . . The Ancestors both outnumbered and outclassed us.

So much cleverer, more adventurous and richer than we were ourselves, the Ancestors were our island heritage, our history, our men of yore, and we crept bashfully about in their long shadows.

We ate our chopped meat and instant mashed potatoes off their plates with their silver cutlery; but most of their furniture was put out of bounds as too good to be spoiled by grubby contemporary fingers—fingers which had been blackened in the process of dutifully polishing the Ancestors' rubbishy pieces of Benares brass. They were impossibly tough taskmasters, these Victorian half-pay officers and frowning clergymen and lawyers. My young father sat up late into the night working in their service, his inherited dog collar clipped over the top of his inherited shirt with its turned and darned cuffs.

"Shush, dear—can't you see that Daddy's busy writing the Family Tree?"

He lived—exactly as I do now—in a mess of papers. He wrote on file cards, on the backs of letters, in school exercise books, in ancestral ledgers. He had appointed himself official secretary to the Ancestors, and there was no Ancestor too obscure, no third cousin too far removed—my father took dictation from anyone in whose veins had flowed a single corpuscle of family blood. He gummed sheets of typing paper together and constructed a diagram almost the size of the drawing-room carpet. From a distance, it looked like a wild plumber's jungle gym of gutterings and drainpipes. Close to, it was a forest of names, dates, arrows and = -signs. It might well have been a Renaissance cosmologist's lifework, a plan of universal knowledge. It was a terrifying document. For what all the branches of the Family Tree—the seventeenth-century yeomen, the eighteenth-century tradesmen, the nineteenth-century gentry with all their fancy dress and swords and medals—boiled down to, on the bottom line, was me.

It was no wonder that the space between the parsonage and the world beyond the hedge seemed oceanic. Our voluminous ancestry made us not so much a family as an entire race. We were not to be compared to people like the

Whites, or the Beales, or even the Habershons, or the Hon. Kitty Brownlow; we were more like the Norsemen, or the Etruscans, or the Phoenicians, or the Manx. No one could possibly have as many ancestors as we did—and we were on first-name terms with the lot. Had we not been impoverished country cousins, we might have dared to drop the "General" and the "Sir" from Edward's name, along with the "Colonel" from William's, but our claims of relationship were proved; we were kinfolks to the great.

There was good reason to believe that our clannish island was the very center of the world. God Himself had assured us of that, in so many words. If the Church Triumphant was at the heart of all things, then the Anglican parsonage was the living heart of the Church. My father's study was the source of all moral and spiritual authority in the world as we knew it. He was the births, marriages and deaths man. His *ex cathedra* statements on politics, social matters, sexual conduct were—it went without saying—the next-best thing that you could get to God's own opinions on these subjects. It's true that there was an impostor living in Pound Road who ran what my father called the "tin tabernacle," also a vagrant Irish priest in the pay of Rome. At various times, as the landscape beyond the hedge shifted, there were Seventh-day Adventists, Mormons, Pentecostalists, Primitive Methodists and people who talked to the dead via planchettes on ouija boards. But no decent or sensible person would get involved with such superstitious lunacies: this was England, we were the Church of England, and that was that.

My father, with his parson's freehold, was our Governor, and he held his office under Royal patent. When visitors from the outside world came to the parsonage, they came as if they'd made a sea crossing to reach us. As comeovers should do, they arrived looking formal, shy and ill at ease.

There would be the scrunch of bicycle tires in the gravel, then an unnatural period of silence, then a ring at the doorbell.

"Oh, drat, not *another* parishioner," my mother said.

"Can you answer it, dear—"

"Are you Out or In?"

"I don't know. See who it is, will you, dear?"

"They really might have the grace not to come at this time—don't they ever *think?*"

But at the door, my mother would say "Oh, Mrs. Beale! Lovely to see you. How are you? *Do* come in!"

A dozen people a day would beach at our door like this. Skulking at the top of the stairs, I watched them with a cold and curious eye—the speechless couples, engaged to be married; the white faces of the bereaved, who always apologized for being there, as if death were an error they should have been able to correct; the loud deserted wives; the unmarried mothers-to-be, shielding their pregnancies like disfigurements; gruff men in bicycle clips who were sorry-to-bother-the-vicar-but; and elderly lone gentlewomen for whom the parsonage was the last remaining place where they could pay a social call. Lingering as near as I dared to the closed door of the study, I heard voices lowered as if the house itself were a church. Sometimes I heard grown-up women crying. My father's voice was wise and even-toned. Its slow, bass seriousness was what people needed when they came to a parsonage; it promised understanding, help and religious mystery.

"Yes," he said. "Yes . . . yes." But there was much more than that. Framed by his own Ancestors, by the institution of the Church, by his unusual personal proximity to the Creator, my father had a great deal of what Victorian writers called "bottom." His *yeses* came from the depths; each monosyllable was a low rumble of compassionate assent. A *yes* from my father would stop a crying woman in her tracks or release a sudden bright cascade of words in the week-old widower. When the parishioners emerged from his study, they looked comforted and changed. I scowled and kept my own counsel about these transformations: I was unimpressible, as islanders are, by another islander's achievements.

There were whacking financial differentials between the parsonage and the outside world. At about £700 a year, a vicar's stipend in the 1950s was roughly the same as the

wage of a skilled laborer living on the council estate outside.
It was a small fraction of the pensions of the real live retired
generals who lived in big houses on the outskirts of the
village, let alone of the incomes of the people with double-
barreled surnames, the directors of London companies, the
doctor, the farmers or the rest of the comfortable middling
classes. We belonged nowhere. We had the money of one
lot, the voices of another—and we had an unearthly godli-
ness which removed us from the social map altogether.

So we learned to exploit our own insularity. Wherever
we went abroad, we were strangers, but we were very knowing strangers. Out on his rounds, my father was always
trying to colonize new tracts of social territory for the
Church; these Raleigh-like voyages of exploration and conquest would, when successful, be followed by a larger landing party from the parsonage. It was a precarious empire:
promising colonies kept on declaring independence and
dropping out of the arrangement, but at any one time we
would have a footing in the council houses, the bungalows,
the old people's flats, the cottages and the big places with
drives and rhododendrons.

By the age of twelve I had become expert at every deadly
English deference and snobbery. On the estate, I learned to
praise all those things which I secretly knew it was correct
to scorn: flights of china ducks going full throttle up the
wall, overfed and molting cats, plastic three-piece suites,
pictures made of bits of old clocks, the new television set
with the *Radio Times* in a special imitation-leather folder,
paper doilies for putting cups of tea on, pots of cacti on the
windowsill and the electric logs in the grate.

"Oh that *is* clever, and what's *puss's* name?"

In these houses I spread condescension like treacle, chattering away in a voice carefully modeled on my mother's
and the Moral Welfare Worker's. No one blew my cover.
Nobody threw me bodily out. I was just "being polite," and
being polite meant that you had to be a prig and lie through
your teeth. I was a paragon of politeness. My lies scaled
new heights of daring; my priggishness shone like a saint's
inner light.

For the farther rim of the village, I had a quite different manner. At tea in Mulberry Lodge, or Chestnuts, or Woodside House, I was boiled and dumb. I projected the little finger of my right hand outward as I held the cup. I nodded and tried to imitate my father's resonant way of saying "Yes." I never commented on the furniture and fittings here, but I took in the heavy chintzes, the little bowls of pot-pourri, the club fenders and firedogs, the engraved invitation cards on the mantelpiece, the smell of flowers and dry sherry, and filed them away for future reference.

"Thank you *so* much for your hospitality," I said as we left. "Thanks awfully."

But from my room at the top of the parsonage I could just see over the hedge to the Common, where the daughters of the Double-Barrels rode their ponies. *Stupid bitches.*

I did have a secret life of my own as a double agent. On the sly I mingled with the comeover kids. They had foreign names like Stew and Kevin and Marilyn and Tracey, and they spoke with a lazy-tough burr in their voices. Up to the age of twelve they fished in the posted waters of the brook, had fights, built dens and pedaled their bicycles round improvised dirt tracks. After the age of twelve, they gave all that up and devoted themselves to snogging.

Kicking stones and swapping obscenities with Kev, I would sometimes see my father, conspicuous from half a mile away in his cassock, ballooning round him like a black spinnaker, trawling for souls.

"Your dad."

"Fuck him," I said, and the word worked on me like a snort of cocaine. "I wish he'd go and stuff that fucking cassock up his arse." These bold denials came hard. They were said with the same excitement and trepidation that the blasphemer feels when he reckons that there's at least an even chance that God will actually strike him dead.

"He's all right," Kev said. Kev's own father regularly beat his mother up, and she was an occasional late-night visitor to the parsonage.

"All right for some," I said, kicking moodily at a dead hedgehog in the road.

At twelve I learned to snog with Tracey. It was passion-
less and apathetic, like doing things to frogs in Science. We
lay in the long grass at the bottom of Lower Common, just
a few yards from where we could hear Kev and Marilyn
learning to snog too. We rubbed and wriggled against each
other for a bit, tried a French Kiss, in which I choked
on Tracey's tongue, then Tracey sat up and fiddled with
her hairdo. I stared resentfully at the ends of my first
pair of long trousers. They were *miles* too wide.
Kev's were "twelves," which meant that they clung tightly round his ankles in the peg-top style that the Teddy
Boys were bringing in. Mine were *twenty-twos*—well,
eighteens, anyway. Hideous public school trousers, like
Oxford Bags. Hating my trouser ends must have given
my face an expression of aroused broodiness, for Tracey
said:
"Show?"
"What?"
"*You* know . . ."
She giggled and pulled a face. The she lifted her skirt
with all its flouncing layers of accessory petticoats. Amazed
and deeply interested, I saw the rigging of belt and sus-
penders that held up her nylons, and her navy blue pants.
She tweaked the front of her pants down and held them
there so that I could see.
I had expected—but there had been no time in which to
expect anything. However, Kev had given me the general
gist of the way things worked down there. Asked to describe it, I would have said that there should be a sort of
dark fleshy tunnel, its entrance probably marked by a pair
of smiling lips. I rather imagined that the lips might look
rouged.
I was appalled by what I saw. It was a dreadful absence,
like the bald scar tissue of an amputation. A few pale hairs
sprouted from the pink skin around what appeared to be a
healed cut.
The pants snapped back, to my immense relief.
"Now you."
Good God!

"Go on, pet," Tracey said. "Undo your trousers, then. Fair's fair."

I couldn't. I blustered and stammered and said sorry, *awfully sorry.* I rode back to the island on my bike, knowing that I'd just had a close shave with the Scarlet Whore of Babylon in person. For several days I quaked every time I heard the doorbell ring, fearing either that Tracey would turn up to demand the payment of her forfeit or, far worse, that her father would come clumping down the drive with serious news for mine. But neither Tracey nor her father braved the hedge, and within a week I was safely away at boarding school. When the next holidays came, I wrote off the council estate as a no-go area and failed to recognize Kev in the Post Office, although the experience with Tracey, artistically embellished, had made me more nearly popular at school than I'd ever been before.

I was getting deep into my teens when, on the far edge of the parish, I found another island, just as socially isolated as our own. Where ours was frowsty and full of English lumber, the other island was glamorously tropical. It was a millionaire's weekend cottage standing on several acres of lawns and woods. No one knew the people who lived there. They never showed up for Christmas drinks at the Double-Barrels'. They certainly never came near the church. The most one ever saw of the owners of the cottage was their new, gunmetal-gray Aston Martin purring through the village with its windows up.

This famous car once purred to a stop for me when I was hitchhiking, and my first anxiety was that its owner would tell the parsonage about how I traveled, thumbing my way to places as far as possible out of parental reach. I needn't have worried. Talking to the driver as he swept us round the Winchester bypass at a hundred and ten, I made my first grown-up friend.

Mr. Rapp had taught Philosophy at Oxford, worked for Reuters, taken over his father's scrap-metal business and turned it into one of the country's biggest manufacturers of aluminum tubes. He drove like Fangio. His bare skull was tanned the color of teak, his beard closely clipped to a circle

of gray round his upper lip and chin. I thought it likely that
he was the cleverest man in England, and at weekends I
cycled slowly backward and forward in front of his cottage,
praying to be noticed and invited in.

The Rapps' bookshelves were full of books that people
actually read: green-backed Penguin thrillers, Left Book
Club editions of Tawney and Crossman, the newest novels
by Iris Murdoch and Kingsley Amis and C. P. Snow, whom
Mr. Rapp always referred to as Mr. Pamela Hansford John-
son.

The Rapps themselves seemed to me at sixteen to have
stepped out of a book. They were like people one read
about, not people one knew. Mr. Rapp, with all his acres,
his amazing car, his tailored shirts and handmade shoes,
voted Labour—a wonderfully unlikely equation in my
world. The whole family, parents and children together,
had just been on the first Aldermaston March against the
bomb, and all wore Campaign for Nuclear Disarmament
badges in their lapels. *Inconceivable.*

They said that they found the Double-Barrels "too tedious
for words," a phrase I clasped to myself and used till it went
threadbare. *Our* isolation in the village was stiff and uncomfortable. It bristled with class tension, class guilt, class
pride. *Their* isolation was lordly. They liked the view but
the people bored them. They made living on an island look
like a handsome and graceful thing to do.

Best of all, the Rapps were Jews. To them, the idea that
the world had been created by a Palestinian peasant just a
few hundred years ago was no more than a quaint conceit.
To go to church every Sunday in order to eat this man's
flesh and drink his blood was an interesting survival of an
old pagan ritual. It was like the business of saying hello to
the fairies in the dell. Lots of people did it, but the Rapps
wouldn't bother.

I heroized them. Their free and easy talk went to my
head. I ached to be a part of their exotic diaspora. Late one
night, Mr. Rapp drove me to the gate of the parsonage.
The passenger door of the Aston Martin closed with a soft,
expensive click, leaving a brief bubble of Havana cigar

smoke in the air. When I walked up the drive toward the Ancestors glowering through their uncurtained windows, I was a comeover from a superior island.

When I tied up in Pwllheli, the pubs were full of talk of the *South Stack*. The total disappearance, in fine weather, of a large, well-found steel trawler was something for every fisherman to worry over and exorcise his own fears by speaking them out loud.

There was the Bermuda Triangle theory. Liverpool Bay was a bad and treacherous place for any ship. All sorts and conditions of boats had gone down there for no good reason. Why, only last year . . .

There was the Gas Bottle theory. One fisherman had heard a bang on the Saturday morning. It was not a big bang, mind. It was a very faraway bang, from somewhere beyond and beneath the horizon. It was so faraway that he could not rightly tell the direction of it, exactly. But it was a bang, definitely. If there had been a leak, or the gas bottles on board the *South Stack* had gone rusty, then perhaps one of the men, lighting a cigarette, maybe, or putting on the kettle for a brew . . .

There was the Secret Submarine theory. Everyone knew somebody who had gone trawling and suddenly found himself being pulled backward, or forward, or sideways through the sea at terrifying speed. He'd had to cut his nets to free himself from the underwater monster or be dragged down to the bottom as the sub dived. There were certainly submarines about—*nuclear* submarines, people said. You never saw them, but they made great, mysterious waves on the surface of the sea, like bulging muscles. Some thought they were "ours," others were sure they were Russians. If they were ours, they were so secret that the Admiralty would never own up when a man's gear—thousands of pounds' worth—was lost to them. Suppose the *South Stack* had not had time to cut herself free . . .

There were other theories too—theories which involved piracy, spies, women. Suppose a man wanted to start a new

life for himself, in Africa or South America: then wouldn't
a fine trawler like that be the perfect vessel to sail away in
into blessed anonymity? And could one discount the IRA?

When I left Pwllheli, still nothing had been found. The
Irish Sea had been combed from end to end and side to side
and not a scrap of wreckage had been spotted. I double-
checked the fittings on my own gas bottles and sniffed the
bilges of *Gosfield Maid* before I sailed. I never heard anyone
mention the *South Stack* again—until last week.

While I was beginning this chapter and describing the
arrival of the Nimrod search aircraft, I wrote a letter to the
Holyhead Coastguard asking if there'd been any further
news. The reply makes sad reading.

The *South Stack* sailed from Holyhead on a Thursday for
two days' fishing in Liverpool Bay. The three men who were
on board were due to show up for a family celebration back
in Holyhead on the Saturday evening. When they failed to
arrive, their relatives rang the Coastguard, who first put out
a PAN broadcast, asking vessels in their area to look out for
them, then, on Sunday morning, put out a MAYDAY call.

> Nimrod aircraft was on scene and searching at 1340
> GMT. Helicopter searching Caernarfon Bay and
> Moelfre Lifeboat searching North Anglesey coast.
> Weather on the Sunday was light Northerly wind
> with slight sea. Search continued until darkness with
> nothing found. The search was continued at first light
> the following morning throughout that day until 1700
> GMT when practically the whole Irish Sea had been
> covered with negative results. Broadcast action was
> carried on for a further 24 hours.
>
> About a week later, a liferaft was found by a yacht
> on passage from IOM to Holyhead about 17 miles
> North of the Skerries. The raft was part deflated with
> flares etc intact. From the finder it appeared to have
> just surfaced. A sonar search was carried out later in
> that area by the Trinity House vessel *Winston Churchill*
> with again results being negative. It can only be
> *assumed* that the *South Stack* caught her gear in an

obstruction and overturned. An enquiry was carried out by the Dept of Transport Marine Survey Office, Liverpool, but as there was no further evidence it was inconclusive.

What the Coastguard is careful to avoid saying is that for such a vessel to overturn as a result of catching her gear in an "obstruction," the obstruction would have to be moving, and moving very fast.

There was nothing unusual in the disappearance of the *South Stack*. Every day the seamen's newspaper, *Lloyd's List*, carries hundreds of such entries in its Casualties columns: boats announced as Overdue, then as Missing; boats known to have foundered on rocks; boats presumed lost "due to stress of weather." Some catch on fire, some spring leaks, some run into hurricanes, and their fates are reduced to a single line of small print. Their names stay posted in the paper for a week or two, then they're dropped to make way for other, more recent, missing ships.

It is the way they go that makes one shiver. "Results were negative." "No further evidence." First you are steaming along under a blue sky, and then you are sunk. For a few minutes you leave a trail of bursting bubbles—then nothing. Not even bubbles.

CHAPTER 3

AN INSULAR WAR

S eesawing in a swell of grizzled waves, with the tide running hard against us, the boat was marking time. It bucked and rolled, shunting the books about in their fiddled shelves, rattling the saucepans in the galley, making the glass frames of the pictures on the walls snatch and lose the sun. There was a lot of motion in my floating house, but no sense of making headway. *Gosfield Maid* felt as if she were tethered to the seafloor on a chain.

Yet I could see the land creeping past the wheelhouse window. I shut my left eye and squinted, lining up a coppice of dead elm trees against the steel rigging of the mizzen shrouds. The trees were making definite but slow progress, while the boat stayed still. The land was a limping ship, making just a knot or two through the water, its decks littered with cars, cranes, containers, scaffolding, apartment buildings—a lifetime of accumulated junk. The long low vessel of England looked dreadfully patched and rickety, and I wouldn't have put a penny on her seaworthiness as she shuffled painfully westward under a charred flag.

This was not a tired hallucination. I had set off in my boat on the assumption that England would have the grace to stay in her charted position. It was *Gosfield Maid* that was supposed to be making all the running on this trip. But within twenty-four hours of my departure, England decided to go off on a voyage of her own. I was pointing east by north for the Dover Straits; England was headed west and south for the Falkland Islands.

I was two miles out of Fowey when the country disappeared into the mist, and I had no idea what she was getting up to in my absence. Trusting to the compass, I felt my way up-Channel by numbers, marking the chart every fifteen minutes with a cross to show where I reckoned *Gosfield Maid* must be. On the extreme edge of my world there was the occasional pale silhouette of a passing ship, and sometimes the boat would give a sudden lurch as it hit the wake of something big that was too far away to see.

Six miles on, I met a pair of scallop dredgers working in consort, raking the bottom for shellfish with what looked like antique bedsteads. The fishermen waved as I went by. The sea is a much friendlier place than the land: when you see someone else afloat on it—at least in difficult weather and away from yachting slums like the Solent—you salute them to acknowledge a solitude momentarily brightened for being shared. You take an inordinate pleasure in what little passing company you can find. I warmed to the little black-and-white guillemots, shiny bath toys, that kept on diving ahead of the boat—there one moment, gone the next, leaving a space in the water as cleanly drilled as a bullet hole.

The warships made themselves heard long before I saw them. I was searching the haze for the loom of Rame Head on the west of Plymouth Sound when the VHF radio yielded a sudden harvest of clean-cut naval voices talking in jargon.

"Roger, Long Room . . . roger . . . roger and out."

"Achilles, Achilles, this is Ajax, Ajax. Do you read, please? Over—"

It was an hour before the warships became actually visible —first as angular shadows, then as gray dirigibles apparently suspended in the sky. Stealing cautiously up on these giants, I felt the walnut-shell littleness of my 32 feet of boat. Slab-sided, beetling, rudely engineered in what looked like bare cement, they made no concessions to the usual curves and frills of marine design. Her Majesty's Navy was a seaborne industrial estate of displaced tenements and factories: it looked as if Slough, Milton Keynes and Newark had taken to the water for the day.

Each ship had a small forest of radar scanners sluggishly revolving on their stalks. Their huge propellers made the sea behind them boil for half a mile and more. I was scared of letting *Gosfield Maid* go anywhere near these wakes: caught in that turbid white water, she would be flung about like a dinghy.

I hung back to make way for a monster ahead. Its guns were masked in tarpaulins, clumsily wrapped Christmas presents, and in the deck space between the guns, men in the uniform of the Royal Marines were at drill, jerking and snapping to their orders.

"Slow-hope *barms!*" I could hear the simultaneous *crunch-crunch-crunch* of the rifle butts and see the limbs of the men moving stiffly in time. They were boys in sailor suits, with spots on their faces and unformed pudge noses. Poor kids, condemned to compulsory games.

"Pre—wait for it! Scent *barms!*"

The enormous ship breezed past with flying colors. The white ensign rippling on a jackstaff at the stern gave the thing an incongruous touch of daintiness: a single rambler rose trained on the wall of a high-rise by some optimistic tenant.

Keeping at a safe distance, I followed the Navy down the broad triumphal avenue of Plymouth Sound. Lined with forts, flagstaffs and monuments to the famous dead, the Sound was a place for ceremonial processions and state occasions. A civilian interloper, I sneaked along the edge of the buoyed channel, fearing summary arrest by the policemen of the water. At Drake's Island the fleet wheeled left for the River Tamar and the naval dockyards; I bore right into the Cattewater, following the antique, but still good, advice of Greenville Collins:

Catwater is a good Place. There is a Place within the
Cittadel and Barbigan, called Sutton Pool, where
Ships lye aground on soft ooze at low-water, by the
Keys side before the Town of Plymouth.

In Sutton Pool I tied up alongside the trawlers by the fish
market. I climbed a slippery ladder, a rope end in my teeth;
stepped ashore and learned that war had broken out.

Even when you've spent just a few hours at sea, it is always
a bit difficult to learn to walk on land. After water, earth is
a sick-makingly unstable element. Your feet keep on en-
countering thin air where there ought to be paving stones;
you have to crouch forward, raising your arms and bending
your knees like a toddler, to balance yourself against the
lurching street.

At first I took the news of the war as another symptom of
this general topsy-turviness of things on land. I didn't trust
it, any more than I trusted the scaly cobbles of the fish
market or its green filigree roof, which was swaying dangerously overhead. It seemed beyond belief.

It had begun six weeks before as a silly diplomatic com-
edy: a bunch of scrap-metal merchants had cheekily raised
the Argentine flag over their campsite on the island of South
Georgia. I had rather enjoyed the exploits of these jingoistic
rag-and-bone men, and thought the questions raised about
them in Parliament had sounded unnecessarily indignant
and pompous.

Yet in the short time that I'd been away from land the
thing had turned from trifling farce to a drama of the most
frighteningly serious kind. Argentinian troops had invaded
the Falklands, and the Governor of the islands had surrendered in Port Stanley after a short skirmish between a detachment of British marines and the Argentinians.
Diplomatic relations with Buenos Aires had been broken
off; a naval task force was about to sail from England to the
South Atlantic to reclaim the colony.

No wonder that the warehouses and shops of Plymouth
were pitching in a tricky sea. There were far too many wars

in the world already—too many bangs and flashes and screams and unattended bodies in suburban streets. Beirut and Belfast were at least explicable: those miserable twin cities were built on enmities so old and loggerheaded that it would have taken a miracle for them not to break out sometime into a state of open warfare. But this Falklands business, as far as I could understand it, was perfectly gratuitous. Two governments were preparing to kill each other's soldiers, to go widow-making, for no better reason than that the exercise would be good for national pride or, perhaps, that it would create a handy distraction from the unhappy tangle of affairs at home.

I sat in a bar full of trawlermen trying to watch television. In dreadful color, behind snow showers of interference, the British Foreign and Defence Secretaries were holding a press conference. They were both speaking in the same unnaturally slow voice; that studied bass, bulging with *gravitas*, which politicians habitually use when they think they're making History. The badly tuned television set gave them the faces of giant goldfish swimming behind the glass, and the lips of Lord Carrington went on slowly opening and closing, opening and closing, as if he were masticating ants' eggs rather than words—soft, fatty abstractions like *Sovereignty, Integrity, Responsibility, Allegiance*.

I trailed out through the darkening city; on Plymouth Hoe I found a joyful hubbub in the Royal Western Yacht Club of England.

"Well, it's four thousand miles at . . . what? Fourteen knots?" The man beside me frowned at his wristwatch as if it were about to come up with the answer.

"It's more than that, Jack. It's more like nine."

"What, *knots*?"

"No—miles. Nine thousand miles."

"Well, then. Nine thousand miles at fourteen knots . . ."

"It's going to be three weeks at least, maybe four, even."

"No—you could do it in ten days. Easily. Those Type 21s go at one hell of a lick. Thirty knots plus."

"Yes, but what about Charlie Slowcoach? It's the landing ships you've got to think of—"

Pink gins on silver trays were moving as fast as Type 21s. Men in dinner jackets and black ties, on the leeside of some formal binge, stood in an important group in front of the fire. Wives in long frocks sat out at separate tables, leaving their husbands free to run the coming war. The men were grizzled and pink. They shared the same old school of the Navy, and were of an age to have served in North Atlantic convoys and seen the beaches of Dunkirk. They were the corvette captains forty years on, and today's news was working on them like a powerful injection of caffeine. They were alight with it. Their voices caroled.

"They've cancelled all leave—"

"They're coming down from Wales—"

"They're sailing from Gib already—"

"*Endurance* is still down there—"

It was an evening to make old men feel young again. There was pure pleasure in their indignation at what Argentina had done.

The man at my elbow was saying: "It's exactly as if Russia had come over and occupied the Isle of Wight without a by-your-leave. *Exactly.*"

"But I thought—"

"Exactly the same. No difference at all. It's British soil."

"Well, is it, quite?"

"Of course it is. Sovereign territory. British soil. The Falklanders are as English as I am. To a man."

As the gins piled up on the bar, the talk spiraled in volume and excitement. We were on to the requisitioning of civilian ships now.

"Trawlers from Hull are going."

"And Brixham too."

"They're going to need cross-Channel ferries—"

"And the QE 2."

"I'd take my tub out there at the drop of a hat," one man said, and opened a floodgate of happy fantasy. Could there, just conceivably, be a place for all of us in England's great adventure? Supposing we set off tonight . . . The catamarans, at least, could make it almost as fast as the warships . . . And someone had a ketch down in the Med—wasn't

that almost halfway to Port Stanley? Imagine the astonishment and terror of General Galtieri's gang when they saw,
approaching them over the horizon, not an armada but an
epic regatta: it would be Cowes Week and Henley and
Burnham rolled majestically into one. The Argentinians
would take fright at the sight of the picnic hampers alone.

"I'd go."

"So would I, Jack, if they'd have me."

"I'm still on the Reserve."

"They'll have to call up the Reserve."

"What about our friend here? Would *you* go?"

"Good God, no," I said, then remembered where I was.
"I only do six knots. I wouldn't get to the Falklands until
about this time next year."

The picture window at the end of the bar framed Plymouth Sound—the pinprick lights of winking buoys, the
bulky blue shadows of ships on the move. Whisky and
the din of the war talk had gone to my head. I'd lost half
the words, but it was a night made for the rollicking sentimental chauvinism of Sir Henry Newbolt and the poem that
every small boy in England used to be forced to recite at
school:

> Drake he's in his hammock till the great Armadas come.
> (Capten, art tha sleepin' there below?)
> Slung atween the roundshot, listenin' for the drum,
> An' dreamin' arl the time o' Plymouth Hoe.
> Call him on the deep sea, call him up the Sound,
> Call him when ye sail to meet the foe;
> Where the old trade's plyin' and the old flag's flyin'
> They shall find him ware an' wakin', as they found
> him long ago!

At least there was no chivalry in the fish business. I was
awakened in the dark by sudden arc lights and a voice
talking through loudspeakers.

"... six fifty ... seven ... seven fifty ... eight.
Any more on eight? Eight, eight, eight, eight—*Wemmidge*."

Maneuvering trawlers were stirring up the water of the

dock, and *Gosfield Maid* rolled and crunched against the harbor wall. Crapulous and underslept, I did my best to nurse the charcoal embers which were still just glowing in the stove in the saloon. The whistle of the kettle in the galley, six feet away, injured something vital in my skull. Moving too fast to shut off the noise, I bruised my shin on the first step of the companionway to the wheelhouse. A small boat never seems smaller than when you have a hangover. It is all obstacles and sharp corners. Its drumskin interior magnifies every sound.

"... whang, whang, whang, whang—*Jorkins.*"

Shaved and necktied, I pulled the broad brim of my felt hat low down over my forehead to hide my bloody eyes and went out to make a brave breakfast of a hot dog and a paper cup of tea from the stall in the market. The predawn auction under the lights was the stuff of which really first-class hangovers are made. It was odd, boring, much too vivid, mildly repulsive and perfectly in keeping with my mood.

The auctioneer, dressed in a white coat like a medical attendant and carrying a microphone on a long lead, was working his way steadily down a line of buckets and trays of dead fish. A dozen fish merchants in raincoats and Tyrolean hats with feathers, their hands deep in their pockets, shuffled along behind him. Every bucket and tray had what looked like a bumper sticker lying on top of it, showing the name of the trawler which had landed the catch. *Our Tracey. Semper Allegro. Jayne Anne. Maaleesh.*

The group assembled round a tray of bleary-eyed Dover soles, fish and men regarding each other with exactly the same indifferent stare.

"Nine fifty, ten, ten fifty—"

Two merchants were bidding against each other. Both had pipes—one a meerschaum, the other a briar. To bid, each man wagged his pipe a fraction of an inch with his teeth. Meerschaum, briar, meerschaum, briar. Neither was alight. The bowls tittupped along in an easy fox-trot rhythm until the briar went doggo at sixteen pounds.

"Sixteen, sixteen, sixteen, sixteen—*Wemmidge.*"

The men trooped on, hunch-shouldered, to perform the last rites over a bucket of yawning ling.

Soon after daybreak I found an open corner shop with the morning's papers stacked in bundles on the floor. The huge headlines looked like schoolboy whoops and yells. There was no fun, apparently, quite like the fun of going to war, and the *Daily Express*, the *Daily Mail* and the *Sun* had announced the Falklands expedition as if a national holiday, with fireworks and free beer, had been declared. There were pictures of the Argentine dictator smiling broadly and making a thumbs-up sign; the message of the headline writers was that nothing would give the British more satisfaction than to wipe that smile off Galtieri's face and crack the joints of both those thumbs. I bought a *Guardian*, which was striking a discordant note of sanity in the middle of all the heady bombast. Its editorial listed the bungled efforts at diplomacy and the bungled collection of intelligence that had led to the crisis. It went on to observe flatly that:

> The Falkland Islands do not represent any strategic or commercial British interest worth fighting over (unless one believes reports of crude oil under its off-shore waters).

This remark—a plain-enough fact, even if insufficiently varnished with the right amount of topical valor—was to be denounced later that day in Parliament by the Liberal Member for Inverness as an outrage that fell only a foot or two short of downright high treason.

Wanting to clear my head at sea for a while, I untied the boat from the quay at nine o'clock and gentled it out through the pack of trawlers. Three small boys were fishing for crabs at the dock-end with lumps of raw meat knotted to pieces of string. One fair-haired child, his face as void of malice as a carton of yogurt, was holding a large live crab in one hand and pulling its legs off, one by one, with the other.

"She loves me—" He pulled a leg out of its socket. "Loves me not. Loves me—"

When he'd run out of legs, he sent the carcass of the crab spinning far out over the water. It was the graceful flick of a Frisbee expert. The crab hit the surface, bounced, bounced again, and sank, leaving a faint dribble of guts to mark where it went down.

The boy saw me watching him. He nodded pleasantly at the splash. "Bloody fiddly."

"What did you say?"

"He were only a bloody fiddly," he said, and went on with his fishing.

Ahead, the world was monochrome, like a smudged charcoal drawing—gray sky, gray sea, gray ships, gray breakwaters, gray cliffs, gray everything. A swell from the far south, relic of someone else's gale, made the oily-smooth water bulge steeply, although there was no wind at all. It heaved and sucked around the long breakwater in the middle of the entrance to the Sound; it broke in an ash-blond fringe around the Mewstone. It was nice to ride this swell out slowly, under engine: its soothing rockabye motion came as a blessed relief after the violent corkscrew rolling of the land.

The evening before, with the retired commanders, I hadn't cared to let on that I didn't actually know where exactly the Falklands were. Later, I'd looked them up in the inky-fingered school atlas in my floating library. They showed as a rash of heat spots off the coast of Argentina, picked out in British imperial pink. By a funny twist of chance, they occupied precisely the same latitude in their hemisphere as the British Isles did in theirs: at 51°46' S, Port Stanley was the Hemel Hempstead of the southern world.

More than that, the Falklands stood anchored off the coast of South America very much as Britain stood anchored off the coast of Europe. You had only to look at the atlas to see that the identity of the Falklanders, like that of the British, was bound up in endless aggressive assertions of their differences from the continental giant across the water.

They were visibly, audibly, our kith and kin. A family of

Falklanders, holidaying in Britain, had been exhibited on television. Even by wintry English standards, they were white. It was the way they spoke, though, that made them so evidently worth fighting for. Their voices had a tinny quality, as if they were being played through a gramophone needle with dust on it, but their accent was loudly Home Counties. They all talked in the voice which, heard across the distance of a *souk*, or a patch of jungle, in some remote quarter of the world, puts you instantly and depressingly in mind of gin-and-tonic, cavalry twill, the next monthly mortgage payment, brussels sprouts, tea cozies, *Journey's End* at the amateur dramatic society, the Magimix in the kitchen and the Queen's head on the stamp.

The Falklanders *were* us, but they were us in looking-glass reverse. Our spring was their autumn. Their Atlantic depressions came to them from the east, spinning round clockwise; ours came at us from the west, spinning counter-clockwise. On the same principle, their bathwater ran out of the plughole in the opposite direction from ours; and if we stood upright on the earth, the Falklanders must have been standing upside down and clinging by their boot soles through the power of suction.

In this miniature inverted cluster, the British had hit by accident on a perfect symbol of themselves. The Falklands held a mirror up to our own islands, and it reflected, in brilliantly sharp focus, all our injured belittlement, our sense of being beleaguered, neglected and misunderstood. As for the Argentinians, they were the last word in Comeovers from Across. They'd got monstrously above themselves, and, as Comeovers deserve, they were going to be given their Come Uppance.

I had on board a copy of E. Keble Chatterton's *The Yachts-man's Pilot* of 1933, whch had belonged to my sailing grandfather. It described the approach to the river Yealm, nine sea miles east of Plymouth: a fussy business which involved lining up a succession of marks to make a dog's-leg course avoiding the rocks to starboard and the shoaling sands to port. *Not to be attempted in strong onshore winds . . . care must be exercised . . .* Chatterton's last line on the place, though, was irresistible: "You are now in one of the most secluded and lovely spots to be found in Southern England." In search of loveliness and seclusion, I motored east through the gray swell and found Chatterton's first set of marks—a church spire followed by a pair of white-painted wooden triangles on posts, one on the shore inside the estuary mouth, the other high up on a hill behind. So far, so good.

I waited while the triangle on the shore moved slowly rightward to join the triangle on the hill, then swung the boat round and squeezed it by within feet of Yealm Head, where the sea slopped and piled on the rocks, blackening the lichens and leaving the exposed granite looking like wet moleskin. The course zigzagged through high bluffs of trees and bracken, going east, then northeast, then southeast, then northeast again, then finally northwest into a deep wooded cleft containing a mile-long pool of dark water like a secret lake. A Victorian hotel stood on a sandy point, half hidden in pines. A dozen early season yachts swung on their moorings. The noise of my engine, echoing in the hollow, disturbed a wading heron, which flapped off up into the woods on boxy wings.

After several minutes of panicky mismanagement, I got the upper hand of *Gosfield Maid*, which had seemed to grow to the size of a cargo ship the moment that she entered the river, and I tethered the boat between two buoys in midstream. In drizzly soft focus, the Yealm was exquisite, just as the late Mr. Chatterton had promised, with its thick country silence, its steep terraces of dripping evergreens and its glassy water, scrolled by the tide and current with loops and whorls of teasingly near-legible sham Arabic.

Below, the saloon was snug and full of comfortable noises: barbecue charcoal wheezed and crackled in the stove, the river muttered companionably in the bilges. Even in this flattest of calm waters, the room felt afloat: the floor shimmied slightly underfoot, the ceiling, walls and furniture had a palpable absence of specific gravity. It was like living inside a soap bubble, suspended, sustained, by a contradictory harmony of tensions. It brought the weightlessness and detachment that are usually confined only to sweet dreams.

Floating, I switched on the wireless in time to catch the beginning of the great Westminster debate. For the first time since the Suez crisis of 1956, the House of Commons was sitting on a Saturday, and the chamber was honoring the occasion with an ominous, unnatural hush. There were none of the usual feeding-trough noises of Parliament in session; just the hiss and rustle of order papers, like static.

The Prime Minister said: "The House meets this Saturday to respond to a situation of great gravity. We are here because, for the first time in many years, British sovereign territory has been invaded by a foreign power." But her cross, nanny's voice made it sound as if there had been ructions in the nursery and the children were going to be sent to bed without any tea.

I stood leaning against the galley bulkhead and looking out through the porthole. The heron had come back again. It was standing not more than twenty feet away, stock-still, head crooked, watching for the underwater flash of a turning fish. The ebb tide, picking up speed now, was leaving two fine plaits of disturbed water behind its legs. Did herons always fish upstream, like dry-fly purists?

"The people of the Falkland Islands, like the people of the United Kingdom, are an island race. Their way of life is British; their allegiance is to the Crown. They are few in number, but they have the right to live in peace, to choose their own way of life and to determine their own allegiance."

"Hear, hear!"

A brick of charcoal hiccuped in the stove. The Prime Minister, reading her ghost-written words, kept on putting emphases in the wrong places. The moment one stopped concentrating on what she was saying it seemed as if she were drifting out of English and into Danish.

The heron's neck uncoiled like a cracked whip, and there was a sudden wriggle of silver in its beak. This brilliant trick eclipsed the Falklands Crisis in a wink.

When next I listened, the radio had drifted off-station

and had to be retuned. A claret-and-Havana Tory voice out of the previous century was saying, " . . . this jumped-up junta of barbarous men . . ." and his words were met by a long indigestion of approval through the benches.

"Our duty now," said the member for Taunton, "is to repossess our possessions and to rescue our own people. Our right to the Falkland Islands is undoubted. Our sovereignty is unimpeachable."

"Hear, hear!"

"We have one duty only, which we owe to ourselves— the duty to rescue our people and to uphold our rights. Let us hear no more about logistics—how difficult it is to travel long distances. I do not remember the Duke of Wellington whining about Torres Vedras."

"Hear, hear!"

"Hear, hear!"

"We have nothing to lose now except our honor."

He was carrying the House with him. After this, any words of caution were bound to fall flat by contrast with these lofty generalities about honor, sovereignty and the Duke of Wellington. There were very few Members now who dared to prick the growing rhetorical balloon.

But the member for Surbiton wasn't happy. He thought that an invasion of the islands at this stage could only lead to innocent people being caught in the crossfire. He had some ideas of his own about how Galtieri could best be dealt with.

"I understand," he said, "that the people of the Argentine are great football enthusiasts—"

The House came back with a low growl of warning.

"The very least we should do," the member for Surbiton said, against the gathering rumpus, "is to ensure the exclusion of the Argentine from the World Cup—"

He was roared and jeered down. The House was marching with drums and trumpets. It trampled on the member for Surbiton and left him far behind.

Beyond the porthole there was a small red cliff of sandstone. Its lips and ledges were bright with freshly opened primroses. The branches of the trees overhanging the water were loaded with budding catkins and the green beginnings of new leaves. Farther up the hill, the gorse thickets were coming into flower. I wondered whether the Falklands autumn, now under way, was, as it were, the autumn that we'd had six months ago or the autumn of months ahead, when these leaves would go tinder-crisp and die. I reckoned that anything to do with the Falklands more probably belonged to Britain's past than to its future, so the naval fleet would be sailing backward, into last year's autumn, or maybe some other autumn belonging to the Duke of Wellington and another monarch.

I listened to the member for Brighton Pavilion saying, "We are determined to make the Argentinian dictator disgorge what he has taken—by diplomacy if possible, by force if necessary. Nothing else will restore the credibility of the government or wipe the stain from Britain's honor."

The outgoing tide made the land at the edge of the water seem to grow. Boulders white with barnacles were surfacing one by one, and fretted banks of mud were rising slowly proud of the river. The heron had gone, but a pair of oystercatchers were strolling fastidiously through the shallows, lifting their legs as if it pained them to get their feet wet.

The member for Wycombe was getting off to a bad start. "I should like to offer a few words which I know will not be popular with the House—"

The House gruffed its assent to this and prepared to give the member for Wycombe a hard time.

"—but they are based on three years' work in Argentina, trying to avoid the eventuality that now confronts us."

"For the Foreign Office!"

"You were working for the Foreign Office!"

"That is right," admitted the member for Wycombe.

"The Foreign Office," shouted the member for Southend East, "was not working for Britain!"

There were cheers from the back benches, mixed in with a very few and feeble cries of "Shame!"

"I'm sorry, but I can't give way again"—The member for Wycombe squealed over the din. "There are alternative ways—"

"No!"

"—in which the interests of the Falkland Islanders can be protected, and I feel that these can be achieved by negotiation!"

"Point of order, Mr. Speaker!"

The member for Epping Forest was on his feet. "Mr. Speaker! At a time of emergency like this, if defeatism of this kind—"

"Hear, hear!"

"—if defeatism of this kind is to be spoken, should it not be done in secret session? Would it be in order to spy strangers in the House?"

"I hope," said Mr. Speaker, "that the honorable gentleman does not."

The member for Wycombe pleaded for "realism," for "careful thought," for "diplomatic efforts," and was duly squashed. But the House was kind to the member for Essex South East, who got the troops on the march again with the right kind of rousing tune. "The very thought that our people," he said, "eighteen hundred people of British blood and bone, could be left in the hands of such criminals is enough to make any normal Englishman's blood—*and* the blood of Scotsmen and Welshmen—boil too!"

"Hear, hear!"

I switched the wireless off, sick of the sound of grown men baying like a wolf pack. It wasn't a debate, it was a verbal bloodletting, with words standing in for the guns and bayonets that would come later when the fleet reached the islands. Listening to it, I felt that I'd been eavesdropping on the nastier workings of the national subconscious; I'd overheard Britain talking in a dream, and what it was saying scared me stiff.

A weak shaft of filtered sunshine was lighting the cushions in the saloon and I went out into the open cockpit to bask in the lovely seclusion of the Yealm. It was not, I saw now, quite what it had seemed in the rain. The thick woods on the far shore concealed an irregular band of furtive picture windows. Like flashers lurking behind the trees in a park, the bungalows and chalets wore dark glasses which glinted in the sun.

Sometime between 1933 and now, the solitude of the river had turned into a real estate agent's desirable view, and I was moored deep in a suburb where nature was a "feature" like a sauna or a fitted kitchen. Its silence was the silence not of seclusion but of retirement—of childlessness, of pottering about indoors, of watching golf on television in the afternoons and having all the time in the world to read the *Radio Times*.

Even so, it was a pleasant place in which to find oneself marooned. One just had to join the retirees and look exclusively to starboard, to the western bank of the estuary and the unspoiled budding tangle of the spring. It was a little inhibiting, though, to find that I was a part of someone else's view. Lacking the captain's hat, the Arran knit sweater and the primrose Wellington boots in which I might have passed myself off as a suitably picturesque figure, I hid in the saloon in my offensive city clothes.

It was dark when I rowed across to the landing stage below the hotel, and the river was icily still. Each paddle-stroke brought up a glittering scoop of phosphorescence— a million firefly plankton at a single dip. An owl was hooting in a wooded bungalow garden; from another hidden house there came a snatch of Mantovani in muffled stereo. I found the landing stage by flashlight and walked back into England on a scented carpet of pine needles.

There were two parrots in the bar of the Yealm Hotel. One was a macaw, anchored to its perch on a chain; the other was a florid man with fierce gray handlebar mustaches —ex-RAF, ex–assistant sales director, I decided, and probably called Wilcox.

"You can say what you like," Wilcox was saying to no one in particular, "but the Hitler Youth did Germany a world of good." He glared hopefully at me, fishing for a cozy bout of argy-bargy. "Of course, it's unfashionable to say that nowadays, isn't it?"

Pepe, the first parrot, said, "Bye-bye, shut up, hullo!"

Wilcox said, "Take your good self, for instance. Did you do National Service?"

Trapped. I said, "No, I missed it by a year. But National

Service and the Hitler Youth weren't exactly the same thing, were they?"

"Shut up, hullo, bye-bye!"

"If we still had National Service in this country today, we wouldn't be in the state we are now. Caught with our pants well and truly down, huh? Pants well and truly down!"

"Bye-bye, hullo, shut up!"

Pepe chewed happily under each armpit in turn, then crapped copiously on the pile of old copies of the *Western Morning News* stacked under his perch. To complete his toilette he settled to vigorously throwing up the feathers on the top of his head so that it looked as if he were wearing a blue-rinse fun-fur wig. Wilcox, less entertainingly, went on about football hooliganism, hard labor in prison, welfare scroungers and how Mussolini made trains run on time.

For fifty pence I bought myself a bath in a fine claw-footed tub upstairs in the hotel. When I stopped moving in the water, I could hear the parrots through the plumbing, going at it hammer and tongs. *Hullo! Louts! Shut up! Maggie! Bye-bye! Argentina! Hullo! Work-shy! Bye-bye! On their bikes! Shut up!* The macaw had all the best lines.

I would have liked to see more of Pepe, but since seeing Pepe meant seeing Wilcox too, I left in search of some other place to drink. At nine o'clock at night, all life in Newton Ferrers was conducted behind closed doors and thickly curtained windows. My footfalls crunched too loudly on the graveled lane, and I was frightened of rousing the local dogs. But no dog barked. I shined the torch on the plaques borne by the gates of the houses that I passed. Most of them were memorials to some former glory of the householder. Here was "Sumatra Cottage," there "Alamein." When I opted for the quiet life in a river-view bungalow on the Yealm, it would be difficult to choose a suitable name for the place. Neither "Aberystwyth" nor "Tomato, Arkansas" struck quite the right note. "Chuck's Diner" and "Saloon Bar" would both cause problems. I supposed that I'd have to resign myself to "Aleppo," which would fit nicely into Newton Ferrers society.

I walked, and walked—evidently in the wrong direction,

since no pub appeared. My pace quickened to that of a route march, and one of those irritating fragments of rhyme that come to plague one at moments like this got stuck in my skull. It went round and round in a loop:

> We don't want to fight, but by Jingo, if we do,
> We've got the ships, we've got the men, we've got
>   the money too.

Left, right, left, right—we don't want to fight, but by Jingo, left and right . . . The torchlight raked the lane and scared the owls from the trees. I marched, singing softly, under my breath, in tune with the times.

The air was dead, and the water shone dully under a waxing gibbous moon, but the midnight-fifteen shipping forecast was bad. An Atlantic depression off the west coast of Ireland was moving quickly east. There were gale warnings out for half the British sea areas, including Plymouth. The gale arrived in time for breakfast, a warm, wet southwesterly blowing up from Biscay. Funneled by the hills on either side of the estuary, it came roaring through like a train. Within minutes, it had transmuted the water into frothy cappuccino. The boat thrummed and shivered on its moorings. Below, it felt as if one were squatting in the sound box of an out-of-tune harp, with every shroud vibrating on a slightly different note and the wooden frame answering the shrouds with a long, low sympathetic groan. Outside, the two thick ropes which held the boat at the bows were as rigid as if they'd been cast in steel.

It was all quite safe, but it meant a spell of enforced retirement from the world. There was no question of rowing ashore; the inflatable dinghy would have been blown straight upstream into the middle of Devonshire. So I gave myself up to a bungalonely life of pipe and slippers, pottering about the library, feeding the stove with charcoal, making a ritual to-do about having elevenses at eleven and lunch sharp at one. At intervals I went above to watch the wind harrowing the water; yesterday's birds, it seemed, had all been blown away.

In the library I found one trophy to copy into my notebook. In Charles Darwin's *The Voyage of the Beagle* there was a disenchanted account of his short stopover in the Falklands:

> This archipelago is situated in nearly the same latitude with the mouth of the Strait of Magellan; it covers a space of one hundred and twenty by sixty geographical miles, and is a little more than half the size of Ireland. After the possession of these miserable islands had been contested by France, Spain and England, they were left uninhabited. The government of Buenos Ayres then sold them to a private individual, but likewise used them, as Spain had done before, for a penal settlement. England claimed her right and seized them. The Englishman who was left in charge of the flag was consequently murdered. A British officer was next sent, unsupported by any power: and when we arrived, we found him in charge of a population, of which rather more than half were runaway rebels and murderers.
>
> The theatre is worthy of the scenes acted on it. An undulating land, with a desolate and wretched aspect, is everywhere covered by a peaty soil and wiry grass, of one monotonous brown colour. Here and there a peak or ridge of grey quartz rock breaks through the smooth surface. Every one has heard of the climate of these regions; it may be compared to that which is experienced at the height of between one and two thousand feet, on the mountains of North Wales . . .

It seemed to me that this passage alone was enough to prove that the "sovereignty," of which the government was making so much, had not been so undisputed as our Prime Minister was now claiming. Indeed, as I learned a week or two later, sovereignty over the land—the physical geography of "these miserable islands"—had already been ceded, in prospect and theory, by the British Foreign Office to the Argentine. What the Westminster government had been trying to retain was a much more limited kind of sovereignty, over the fortunes and futures of the eighteen hundred British-passport holders who were the islands' tenants.

The behind-the-scenes story of these negotiations was preposterously comic. The men from the Foreign Office had shuttled between London, Buenos Aires and Port Stanley on an impossible mission. They had been instructed to dream up ways of making the Falklanders learn to love Argentina, so that when the new lease was drawn up the tenants wouldn't protest too loudly against their incoming landlord. The diplomats themselves got on fine with the Argentinians and enjoyed their trips to Buenos Aires; they found the Falklanders intractable, stick-in-the-mud and woodenly provincial.

The British diplomats and the Argentinians got together and set up a sort of carrot factory to produce tempting morsels to dangle in front of disdainful Falkland Island noses. They tried cheap package holidays in Argentina, and got no takers. They set up football scholarships, so that the children of the islanders could learn to pass and dribble at the feet of Argentina's international stars. The parents refused to let their boys travel abroad. The diplomats played their ace—a Scout and Guide exchange scheme, with singsongs in English and Spanish around campfires. The camp in the Falklands was rained out, and the one in Argentina never materialized.

Nothing worked. It was a pity that the Foreign Office men hadn't read the poems of T. E. Brown, hadn't reckoned with the mixture of smugness, stubbornness and ferocity with which an insular people will defend its identity. The Falklanders were just as proud and cussed as the Manx. They sat tight on their foggy islands and saw themselves as occupying the center of the world. They despised the people from Across, with their foreign language and foreign politics. They loathed the British diplomats with their superior voices and hoity-toity manners, and saw them as traitors, bent on selling the islands over the sea.

It was at this absurd impasse that General Galtieri, Admiral Anaya and Brigadier Dozo had launched their invasion. Having wined and dined so happily with the Foreign Office men, they had expected only irritable noises from Britain. After all, the British Government had spent years trying to quietly rid itself of the Falklands, and Mrs. Thatcher might even be secretly grateful to Galtieri for taking the initiative and relieving her of this unwanted piece of British baggage.

Galtieri could not have been more wrong—and there was another clue in Charles Darwin's description as to why the Argentine dictator had made a tragic miscalculation. The very bareness and monotony of the islands themselves, together with their tiny population, gave them the lucid purity of a symbol. Their blankness was their point: you could make them mean nothing or everything. And England had run out of symbols. Over this windy weekend, it was busy writing meaning into the Falklands, making that undulating, desolate land *signify*. Between Friday morning and Sunday afternoon the Falkland Islands accumulated a huge bundle of significations. They meant Tradition, Honor, Loyalty, Community, Principle—they meant the whole web and texture of being British.

I couldn't get much of a picture out of the TV in the saloon, but it was enough to show that in General Galtieri we had found a worthy enemy, a monster that every clean-living Englishman could love to hate. Galtieri was an odiously pretty man. His soft and petulant Valentino lips betrayed the distorted sensualism of power. It was uncannily easy to imagine that face creased with pleasure in the exercise of the rack and screw. Those misplaced feminine features, that braided stewardess' uniform—to the English, who dislike and fear male beauty for reasons safest left in the closet for the moment, Galtieri was a gift. The cruel, sexually ambiguous cast of his face seemed enough in itself to justify our unbridled distaste. His televised image was infinitely, luxuriously more hateable than that of Hitler, who had always been dangerously disadvantaged by his strutting, cowlicked, little man's air of being on the verge of turning into a music-hall figure of fun. We used to jeeringly call Hitler "Adolf"; no one would dream of *tutoyer*-ing Galtieri as "Leopoldo." In the new kind of warfare, where television cameras are used as offensive weapons, a suitably loathsome face is a very useful adjunct to an improper foreign policy.

By mid afternoon, the depression was centered somewhere over the English Midlands. The wind paused, the river flattened. There was an abrupt silence, then a thrush began to sing in the trees close by the boat. Wood pigeons gobbled. A fish jumped. I was getting the dinghy ready to row over to the village when the wind came back, this time cold and dry from the northeast. Gusting slantwise across the river, it leaned against the eleven-ton bulk of the boat and made pens, papers, ashtray, matches slide gently off the edge of the table down in the saloon. It blew all night. I lay in the bunk in the fo'c's'le reading Darwin by lamplight, tipped by the wind at a slight, oblique angle to the rest of society on the shore.

On Monday, the first ships sailed from Portsmouth. I watched them go in old-fashioned black and white. The movement of the boat, restless on its mooring, made the picture shatter every few seconds, then put itself back together. That hardly mattered, because it was such a famous picture—a picture as famous, at least in England, as *Mona Lisa* or *The Boyhood of Raleigh*. It showed pipe bands, bunting, flags, kisses, tears, waved handkerchiefs. Thousands of little Woolworth Union Jacks fluttered on the quay in time to the oom-pah, oom-pah of martial music. The camera dwelt in close-up on the faces of the girls, on the sooty trickles of mascara on their cheeks, on hooded infants held up on grandpas' shoulders. It tracked across to the boys on deck, who looked as if they should still be in school as they waved their caps in the air and the wind rucked up their pigtail flaps around their bare necks. As lines were cast off, the camera homed in on the margin of black water between the dock and the gray hull of the ship, widening slowly from a pencil line to a canal. And they were off. Girls, their shoulders quaking, searched for their powder compacts; the grandfathers frowned at a memory; the infants shook their happy flags like rattles. The colors of the saloon aboard my own boat were running together; I was dabbing my face and blowing my nose with paper from the kitchen roll in the galley.

Absurd. It was like crying over a bad movie in an empty cinema. I had thought my own skepticism about this political adventure was waterproof; not so. The insidious British genius for impromptu ceremonial could dissolve a skepticism like mine in a few moments. The families on the shore, the receding ships, the bands and streamers had me blubbering with silly pride in Queen and Country. It was lucky that no recruiting sergeant was on the prowl around the Yealm that afternoon—he would have had a tough time getting rid of me. Never mind my flat feet and falling hair, never mind my middle-aged belly, I'm your man, I'm here!

I switched off the set, angry with it, angry with myself. This was not how a detached coaster ought to feel: it was an involuntary throwback, like a genetically inherited disease—some sort of patriotic dystrophy whose course was triggered by the sound of bugles and the ripplings of flags.

But the Ancestors would be smiling in their chipped gilt frames. Colonel William, Major General Herbert, General Sir Edward and the rest hadn't had much to smile over in the last forty years. Humped about by moving men from parsonage to parsonage, council estate to village and back to council estate again, they had never looked happy with their billets. Medaled and uniformed, as spruce as if they'd just stepped out of bandboxes, they had silently suffered this century behind their glaze of varnish and watched the family fortunes crumble. They had, presumably, perked up a little for the two World Wars, but they had spent my lifetime looking increasingly offended at their own spectacular irrelevance. They'd turned into fossils, beached up on the shore of a world of trades unions, winds of change, atheism, jeans, video clubs and one-parent families.

At long last there was something on television for them that they'd understand. Great-great-grandfather Herbert, who'd put down a rising of Looshai tribesmen in Bengal in '59, was back in his element this afternoon, suddenly in touch again with the rising generation, just as the rising generation, lectured by Mrs. Thatcher on how they must return to "Victorian values," were suddenly, magically, back in touch with their lost forebears.

I have in front of me a letter written from aboard the QE 2, a day or two after embarkation for the Falklands, by a twenty-one-year-old subaltern in the Welsh Guards to his mother.

> Dear Mummy,
>
> . . . Everybody on the ship is dedicated to the repossession of the Falkland Islands. We are all supremely confident in our leaders. . . . I hope that I will some day return to see the green fields of England but my main aim is to do my duty to my country and my men. . . .
>
> You must thank everybody for organising parties for me down to making encouraging remarks—it is all very good for morale. Especially thank *you* for everything you did getting me on my way. *Don't* worry about me—worrying gets you nowhere. My life is in God's hands and to a limited extent my own hands. However I would not be sailing to the South Atlantic if I didn't think that what we are doing, and about to do, is entirely right. . . .

Even when one has allowed for some regimental ghost-writing, this is strange language coming from a man born in 1961. It is a letter written in a dream. The prospect of war has floated its author clean away from England of the 1980s. He is writing from a realm of such plucky unrealism and moral simplicity that it would be hard to locate it in any actual period of history. When a real Victorian, my own great-great-grandfather, embarked for India as an ensign in 1840 at the age of twenty, he too wrote to his mother from his ship:

My dearest Mother,

    As you requested I write the last thing. The Pilot is
just going to leave the vessel. We have a fair wind
and everything appears as if we should soon be
comfortable. Robert has just left the ship and will tell
you all. Give my most affectionate love to my father,
sisters and all the rest of the party. Believe me to
remain, Ever your most affectionate son . . .

The tone of the new Elizabethan is infinitely more elevated
than that of this young Victorian. When the Empire was a
matter of political fact, the dangerous business of policing
it was just a job that young men of the middle class were
automatically expected to do. They had little or none of
the zealotry, the heady sense of being on a religious and
national crusade, that the Welsh Guards officer brought to
the phantasmal imperial exercise in the Falklands when the
real Empire had disappeared long, long before he was born.

Everyone was embarking for somewhere. On the rising tide
I rowed the dinghy up into the village and loaded it with
pacific supplies like bags of charcoal for the stove, new wick
for the lamps, a mackerel line and, in case the mackerel line
came to no good, some tinned sardines and steak-and-
kidney pies. At midday I embarked for—I wasn't sure
where. I crept as quietly as I could, with the engine keeping
up a stream of warlike remarks, down the Yealm into a brisk
blue day on the open sea.
    I had been singlehandedly in charge of the boat for less
than a week, and was shivering with adrenaline and nerves
as I did everything to Commander King's ghostly orders. I
checked the shrouds overhead to see they were clear,
wound up the heavy sails on their winches, tidied the foredeck, wrapped ropes round cleats, until the whole boat was
tuned and taut, braced against the wind and plowing splash-
ily ahead. She did not sail like a yacht: her trawler hull
drove heavily, bullishly, through the water, shouldering it

aside and raising plumes of sunlit spray over the bows. She didn't so much lean to the wind as yield to it unwillingly, exposing as little of her hull below the waterline as she possibly could.

With the reactionary engine shut down, I listened apprehensively to every sound in the sudden quiet. Ropes creaked and banged in their wooden blocks. The freshwater supply slopped and gurgled in the fifty-gallon tank under the cockpit. The chains of the steering gear rumbled with every small adjustment to the wheel. The short, sharp waves marched steadily alongside, breaking against the hull in a continuous low hiss. Once, I caught the noise of an intruder's footsteps, but it was only the rhythmical *flop-flop-flop* of loosely packed books in the saloon shelves.

Gosfield Maid lumbered along under sail at about four sea miles an hour, but it felt as fast and heart-in-mouth as flying, with the water foaming past under the gunwale and the boat's wake breaking up behind her like a jet trail. I was utterly absorbed in the anxious business of simply staying afloat, living from moment to moment and from wave to wave.

Anxiety kept me very much busier than I need have been. I was frightened that the compass was wrong, that the tidal current would carry the boat miles off course, that fog would come down, that I'd lose my landmarks, that the wind would blow up into a gale, that I'd spring a leak—that somehow or other, this intense, private, shivery pleasure was eventually bound to turn into a string of bubbles.

I had the floorboards up to check the bilges. They were dry. Were they too dry? I blackened the chart with crosses, and kept on dashing out into the cockpit with the hand-bearing compass to see if Bolt Head and Prawle Point were still where I'd last left them, or whether they'd made a break for it and escaped over the horizon. From three miles off, the Devon coast was still winter-brown in the April sun; its headlands, cliffs and outlying rocks looked like a crumbled and half-eaten fruitcake on the edge of the sea.

The egotism of a man by himself in a boat is bolstered by everything that he can see. Out on the water, you *are* the centrifugal point of the world through which you move, carrying the great disk of your horizon with you as you go. The first lessons in navigation entail an almost-scientific proof of the magnificent fallacy that the universe has been constructed for your convenience alone.

Bolt Head and Prawle Point are important for their *relative bearings*—their bearings in relation to you, which alter with every move that you make over the seafloor. The land in general turns into a wonderfully protean material: cliffs slide in and out from behind one another; new hills slowly enfold themselves round cities; houses and trees wander about the landscape, meeting and separating, while you stay fixed on your own lumpy patch of water.

This is just a prelude to the higher egotism yet to come. I had on board a sextant which I meant to learn to use sometime, together with Maria Blewitt's *Celestial Navigation for Yachtsmen*. The book began by sketching out an intoxicating fiction:

> We navigate by means of the Sun, the Moon, the planets and the stars. Forget the Earth spinning round the Sun with the motionless stars infinite distances away, and imagine that the Earth is the centre of the universe and that all the heavenly bodies circle slowly round us, the stars keeping their relative positions while the Sun, Moon and planets change their positions in relation to each other and to the stars. This pre-Copernican outlook comes easily as we watch the heavenly bodies rise and set, and is a help in practical navigation.

Forget Copernicus? I had spent my life trying, pretty much in vain, to remember Copernicus. I was delighted by this navigator's view of the universe, in which everything was just as it seemed to be, with the sun, moon and stars as mere satellites, tastefully disposed about the globe, and man the navigator at the epicenter of the whole ingenious piece of clockwork. *Geocentric* and *egocentric* are one small typing error apart; in celestial navigation, I had at last hit on a cosmology I could live with.

"Sometime, old boy," my father said, "you're going to have to learn that the world does not revolve around *you.*"

Thirty years on, I was learning the very opposite. With the headlands changing places and the sun going west, the world was turning round the axis of *Gosfield Maid* and I was back to Ptolemy.

Far out on the rim of the world, and in some danger of dropping off it altogether, there was the faint angular silhouette of an enormous ship. I couldn't tell what it was— maybe an aircraft carrier, maybe a cruiser, but it looked big, naval and Falklands-bound. Seen from the center of things, its distant shadow was comfortingly insubstantial, anyway; an irrelevant distraction from the really important business of ropes, compass points and log readings.

I had never known a privacy so deep and self-contained as this. It was temporary and spiced with fright. It was bounded by Devonshire on one side and the task force on the other; but for the moment at least it felt absolute: an isolation, and an equilibrium, often dreamed of but never experienced till now. Lurching airborne through the sea, with lots of sunshine, a good library and the kettle just coming to the boil, I thought: I wouldn't half mind spending eternity along these lines.

But the wind was fading and *Gosfield Maid* was down to three knots, then two and a half, against a foul tide that was picking up in speed as the English Channel tried to empty itself into the Atlantic Ocean. Off Start Point, twenty-four miles and seven hours out of the Yealm, I gave in and got the engine going. It came to life with a burst of patriotic blather.

The sea here was suddenly troublesome. Start Point sticks out into the tidal stream, a mile-long breakwater of solid granite. When the tide is running, it piles up against the headland and pours round its end in a confused mass of white water—eddies, whirlpools and frothy, pyramid-shaped waves. When a strong wind blows against the grain of the tide, the place is dangerous, a sickening switchback ride over an indignant and frustrated sea which will do its best to spit you out and suck you down at the same time.

There was not enough wind to do that today, but there was a broad stretch of water ahead, rippling, off-white, like a field of grazing sheep. As soon as it came into sight, the boat began to slew and stumble through the waves, even though their tops were barely breaking. Following the instructions in the pilot book, I tucked myself in within a half-mile of the shore, waited until the lighthouse shifted round from northeast, through north, to north-northwest, and steered for it, aiming to shave past the rock with fifty yards or less to spare.

All tide races are supposed to have an "inside passage"— a ribbon of water close inshore through which you can sneak past the race without getting caught in it. Such inside passages exist only in the right weather. Some are just diluted versions of the turmoil to seaward. Some are avenues of calm as wide as the Champs-Elysées; others are narrow alleys in which a boat is squeezed tight between the race and the rocks. They are all places where your heart quickens and you keep your fingers crossed as you go in.

The inside passage round Start Point *was* there that evening—a broad, sluggish channel, its seaward bank marked by a ragged line of scum. It led into what was left of the sunset; a few low cloud banks smeared with ocher and mauve. Everything was darkening fast: Start Bay was turning to a lake of ink, and lights were coming on in the straggle of villages along the shore. I steered for the fading obelisk on the hill over the entrance to the River Dart until I lost it in the dowdy sky. Then there was just a confusion of colored lights. Crab boats, returning to the river at different angles, showed as winking dots of red, white and green. The trouble was that the rest of the world was afloat too. Pubs, cars, lampposts and front rooms were bobbing about among the crabbers. Observing the international collision regulations, I gave way indiscriminately to nursing homes, Volvos, bungalows and guesthouses as they steamed past my bows, before I found the metrical flash of the Kingswear light which guided me into the river between a pair of invisible castles.

By night, Dartmouth was a dazzling incandescent city. It blazed on the water, a mile-long pool of blinding reflections so hard and bright that you could nearly hear them clink. They shattered and regrouped in the crisscross wakes of fishing boats and ferries—a Manhattan of lights on the hop. I left *Gosfield Maid* chained to a buoy in midstream, rowed through the middle of the loud reflections, found a seafood restaurant on the waterfront and basked in my luck at happening on such unexpected splendor.

But day broke on Boots the Chemists' and on Barclays Bank. It disclosed an English seaside town, bunched and squat, with too much pastel pebbledash and too much tea-shoppe half-timbering. The jam of traffic on the streets was as quiet as sludge, patiently shifting, a few feet at a time, through narrow conduits of low brick villas and tall advertisments for low-tar cigarettes. On a green hill of razored lawns to the north of the town, the Britannia Royal Naval College lorded it over Dartmouth. I studied it through binoculars. No one seemed to be at home, although some wheeled cannons were parked on the gravel near the front door. The College didn't look a very friendly place. Its bland white facade and banks of bare uncurtained windows gave it the supercilious expression of an officer staring fixedly over the tops of the heads of the Other Ranks. Searching the grounds, I found a gardener marching a power mower uphill, another cannon, pointed strategically at Marks & Spencer's in the town, a bed of obedient and well-drilled roses, a blue naval Land-Rover and a horse. Perhaps everyone had gone to the Falklands.

In the town, I tried ringing the College number and found that the cadets were away for their Easter holidays, but that the Captain was in residence and would be happy to see me. He would, he said, find a chap to show me round. Thinking of those lawns, the ruled parallel lines of green left by the mower, the nap of the turf trimmed to the quick, I decided that I'd better get a haircut first.

I had hoped to find the College barber and persuade him

to disguise me as an officer and gentleman, but I got Kath
in a small and smelly Unisex Salon. She wore her name on
a badge pinned between her breasts, which were unusually
large and tended to get in the way of her craft.

"Here on business, are you?"

"Sort of. Not exactly." I could hardly breathe for breast,
as Kath soaped and kneaded my skull. Given our intimacy,
I felt that this was a lame and dumb reply. Washed, cradled,
patted, pummeled, I confided in Kath and tried to tell her
what I was doing.

"Oh . . . *travel.*"

The air in the salon was hot and chemical. Wriggling free
of the breast for a moment, I inhaled a sick-making lungful
of acetone, peroxide and synthetic jasmine.

"I'd like to travel."

To travel. An intransitive verb. A state of being, not a
journey to a destination.

"Where to?"

"What, dear?"

"Where would you like to travel *to?*"

"Oh—you know. Abroad." She was on to the scissors
work now, snipping away behind my ears, her coral slacks
a bright splash in the mirror. "You get fed up, don't you,
staying in one place all the time? Specially in Dartmouth.
You should be here in the winter—it's a real dump then."

"Where have you been so far?"

"Well . . ." Kath stood back from her handiwork, her big
and rather piggy face heavy with thought. "I went to Sheffield in November. I got an uncle and auntie living there.
In Sheffield."

"Yes, I know Sheffield. That must have been a change
from Devon. The North's so different from the South, isn't
it? What did you make of it?"

She snipped and put on her thinking face again. "It were
a lot cheaper than here," she said.

Cuttings of gray hair were falling into the lap of the
surplice which Kath had dressed me in. I thought: *surely
that's not mine?* It struck me that the curious style of babying
which goes on in a Unisex Salon is exactly the same treat-

ment that gets meted out to the senile, and perhaps it was my elderliness which had entitled me to the insistent nuzzling of Kath's breast against my ear.

"Well, meat—things like that—*they* was cheaper. But fruit—that was round about the same."

Up on the barbered hill we sat out on the terrace of the Captain's House, taking tea.

"There's no romance in the sea," the Captain was saying. "It's interesting, of course. Fascinating, even. But it's not a place for the Walter Mittys of this world."

We'd been discussing the schoolboys who came to Dartmouth as officers-in-training, but I had the uncomfortable feeling that this talk of romance and Walter Mittyism might, just conceivably, be directed at me.

"Do you get a lot of prospective Walter Mittys, then?"

"Not a lot. Some. Either it gets knocked out of them in their first few weeks here or they don't stay the course and go off and work in . . . advertising, or something."

The Captain's crisp, open-air, naval voice came straight out of British war movies of the 1950s starring John Gregson and Kenneth More. It suggested unflappable calm in times of peril and boundless common decency and common sense. You could hear it saying things like "Buck up, old girl —we'll soon have Jerry licked" and "All right, Number One; I'll take her over now." Like the rest of the Captain, his voice was perfectly tailored to his job. Fiftyish, grizzling round the temples, tidy-featured, he was a national archetype; the sort of Englishman whom one could sell in Texas or Saudi Arabia as a masterpiece of authenticated provenance. There was just one detail which seemed to be at odds with the rest of him: against the background of his fine-check Viyella shirt, he was wearing a brilliant gold silk tie. Looking at that splendiferous tie, I wondered if perhaps there was a streak of Mittyism in the Captain's wife.

Of course, the Captain said, the College had changed a great deal since his own days there. It was far more democratic. One saw a lot of chaps nowadays from state-run schools.

"A lot? How many?"

"Oh, I haven't got the figures offhand. But we get quite a few coming in now."

Certainly the college was very democratic in its academic standards. A handful of O levels and one scraped pass at A were enough to qualify a boy as an officer-in training. ("We don't call them 'cadets' nowadays.")

"We're not after intellectuals. We're looking for leadership potential."

Talking to the Captain, I felt that I was being interviewed for a place in the College and was being found wanting on every count. Words went flat in my mouth. I didn't know how to crack the dry little jokes that would have made things easier between us. When I referred to the Falklands adventure as "a pretty Walter Mittyish sort of exercise," trying to milk our one common allusion for as much as it was worth, the Captain stared at the sky with a smile of forced politeness.

Below us, the River Dart was landlocked by the hills. Boats which were too small and far away to see were decorating it with feathery wakes. I wished that I were afloat instead of stranded here out of my element, feeling cowed and clumsy in the Captain's headmasterly presence.

The "chap" who had been detailed to show me around was a uniformed Lieutenant Commander who had, in the service phrase, "risen from the ranks," as if the process were closely akin to miraculous ascension. "I'm Mike," he said, and his voice had kept the local coloring of what I took to be Cheshire or the Pottery Towns. I liked his slight stoop, his meat-plate hands, the way his uniform hung on him like someone else's cast-offs. He made being a naval officer look like a proper job and not something that just happened to you, like being a debutante or a manic depressive.

The empty College smelled of polish and carbolic soap, with a faint residual trace of changing-room; of wet towels, jockstraps and dubbin. Its floors were called "decks," and its architect had fancifully framed and paneled it like a ship in

varnished oak. We marched, out of step, down a corridor
tiled in institutional sea-green and inspected the Seamanship and Navigation rooms. I looked, with as much interest
as I could muster, at knotted ropes in glass cases, at colored
wall charts. I read:

> A dredger shows two vertical red lights (balls by day)
> on her foul side, and two vertical green lights
> (diamonds by day) on her clear side.

But it was the smells, which no carbolic could mask, that
kept me silent and preoccupied. There was the broken soil
and bruised grass of the rugger pitch. Blanco, chalk dust,
gun oil, licorice, stale flannel, passed gas. The badgery
musk of adolescent boys herded into classes, teams, sections
was ingrained in the woodwork of the place.

"I'd expected a sort of nautical university," I said; "but it
feels just like a school."

"They used to come here at thirteen, of course. Now
they come in at eighteen or nineteen, and I don't know . . .
I sometimes think the College hasn't quite adapted to that
—they still tend to get treated as if they were thirteen."

The walls of the Quarter Deck were hung with royal
portraits which had the impressive awfulness of painted ef-
figies of saints in a Maltese Easter procession. We were
followed across the parquet floor by the waxwork eyes of
Prince Edward, Prince Charles, Princess Anne and Lord
Mountbatten. The bold crudity of the paintings was in
sharp and significant contrast to the fussy perfectionism of
the ship models. They sailed under glass, every hatch coam-
ing and coil of rope fastidiously to scale. Some were tended
by manikins two-thirds of an inch high, who were working
their anchor winches, scaling their ratlines and furling sails
on their yards. Tiny officers on 1:100 bridges squeaked tiny
orders to their tiny men. This modeling of life in miniature
seemed to me to be of a piece with Dartmouth at large; the
College felt as if it had been designed specifically to stop
young men from growing up.

"Would you have been happy to come here when you were eighteen?"

"Me?" Mike stood hunched, hands-in-pockets, intransigently life-sized. "I expect I'd have thought it was murder. But they're used to it. They've nearly all been to boarding school. It's the ones who haven't been who find it a bit tough."

"I went to boarding school, and I'd have hated it—it would have been everything I wanted to run away from."

We went upstairs to the Poop Deck, where the dormitories were. The officers-in-training slept twenty to a room in tiers of bunks, their Navy-issue blankets nipped round the mattress ends in regulation "hospital tucks." No space for private thoughts and feelings here: the bare quarters looked like a place of punishment.

"My worst memory," I said.

"Oh—it teaches them to live together. Doesn't do them any harm."

"I wouldn't be too sure of that."

I stood leaning on a cold radiator under a high window, looking out. The river below was muddled with another river, a hundred miles or so away from here; the Severn, like simmering caramel, spilling over its banks into the water meadows and playing fields on the far side. It yanked up winter trees by their roots, swallowed unwary cats, carried away people's garden sheds. Frogmen were forever searching it for bodies near the town bridge, a favored suicide resort. From the barred dormitory window, the river looked so wild and free that it was easy to see what made the jumpers do it.

"They share cabins after the first year."

There was a small locker by each bunk. I opened the door to one of them. A *Playboy* centerfold was thumbtacked to the inside along with a Polaroid snapshot of a woman of about my own age holding a panting golden Labrador on a chain. Nothing had changed, except that the pin-up had grown a lot skinnier since my day and Mother's picture was in color. The one missing item was a graph-paper chart on which you could cross out the remaining weeks, days, hours and minutes to go before the end of term. I shut the locker, feeling breathless and tight about the chest.

"It's a pity that the lads are all away," Mike said.

No, it wasn't. The lads were crowding far too thickly round for comfort as it was.

"I'm so sorry—" I made a pantomime of looking at my watch. "I'd completely lost track of the time."

"The Captain said to show you the beagles and the Royal garden—"

"Tell him I loved them," I said. "They were wonderful—"

"You're sure?"

"Certain, thank you. I just have to go—"

On the way downstairs—we must have been on the Orlop Deck—I heard a light, cruel tenor voice baying "Fa—a—ag!," the scramble of feet on a flight of stone steps, and a feeble asthmatic wheeze in my own lungs. By the time we reached the graveled drive with its memorial cannonry, I wasn't so much leaving the Britannia Royal Naval College as running away from it in a fit of blind funk.

No secrets were permitted. In stern Protestant tradition, everything was above board and exposed to public view. On the dormitory windows there were bars but no curtains; the long uncarpeted room held twenty-four narrow iron bedsteads spaced, by order, at eighteen-inch intervals. This was just sufficiently close for your neighbor on either side to grab your genitals without polite preliminaries.

You wank me, I'll wank you. There was no more homosexual affection in the exchange than there was in fives or boxing: it was a compulsory game designed to teach the new boy that his private parts were private no longer. From now on, nothing was private. What else would you expect of a *public* school?

The doors had been removed from the toilet cubicles. Boys squatted in the row of open stalls, their trousers collapsed around their ankles, showing bald knees and moon faces as they emptied their bowels. At 7:15 each morning they queued in naked lines for the cold showers, while the duty house monitor—another, older boy of seventeen or eighteen—stood by in a dressing gown, on guard.

"Get *under* it, Pearson! . . . Reynolds, soap your shitty arse, will you?"

The younger boys were "fags"; fags by name rather than fags by nature, since in England in the 1950s the word had not yet taken on its American meaning. A fag was simply a monitor's personal servant. He swept the monitor's study, cleaned his shoes, pressed his trousers, laid out his books, woke him with morning tea, and was permanently on call for chores and errands.

"Fa—a—ag!"

In the Lower Common Room, the fags sprinted for the stairs. The last to arrive in line at the shadowy corridor of monitors' studies, with their superior scent of Woodbine cigarettes, coffee and old leather, got the job. I had asthma and was a hopeless runner, so the last in line was usually me.

I was no Jeeves. I fetched the wrong cricket pads from the pavilion, the wrong brand of gramophone needles from the music shop in town. I left smears on most of the things I did. When I ironed trousers, their creases turned, despite my best efforts, to a maze of intersecting lines like a railway junction. When I made cocoa for the monitors, the milk foamed in the pan and congealed on the stove in a mess of black gunk. Three or four times every term I was ritually beaten for being "slack."

"You are a very *low* person, Raban."

"Yes, Owen."

Owen was Head of House, a far more impressive figure, with a far wider range of punishments at his disposal, than any master.

"What are you, Raban?"

"A low person, Owen."

"You're so low that I can hardly see you, Raban. You're a wet squit."

"Yes, Owen."

"So take your horrible low wet squit presence out of my sight."

To begin with, there was an internal blaze of hurt and

disbelief, like a bursting appendix. But after a few months the day-to-day terrorism of boarding school settled into an acceptable, at least survivable, normality. I knew well enough that beatings, crushings and physical humiliations were all in the curriculum if you were going to be properly educated as an Englishman. They were an essential part of the privilege for which our parents were making their well-trumpeted financial sacrifices. My own father had been at the school, in the same house, twenty-three years before me. I found his initials, J. P. C. P. R., scratched into the stone window frame of the Lower Common Room. He had regaled me with a memory, curiously cheerful, of being tossed in a laundry basket until his leg had been broken. King's had made a Man of him, and it was going to make a Man of me.

The school, in the cathedral grounds at Worcester, had started life in the Dark Ages and claimed the Venerable Bede as its founder. But its character was wholly nineteenth-century, a shoestring model of Thomas Arnold's Rugby. Since the middle of the nineteenth century it had been preparing the sons of clergymen, solicitors and the better sort of tradesman for the tough business of Empire. Wherever the map was still colored red, there were Old Vigornians. They were not grandees but functionaries: adjutants, A. D. Cs, civil servants, schoolteachers, tea planters, shipping agents . . . the gruff, uncomplaining men in the middle of things who sported an Old School tie that no one who had been to Winchester or Harrow would recognize.

Bulletins of their doings, apparently borne in cleft sticks, reached the school magazine, their tone breezy and facetious. There was the instantly identifiable style of the lonely O. V. keeping his pecker up in foreign parts:

> **Anyone for Tennis?** H. P. B. "Tug" Willson (School House, 1941–46) reports that he is now settling down to his new job as Assistant Manager of Crombie & Prettejohns' Commerical Bank in Bulawayo, which is *not*, as he points out, where the nuts come from. "Tug" observes that rugger, Bulawayo style, fails to

match Vigornian standards. His tennis, as a result, is
rapidly improving, and any O.V.s in the Bulawayo
area who would like to try their forehands on the
Bank's well-lit asphalt courts are invited to get in
touch.

The O.V.s were all around us. Their names were engraved
on the pawnbroker's hoard of silver cups, which it was the
duty of the fags to polish up on Sunday mornings in the
interval between cathedral Matins and lunch. The walls of
the house refectory were stacked solid with their photographs. They stood, sat and squatted cross-legged in teams,
holding rugger balls, cricket bats, oars and hockey sticks.
The older O.V.s were in sepia—boys already looking as
grim as middle-aged men, wearing linen shorts that came
down below their knees. Their stares were blank, their faces
masks. They were our future. Their tradition of duty, service, knuckling-to and playing the game was being passed
intact to us, a millstone inheritance.
    At evening prayers we sang:

> The day Thou gavest, Lord, is ended,
> The darkness falls at Thy behest . . .

Owen, a cathedral organ scholar, was at the piano, keeping
up a weepy, throbbing, juicy rhythm in the bass. Major
MacTurk, our housemaster, late of the Scots Guards, led
the singing. His black walrus mustache was going to salt-
and-pepper at the tips, and his ears and nostrils sprouted
fierce little curlicues of hair.

> The sun that bids us rest is waking
> Our brethren 'neath the western sky,
> And hour by hour fresh lips are making
> Thy wondrous tribute heard on high.

Our brethren 'neath the western sky were O.V.s every one.
Sunset over Worcester was sunrise in Fiji and the Gilbert
and Ellice Islands. On isolated hill stations, in mission

schools and trading posts, our brethren were emptying their
tin bowls of shaving water and knotting their O.V. ties,
assisted on every hand by native fags. The hymn, together
with my heroic and somewhat simplified view of the reali-
ties of the British Empire, always made my eyes prickle
unmanfully, thus disqualifying me from a Vigornian vocation at the very moment when the vocation itself tugged at
its strongest.

Like most of the masters, Major MacTurk conspicuously
retained his wartime military rank. For the school was
staffed by men who were officers by inclination and teachers
only by necessity. From Monday to Friday they strode
about the school like fugitive crows in their threadbare university gowns. In class, they slogged through Caesar's *Gallic
Wars*, the Tudor kings and queens and French irregular
verbs. No one could accuse them of unseemly enthusiasm.
But on Saturday mornings, when the school Corps assembled in uniform, they came out in their true colors. In full
battledress, their campaign ribbons glowing on their
breasts, they twirled their swagger sticks and *grew*. Colonel
Shepherd added three inches to his height; Captain
Thomas turned from a tenor to a baritone in his Saturday
Black Watch outfit; Major MacTurk, already frighteningly
large in my world, swelled up like some mythical avatar of
War, his mustache points freshly waxed, his eyebrows as
black and spiky as a hedge of thorns.

The moment the bell sounded at eleven, the school became an Army company. Blancoed and bereted, equipped
with rifles salvaged from the Boer War, we drilled on the
parade ground in deadly earnest. The Corps was not a
game: it was, more effectively than Greek or Latin, an
educational foundation stone, a serious preparation for the
life that was supposed to lie ahead of boys who went to
King's. The school kept Sandhurst supplied with a steady
stream of officer cadets, and to do National Service without
winning a commission was regarded as mildly disgraceful.

At thirteen-going-on-fourteen I was a daydreaming academic washout, but I could strip a Bren in sixteen seconds,
calculate the trajectory of a bullet, with all due allowance

for dead ground, charge a stuffed sack with a bayonet, and interpret an Ordnance Survey map in terms of its possibilities for gunnery and tactical surprise. In the Corps, the slovenly and inattentive child came within a whisker of making the grade. There was a good deal of derision in the Lower Common Room when I was, to my own astonishment, promoted to lance corporal.

Major MacTurk said: "If you didn't have asthma, Raban, and generally pulled your socks up, one might even begin to think in terms of Sandhurst, but alas—"

He might as well have pinned the Military Cross to my chest. Once a term, on Field Day, I got a taste of what it might feel to be a true Vigornian. We were bused out to Bromyard Down, an undulating land, with a desolate and wretched aspect. Wheezing only a little, I led my section in V-formation through the spiny gorse and made them wriggle on their bellies in single file. The foggy silence was broken every so often by the petulant small bangs of blank .303 cartridges and the loud voices of officers proclaiming the injured and the dead.

The officers had commandeered every bump and knuckle of high ground, from where they ran the war with whistles and enlivened it with thunderclaps. It was an old-fashioned, low-tech war. Fighting was at close quarters, some of it hand-to-hand. From sandy foxholes, covering fire was provided for acts of suicidal heroism. It belonged somewhere between Spion Kop and Mademoiselle from Armentières.

The casualties were carried away on stretchers by the conchies in the Red Cross—day boys whose (mostly Quaker) parents had objected to their compulsory service in the Corps, and who were reckoned to be beneath contempt. The living fought on into the dusk, mounting pincer movements, recce patrols and snatch raids for prisoners, who were frequently tortured during their interrogations.

This enforced military apprenticeship at least produced a fund of metaphor with which to explain and ratify the experience of boarding school. For most of the five years that I spent at King's, I saw myself as a prisoner of war, detained by Germans in a comfortless Stalag for the duration. The ferocious bullying, the removal of the most basic privacies, the treatment of physical weakness as an offense worth punishing, were simply what one expected to endure at the hands of the gooks.

I knew all about gooks. I escaped into the literature of escape—the paperback memoirs of the British prisoners who had dug tunnels, built wooden horses, gone over the wire in laundry trucks during the War. In the early 1950s, scads of these stories were published every year, and I read every one of them, greedily, lost in the romantic fiction of running away. Many of the most commercially successful of these books were unsatisfactory for my purposes, since they dealt with escape on a mass scale—twenty or thirty men at a time scrabbling their way through the earth to freedom. My interest was in the one-man tunnel, the solitary break planned without reference to the Escapes Officer, and these were so rare that I had to invent most of them for myself.

In the moonlit dormitory I lay half-awake, with bells from the cathedral ringing the quarter-hours. The gooks slept. Working effortlessly, I carried away paper-bagfuls of soft soil, which would later be surreptitiously scattered over the rose beds in the school gardens. I shored up the night's work with slats of wood torn from a tea chest that I'd spotted earlier that day outside Matron's door. My nails were broken and I had earth in my hair, but I was already under the first line of wire. Ten yards more, and I'd be under the perimeter fence. Twenty yards beyond that, the pinewood began. The gooks, with their searchlight mounted on the eastern watchtower, would never spot me as I sprinted (asthma miraculously cured) through the trees. *Auf Wiedersehen!*

Ten years later I came across what I took to be the key to this compulsive fictionizing, these sweet dreams of heroic warfare and flight, when I read Vladimir Nabokov's afterword to a reissue of *Lolita*. The germ of the novel, Nabokov said, lay in a newspaper clipping about a captive ape in a Californian research institute. Given paints, brushes and paper, the ape spent a year producing indecipherable blobs of color. Electrodes were attached to its brain. Its tormentors tried to encourage it by subjecting the animal to a perpetual exhibition of simple pictures of female apes, bananas, tall trees and other likely objects of fantasy. At last it came up with the goods. Sheet after sheet of paper was painted with shaky black parallel lines. The chimpanzee was drawing the bars of its own cage.

I wasted the greater part of my time at this school in drawing the bars of my cage. I went there at eleven, on a state scholarship, and was mercifully withdrawn from it when I was sixteen.

Now the whole country was out on a field day.

The saloon, lit by the flickering gray moonshine of the TV, rocked comfortably at anchor. Crouched forward, cupping my jawbone in my hands, I was engrossed in the shuffle of bizarre pictures on the screen.

Vertical-takeoff fighters dithered grotesquely aloft, making the air below them boil. Marines with bodybuilders' muscles and elaborate tattoos were doing physical jerks in an improvised gym. They were naked except for their uniform undershorts, which consisted of two Union Jacks, one fore, one aft. The crux of the frontward flags bulged with impressive genital equipment. More soldiers, their faces menacingly camouflaged with boot polish, or perhaps woad, were at bayonet practice, making horrible noises as they charged the sack. The show came to a climax with a wide-angle shot of another saloon, now an Other Ranks mess, packed with several hundred singing men.

> It's a long way to Tipperary, it's a long way to go!
> It's a long way to Tipperary, to the sweetest girl I
> know . . .

This was, by field-day standards, surprisingly tame, and was probably a special request of the TV crew: the songs I remembered were all ones of unrelieved dirtiness, like the pathologically fecal "In Mobile."

The reporter's voice was as strange as the pictures themselves. It was an earnest pastiche of the Britain-can-take-it style of Movietone News in the 1940s. It left unnatural dramatic gaps between the words of the script; it was over-loud, as if the reporter were addressing a camp meeting instead of a clip-on mike in his shirtfront; like the singing, it was exaggeratedly *ff* and *allegro con spirito*.

I felt like an eavesdropper watching this bulletin from the task force being transmitted from a secret position some-where in the Atlantic. The program was, I suspected, not designed to be seen by me or by anyone in the British Isles. It was certainly not news in the ordinary sense, but a form of warfare in its own right. Its targeted audience was Argen-tinian, and the reporter's overemphatic delivery was proba-bly intended to make his words more easily translatable to the people to whom he was really speaking—the General, the Admiral and the Brigadier in Buenos Aires.

The first objective of the voyage of the task force was evidently to scare the invaders away from the islands by showing them bloodcurdling television pictures of what was going to happen to them when the ships arrived. This was assault by photomontage, with flags superimposed over phalluses and songs over airplanes, gun muzzles and bayo-nets. The theme of sexual prowess and conquest was rudely explicit: the Argentine forces and their effete *supremo* were going to be raped by the greater potency of the British.

As we sang on the bus to Bromyard Down—

> Hitler has only got one ball!
> His other one's in Leeds Town Hall;
> Himmler
> Has something sim'lar,
> But poor old Goebbels
> Has no balls
> At all!

No one now could accuse the British of lacking balls: the precious objects had been exhibited on television, tastefully wrapped in the national flag.

There was another novelty in the broadcast. Everything was happening in the first person plural. "We" were steaming south, "we" had declared a two-hundred-mile maritime exclusion zone around the Falkland Islands. The blackface marines were "our boys" (or, as the Prime Minister chose to refer to them, "my boys"). A week before, no anchorman or commentator would have dreamed of risking this cozy pronoun: the State was perceived as a fragile assembly of conflicting parties—Government and Opposition, management and unions, North and South, those with jobs and those without them. But war was working its old black magic, restoring the image of the State as an extension of the self. Britain was beginning to sound exactly like School House.

"We," said Peter Snow, the housemasterly presenter of the BBC's *Newsnight*, "are, at a guess, roughly *here*." He moved some ship models about on a gray plasticine ocean.

Would you be so kind, I thought, as to leave *me* out of this?

Snow's model ships were already three thousand miles away. *Gosfield Maid*, on a reciprocal course and making five, sometimes six knots, was modestly increasing the distance. The task force became as remote as a legend, and what little news I got of it had the cracked ring of archaic fiction.

When you set up house on a boat, however soft and urban you may be and however crowded the coast you sail past, you soon find yourself turning into Robinson Crusoe. Four things matter: food, water, fire and weather. Inside your timber stockade, you begin to construct your civilization from scratch. You start by keeping warm and end up with do-it-yourself theology.

I was in the early stages. I hoarded charcoal. I fished over the stern. The April mackerel were sad things, with tarnished scales and heads too big for their bodies. I bought blotting paper and mustard and cress seeds and set up a kitchen garden in an old office In tray which I screwed to the wheelhouse roof. Hours leaked away in the search for a quay with a freshwater tap and a hosepipe with which I could fill the fifty-gallon tank under the cockpit.

But it was the weather and the tides that kept me in a

state of dazed preoccupation—the same trancelike absorp-
tion that a writer feels in the middle of a book when
he finds himself swallowed in his own plot, no longer the
author of circumstances but a creature of them. Living
in a city, I'd hardly bothered to notice whether it was
raining or shining. Weather was something that just *was*,
and I couldn't have been less interested in its whys and
wherefores.

Now I studied it as intently as any text that I'd pored over
in the past. I watched the Atlantic lows winging their way
in from south of Greenland—unstable, whirling cones of
disturbed air, filling, deepening, changing track, spawning
more depressions in their wake. Spinning against the clock,
they brought the powerful, salty southwesterly winds that
whipped the sea up into untenantable hills of froth and
spume, took slates off roofs and made the water even in
sheltered harbors slop and gurgle round the quays, slamming boats into walls and tossing them frivolously about on
their moorings.

I learned Buys Ballot's Law. Face the wind, and you'll find
low pressure to your right and high pressure to your left
(the reverse, of course, applies in the Falkland Islands). It
was the high pressure to the left of England that I began to
dream of wistfully as I'd once dreamed of unattainable girls.
Please, God, give me a kindly ridge of it, just from, say,
north of the Azores to somewhere a little west of Ireland.
The northwest wind would be cold, but it would come from
the shore, the sea would be flat and *Gosfield Maid* would
whistle up-Channel to the Dover Straits with her sails wide
out to starboard.

I watched the drum on the barograph in the saloon revolve at a tenth of an inch an hour, its inked stylus leaving
a thin blue line on the paper as the vacuum cylinder swelled
and contracted with the changing atmospheric pressure.
Very soon I found myself subscribing to a theory of natural
magic. On the rare morning when the barograph needle
had climbed overnight and was holding steady, so I discovered a buoyancy of spirit in myself, a sudden rush of cheer-
fulness and hope for the day. As the needle dipped, my

mood darkened in sympathy, and I could feel myself sinking down the inky slope on the graph paper.

Galebound at 995 millibars and falling, I sat up in the wheelhouse under a sky of heaped slag and asphalt, lost in the small print of *Reed's Nautical Almanac*. The boat was parked in the busy middle of Brixham harbor, but Brixham itself was no more than a pale frieze of terraces in scabious pastel on the extreme periphery of things. I was more concerned with the moon.

It had been a full moon last night, so with sun and moon in direct line, the tides were running strongly, surging past headlands, then slowing up as they swerved in to fill the bays. High Water Dover was at 0204 and 1420 hours on April 12; the stream ran north and east into Lyme Bay from six hours after until an hour before HWD, so I could ride on a fair tide from 0804 to 1320. But suppose, suppose . . . Lyme Regis was thirty miles along the bay, anything between five and seven hours by boat, and with High Water Lyme at 0949, the harbor there would be a gully of dry sand long before I reached it on that tide. Think again. Try working the next lunar bulge . . . Leave Brixham at 1500, breast the steadily weakening tide until it turns in my favor at 2020, and make Lyme in time for High Water at 2203, with the harbor brimming and plenty of depth and space in which to swing the unwieldy bulk of *Gosfield Maid*. Two flashing red leading lights mark the route in between the piers; sixteen miles to the west, a red light flashes every ten seconds on Straight Point . . .

My notebook turned into a tangled bird's-nest of prophecies and speculations as I tried to fit my own life into these great movements of air and water. I logged the shifting barometric contours, the speed and direction of the winds, the phases of the moon, tidal heights and tidal streams. It was not a scientific exercise. It was more like Hindu astrology, a search for the single auspicious moment when you and the universe are in perfect conjunction and fortune smiles. But my stars were out of sync. When the air was right, the water was wrong; when the water was right, the air was wrong. The boat skulked in dock on its chain, growing slimy green maidenhair under its bilges. I consulted the arcane books, made more prophecies, and tended the mustard and cress on the wheelhouse roof, waiting for the break.

Happy conjunctions were rare, and lasted for the six-hour length of a single tide at most. I learned to trust and seize them when they came. The wind blew off the hills to the north. The sun slid temporarily free of the banks of sullen cloud and put on a display of alchemy, transmuting the sea from lead to chased silver. All sails up, the boat slogged ahead, leaning a little away from the wind. I sat up in front on the hatchway over my bedroom, listening to the log-fire crackle of the breaking foam on the bow wave and watching out for the old bleach and fabric-softener bottles with which the crab and lobster fishermen marked their pots. Properly afloat again, I was up to 1024 millibars and steady.

In this mood, England was as far away as the task force. I was running my ship, and I left Mrs. Thatcher to run hers as she pleased. Immersed in the business of ship's husbandry, I barely noticed what was going on, even when I was on shore. The previous day in Brixham I'd noticed a freshly spray-gunned graffito on a wall at the end of a street. In letters six feet high it said SMASH ARGENTINA! For a second or two I took it for a football slogan, before I remembered.

Two messages from the period.

One was a postcard addressed to me in London. The front was a photograph of the Saint-Gaudens monument to Colonel Shaw and his doomed regiment of black soldiers which stands in front of the State House at the top of Boston Common. The wife of a Harvard professor wrote:

> When are you next coming over? Maybe you'd better emigrate—people here think your country has lost its wits.

The other is the first letter home from the *QE* 2, written by the young Welsh Guards subaltern to his mother. In his last paragraph he looks forward to his arrival at the task-force rendezvous, Ascension Island, where his mail will be waiting:

> No doubt I will pick up Colonel Sinclair's knife in Ascension Island—how many Germans did he kill with it?

CHAPTER 4

HUNTING FOR
FOSSILS

The coastline of southern England softens steadily from west to east. Angular blocks of granite, intransigent in the face of sea and weather, give way to outcrops of soft sandstone. A couple of distant ice cream scoops of chalk mark the point where Devonshire begins to peter out into Dorset. Then it's limestone country. Smoothly curving hills lie low on the horizon. The bare rock—porous, friable stuff, like badly fired pottery—is the color of storm clouds. It dissolves in the rain. Watercourses eat into it like acid, their branch patterns standing out on the landscape. The Jurassic Lias is full of remains, as thickly packed as a common grave with skeletons of creatures that used to live in the sea.

This is England's vulnerable underbelly where people scare themselves to sleep with dreams of strangers and invasions. Here in Dorset a pet monkey swam ashore, the lone survivor of a wrecked ship. The local vigilantes put it to death because they thought it was a French spy (though that story is part of insular mythology—I heard it again in

Northumberland, where the monkey was a Spaniard). Sixty miles away from Europe is just far enough, and near enough, to foster belief in monsters aboard.

In Lyme Regis, *Gosfield Maid* lay against the Cobb, the stone breakwater which enfolds Old Lyme in the crook of its protective arm. The outgoing tide left the boat high and dry, leaning against the wall, its masts roped to bollards on the quay to keep it from falling over into the harbor. Arriving alone and out of season, I fell into the good company of the fishermen, who found a space for me, took my lines, nursed *Gosfield Maid* alongside and came aboard to inspect and approve my ship's carpentry while I stood by, tending bar.

My visitors were the first people I'd met who were not in the least impressed by the saber-rattling which was going on in newspapers and on television.

"What's the point of un?" said John, the owner-skipper of the trawler *Whynot*. "If the government had of wanted a *good* war on their hands, they could've fought the bloomin' French. We should have had a war with *they*, over the seine netting and the fishing limits. But *Argentina* . . ." He shook his head over the idiocy of our rulers.

"They sold we right down the river. First it was Iceland and the cod fishing, they give in over that. Then it's France and the Common Market. Now they got Russians in Liverpool Bay. In bloody great factory ships.

"I was up to London, to Parliament. We was all there, from Lyme. Didn't do no good, though. The politicians, they just give our livelihood away—to the French, the Spaniards, the Portuguese, the Russians . . .

"There's no fish left, hardly, in England now. You see a Dover today, he's a shadow of what he used to be, a little-bitty thing of gristle and bone, all head, no flesh to him. That's seine netting. Or you take sprats. Ten year back, I've had this harbor full of blood after the sprat fishing, the water *red*—even the sand were red. You'd never see that nowadays. The French took they, and they took the fry too, with nets so fine that nothing, not the little babies even, gets away.

"They lets all that go by on the nod, then they goes off to fight a war with Argentina over they Falkland Islands— *lovely job!*"

Nevertheless, John was a fish plutocrat. Jeaned, booted, with gray muttonchop sideburns and Zapata mustache, he was king of the Cobb. He'd begun as a farm laborer, fishing in his spare time for roach and chub in the muddy Somerset rivers. Then he came to Lyme, bought a leaky 9-foot dinghy for £5, and set pots for crab and lobster in all weathers. He'd been laughed at by the locals, who promised him that the next time he took his absurd little cockleshell boat out to sea would be the last.

"They used to joke about how I were going to turn into bait for the crabs."

These ribbing sessions were overheard by a lonely retired man who lived in a cottage above the Cobb and used to sit by himself in the fishermen's bar.

"Laughing at a tryer. Old Varnes, he wouldn't *bide* that."

So Mr. Varnes lent John the £400 he needed to buy a proper boat, an 18-foot launch properly equipped for crabbing. John paid him back with fishing trips and a £10 note every Friday night.

"We'd go out, with Mr. Varnes sitting up in the front, smoking his cigarettes and eating scallops raw, out of the shell. That's all he ever did—smoked, and ate his 'queenies.' He wouldn't say a word to me, and I wouldn't say a word to he, from one end of the day to the other."

A year later there was a new boat—a 24-footer. Varnes sat in front, coughing, smoking and sucking scallops out of their shells. John was now the most successful crabber in Lyme Bay, often working in the dark, in seas rough enough to keep everyone else ashore. With Varnes's help, he bought a 36-foot trawler, from which he was able to shoot strings of pots and fish offshore for whiting, plaice and pollock. When Mr. Varnes died of lung cancer, John was his sole heir. He'd been left £17,000—enough to commission a boatbuilder in Bideford to make him a fine wooden 48-foot beam trawler.

Now, with the *Whynot*, a cockle barrow at each end of

town, a fishmonger's shop and a kiosk on the Cobb, he was rich. In Mrs. Thatcher's England, John was an exemplary figure of self-reliance, industry and business acumen. Coming up past fifty, he still kept that innocent entrancement with the secret watery world of the fish of the boy who had once haunted the riverbank, waiting for his colored-quill float to tremble and go under.

"With fish as scarce as what they are, you always got to be *thinking* fish. The others, they'll go where they caught plaice last week, or last year. That's not good enough—not now it isn't. Me, I go out, and I say to meself, 'Where's he *to*, then? If I were a plaice, where'd *I* be?' "

"So where are the plaice now?"

"Right inshore. On the rocks. They're feeding off of these little mussels, see? Building theyselves back up after spawning. Today, now, you got to go in close—closer'n most people like to, till you can *feel* the bottom under the keel. That's where the plaice is now. But next week he'll be gone, back to deep water. Next week, or the week after."

Even his holidays were spent fishing. For five weeks each summer, John took his wife to the island of St. Lucia, where he fished for tuna in the hard-drinking company of the Haitian Ambassador.

It was a Horatio Alger success story, from farm boy to tycoon. It was authentically English and long-shadowed in two essential respects—in the sad, solitary, silent figure of John's benefactor smoking himself to death in the cuddy, and in the prospect, not far off, of a sea so thoroughly trawled and netted by comeovers that its stock of fish would be exhausted. But in the interval between the death of Mr. Varnes and the death of the Channel as a fishery, John was one of the happiest Englishmen alive.

I was taken crabbing by Geordie and Ken, who woke me at 0830 hours by bringing a dead squid to my bedside. Geordie was trying to operate the squid like a glove puppet.

"Wakey, wakey!"

A day that begins with a face-to-face confrontation with a talking squid can only get better as it goes on.

"In Italy they eat that," Geordie said. "It's what they call a calamari."

"Cally-what? Go on—!" Ken said, leaning against the lintel of my bedroom.

"They do, the Italians. It's a delicacy, squid is."

"I wouldn't eat nothing like that."

Geordie, who had lived in Lyme for thirty years but was still known as the comeover from Newcastle, had a small crab boat with a cramped wheelhouse up in the bows. Ken was his odd-jobbing crew, a man with a vacantly handsome face which came to life only when he talked about emigration. Some day soon, when he'd saved up a bit of money, this year perhaps, but next year certainly, Ken was going to Tasmania. He didn't seem to know much about Tasmania, but he'd seen an article about it in a magazine, and had decided that Tasmania was his manifest destiny.

"What are you going to do when you get to Tasmania, Ken?"

"Sheep. I'll have a sheep farm—prob'ly."

He spent much of his time standing on the end of the Cobb, staring at the sea as if he could see past Australia in it. *Anywhere but here . . .* In the saloon of *Gosfield Maid* Ken discovered a book I had written about Arabia. He didn't open it but devoted a quarter of an hour to an intense perusal of the photograph on the dust jacket, which showed a many-arched palace with water gardens. I watched Hobart slowly reshaping itself into Abu Dhabi in his eyes, and saw Ken drilling for oil, Ken riding a camel over mountainous dunes of sand, Ken robed in a djellabya, Ken camping out alone under a desert moon. My version of his future seemed as plausible as his own.

Lyme Bay was windless and misty. Its only landmark was a hillock of limestone called, with more grandeur than it deserved, Goldencap. The crab and lobster pots were all laid out on compass bearings from Goldencap, which kept on fading out, then showing again as a brushstroke of gray in the bright mist. Geordie steered the boat while Ken tended the power winch and baited up the "inkwell" baskets with crucified skate.

We motored around the bay, hunting for the plastic detergent bottles which buoyed each string of pots. At each stopping place, the boat flopped about in the light swell, the winch moaned and Geordie heaved the pots aboard. He leaned over the side saying "Not a lot, not a lot," as another inkwell broke the surface with its bait largely intact and a single fiddler crab crouched in the corner.

Geordie, with more kindliness than the boy in Sutton Harbour, threw the fiddlers back into the sea with all their legs in working order. "Go home, fiddly!" he said. "Phone your mum!"

The crabs were brownies, peelers, spiders and fiddlies. Lobsters were just "beautiful black ones." But there were very few beautiful black ones: many pots came up empty, some had a few inedible fiddlies, and a single brown crab was a good catch.

After Ken had winched up two strings of empty pots in succession, Geordie said: "Looks like the amateurs have been out."

I had come across the "amateurs" before. In the last five years the amateurs had been increasing in number as the unemployment figures rose. They came mostly from well inland, from towns and cities where they scraped by on Social Security. They had turned to the sea as the last place where a man without capital might make an independent living.

All the plant they needed could be had for less than £1,000—the secondhand inflatable boat, outboard motor, pots, buoys and nylon nets. The amateurs started up in business just like John of the *Whynot;* but where he had begun in flush times, when there was room on the sea for everyone, they were coming too late, to a sea which was rivaling the land in making men who worked on it redundant.

On the south coast, the amateurs laid pots. On the northeast of the island, off Blyth, Alnmouth and Berwick, they netted the mouths of the rivers for salmon. The professional fishermen, already squeezed by falling stocks, hated the amateurs. An empty pot was clear evidence that an amateur had stolen a beautiful black one out of it. The professionals, like robins, had intricate territories of a kind that no landsman would understand. Everyone had his own private patch of sea, marked out by compass bearings and transits of tree-over-church and rock-under-chimney. The amateurs saw the sea as a featureless free-for-all, and ignored all the consecrated boundaries.

I felt for the amateurs. They had, after all, behaved exactly as they had been exhorted to by the British government. They had got on their bikes. They had set themselves up in legal private enterprise. Because their boats were terribly inferior to those of the professionals (they were sometimes just stripy beach toys), and lacked professional gear like diesel winches and depth-sounders, their job was absurdly difficult and dangerous. Knowing little about the sea, they were easily caught by tricks of tide and weather. Instead of being taken in hand as innocents, they were treated as enemies and pirates. Their boats were sabotaged. While professional pots were always "stolen," amateur pots, when found, were righteously "confiscated." To the puzzled amateur who had resorted to the sea, much as I had done myself, because it looked like freedom, it must have been a heartbreaking business. If even the sea was a closed shop of fiercely guarded jobs and rigid demarcation lines, where else was left? Tasmania. A picture of open country and blue skies seen in a magazine.

Ken was an out-of-work plasterer. He was lucky to have been taken on, for pin money, by Geordie. In any case, he lacked the kind of practical-mindedness that was needed to go into business as an amateur. Ken didn't make things happen; they happened to him—like his first marriage. He'd had a safe, safely institutionalized job as a deckhand in the merchant navy until "I got pissed one night and got a bird in the club." Now, with his second wife, two children and a council house, he was encumbered with a world too big, too expensive, too complicated for him to understand, let alone control. Twice he said to me, "I'm only thirty-eight," in a voice full of grievance and bewilderment.

Tailing the rope from the winch, he eyed the water moodily. Gorged jellyfish, tasseled like lampshades, colored pink and violet, drifted past the side of the boat. "Fucking jellies," Ken said. Then, "I got to write off for the papers."

"Papers?"

"For Tasmania. There's a lot of forms to fill in. Bureaucracy."

We were close inshore, between Charmouth and Lyme, where ledges of soft blue-gray rock slipped into the water at such a shallow angle that it was hard to make out where the rock ended and the sea began. All over the bay, more ledges were surfacing as the tide sank away from them, and I was almost certain that I'd spotted the place I'd been looking for—a depression in the low cliff where the layers of rock had split apart as they were squashed into a soup-bowl curve. The big shoulder of limestone on the Charmouth side, the shale-falls, the sagging fringe of overhanging turf—nothing had changed, except that it was now all on a smaller scale that it had seemed then.

"I used to come here thirty years ago," I said. "When I was nine or ten, with my parents, collecting fossils."

"Fossils—" Ken spoke of them in the same tone that he used for jellyfish. "They sell them up in the town, to the tourists. There's more money in fossiling now, I reckon, that what there is in crabbing."

Geordie headed the boat back to Lyme. The long morning's work for two men had produced one bucket of brown crabs and four lobsters. Geordie would get about £20 for the entire haul.

"Not a lot," he said. "Not a lot."

I felt like a burglar. I found a hammer and a caulking punch in the tool locker, hid them in my overcoat pockets, and left the boat to go for a raid on the ancient past. But the present obtruded: in the newsdealer's where I stopped for a tin of tobacco, the headlines on the papers were deep and bold.

STICK IT UP YOUR JUNTA!

This was the *Sun's* illuminating ray, cast on the peacemaking efforts of the American Secretary of State, Alexander Haig, who had spent the last week shuttling between London, Washington and Buenos Aires. It was the tabloid newspapers' view that the United States was now behaving like a soppy spoilsport. The editorial writers had a best-selling war on their hands, and they were not going to be cheated out of it by a sleight of yellow-bellied diplomacy. They had launched a series of patriotic competitions. Readers were invited to submit "Argie" jokes and to "Sponsor a Sidewinder."

I had encountered bloodthirstiness and bigotry before. In Syria I had made friends with a man who kept under his bed the rotting remains of the head of an Israeli soldier whom he had killed on the Golan Heights. In Tennessee, I had had it patiently, solemnly explained to me that the Negro was a penance, created by God to remind the white man of his Original Sin. Both these were confidences, told in private, in eccentric foreign parts. In Lyme Regis, I saw hatred mass-produced, bigotry put up for sale under the benign eye of the government whose cause the bigotry was designed to serve. It was, on the whole, rather less attractive in prospect than the Jew's head in a sack which I declined to view, although I told Ibrahim that I felt privileged to be offered such an opportunity. It was no privilege at all to see the *Sun*, the *Mail* and the *Express* gloating over the bloodbath to come.

The strangeness of the country was made stranger by the fact that, although every footstep here was a footstep I had taken thirty years ago, I couldn't quite remember whether I actually remembered it. I crossed the half-moon of sand in front of the beach huts and the public lavatories. I left big, sloppy prints on the edge of the water, which was sluggish and purple with weed. In the sea air, slightly sweetened by a tincture of stale urine, I thought I smelled egg sandwiches, orange peel and fizzy lemonade, though the beach was deserted. Maybe lavatories for me were what madeleines were for Proust.

Then the ledges of rock began—long, slippery tongues of stone, with threadlike pools of sea between each ledge. You could take them at a steady lope, on tiptoe in sand-shoes, skipping from ledge to ledge, flying high over the starfish, sea anemones and rock blennies. You could, once. But frightened of breaking something, I clambered, skidded, got my feet wet and didn't dare to jump. The ten-year-old raced on ahead; the thirty-nine-year-old plodded behind, trying to remember the way.

I found the depression in the cliff. My father had parked the Bradford Jowett a mile inland, at the end of a rutted track. We carried our picnic stuff, the cardboard boxes, the mallets and stonemason's chisels across two fields down to the shore.

Rock Drill. The fossils embedded in the limestone had Old Testament names. Then the Ammonites together with the Belemnites did rise up against the Trilobites and they slew them. They were beautiful things. When you split the rock right, it swung open on its secret like an unlocked door, revealing inside a whorled ammonite with the metallic luster of a casting in bronze. Then you had to ease it out with delicate surgery, tapping, prising, tapping again, until the mummified shell came cleanly away in your hand, in mint condition after fifty million years, according to *Fossils for Beginners*. Trilobites, a sort of giant sea wood louse as big as a side plate, were a lot harder to extract. They usually shattered at the first tap, going from flesh to dust in a couple of seconds. The bullet-headed belemnites simply dropped out of the rock, came by the dozen and were thought too boring to bother with.

We filled the cardboard boxes with ammonites, gently swaddled in old pages from *The Times* and with promising chunks of rock which would be operated on later at the parsonage. Boxes on heads, the family chain gang toiled back up the hill to the car, stumbling under the weight of their prehistory.

Every summer holiday we trekked from site to site, digging up more of the past—fossils from Charmouth, shards of pottery from plowed fields near Roman villas, the brittle and yellowed pages of old parish registers in county record offices. In search of more ancestors, we peeled the moss off the lettering of tombstones in country churchyards, uncovering dead Bakers, Buncombes, Cockburns and Rabans— forebears hardly less remote in time than the ammonites and the trilobites. My father, searching for the buried roots of the family tree, worked his way patiently through the sedimentary layers of the eighteenth century, passed 1700 and headed for the Restoration and the Civil War. Tapping out his pipe on the broken base of an Etruscan pot salvaged from a gravel pit, using ammonites as paperweights, he stayed up into the small hours annotating and collating his summer research.

Where would it end? I saw this thin and spotty trail of blood leading back forever—to Anglo-Saxons in mead halls, to helmeted centurions, to naked creatures covered with hair and waving clubs. One day the fossils, the pottery and Colonel William and General Sir Edward would compose an unbroken arc of pure ancestry. Our pedigree family would be back in touch with the first things, waddling on scaly stomachs out of the sea. *These fragments I have shored against my ruins,* wrote Eliot in *The Waste Land,* and this great antiquarian truffle hunt was just such a shoring-up job on the fading family fortunes. In England in the 1950s, suddenly exposed to the cold winds of socialism, village atheism and genteel poverty, we needed History, measured by the quire and the ton, to prop us up.

And now I was at it again. There was no one on the shore except for a matchstick man and a dog in the far distance. With hammer and caulking punch, I chipped at the limestone, knocking my way back into 1952. The rock felt harder than it should have done: the punch slipped and scraped on it. I banged my thumb. There were ammonites there—the gray stone was paisley-patterned with their spiral imprints. But too many people had been here before, and there were no beautiful black ones. It would take a charge of dynamite now to find what I was looking for. When it started to rain I packed up. Not even one lousy belemnite. The wet ledges were treacherously greasy underfoot and the raindrops fell on my bare skull in a steady patter of icy surprises.

My father looked up from under his ruffled black thatch of hair. Freed for a fortnight from his clerical dog collar, he wore a moss-green terry-cloth shirt open at the neck, and the khaki shorts and army socks in which he had lately chased Rommel across the North African desert. Mallet in one hand, cold chisel in the other, he said in his breezy on-holiday voice: "Giving up the ghost already, old boy? If you can't learn to stick at a thing once you've started it, you're never going to get any results at all, you know."

In Lyme Regis, I bought an ammonite in a souvenir shop. It had been thickly varnished, encased in plastic and made into a novelty key ring. At £3.50 it was History on the cheap, perfectly in keeping with the spring of '82.

At low tide John was putting his caulking punch to its proper use on the *Whynot*, banging strands of tarred hemp into the seams below the waterline. The fat blue trawler, canted over on its side in the dry harbor, looked indecently exposed out of the water. The technical term for the full width of a ship's stern is the "buttock"; and there was something disturbingly gynecological about the way in which John was studiously absorbed in patching up his boat's broad nether parts.

"I got something to show you," he said from the shadow of the *Whynot*'s barnacled bottom. We went up the ladder, scaled the steep hill of the deck, hauled ourselves into the wheelhouse and swung our way along from handhold to handhold like monkeys, down into the dark, fish-smelling bowels of the trawler. John shined a torch along the cloister of massive oak frames; I followed him past the engine into the stern, where I hung from a slack rudder chain.

"See there?"

The torch beam was dickering about on what looked like a ruined toy theater whose actors and scenery had been gruesomely disfigured by oil and fish scales. It was only just possible to make out what the thing was—a grotto of plastic stalactites and stalagmites, with a haloed six-inch Virgin Mary and a bespattered male puppet in a cloak standing a few steps behind her.

"*He* was in here when I bought she—I didn't like to chuck un out."

Inside the shrine there was a bulb and a switch; at the back, there were the furry green remains of a battery.

"She come from Brittany, original. I reckon they Frenchies, they'd all be Roman Catholics, wouldn't they?" He pointed the torch at the cloaked man. "Who's that—Jesus?"

"I don't know. It might be Peter, I think . . . the fisherman."

Together we stared ignorantly at this neglected relic. I wiped the Virgin down with a Kleenex.

"He gives me the creeps sometimes," John said, "coming down here at night, when you're at sea . . ."

I found it spooky too—the thought of the Breton fishermen on their knees, praying for the tempest to be stilled or for a fine catch of haddock. Their plywood shrine with its grubby statuettes looked like a queer survival from some lost pagan world. Aboard this secular ship it was just the same as an abandoned church in a modern city; a sad thing which stirred memories. You didn't believe in it, but you couldn't bring yourself to chuck it out, and sometimes it gave you the creeps in the night.

From Lyme Regis I set out to find my parents. High Water was at 0923, and at a quarter past Geordie and Ken helped me haul the boat's head round to face the sea. The wind was blowing from the north, just hard enough to frost the water outside the harbor; the only marks on the blue sky were distant jet trails; the barograph needle was at 1015 millibars and rising slowly. With all sails up and the engine going, *Gosfield Maid* rumbled off across Lyme Bay as sedately as a tram.

Stick it up your junta, stick it up your junta, stick it up your junta . . .

It would have been nice to silence the engine's idiot jabber, but with seventy sea miles to go, and the tide to catch, I couldn't afford to dawdle. For the next five hours, the westgoing tide would be holding the boat back, but in the forty-mile half-moon of Lyme Bay the tidal streams are list-less and fainthearted, neither much of a hindrance when you're against them nor much of a help when you're riding with them. Farther ahead, though, there were tides of such brute force and speed that *Gosfield Maid* would be stopped in her tracks if I misread the nautical almanac. So I let the engine rattle away down in the basement.

No surrender, smash the Argies, stick it up your junta.

In the meantime I sat up at the chart table, rechecking the courses that I'd laid the night before and studying the showers of small arrows on the tidal diagrams in the alma-nac. At 1130, Portland Bill showed on the port bow as a low island in the middle of the sea. It was not quite in the right place. A compass reading on its southernmost tip put it more than five degrees too far round to the southeast, or put *Gosfield Maid* about two miles north of her charted course. From the sea, the land always seems so unreliably fluid that one's first instinct is to assume that hills, cliffs and cities have deserted their stations since they were last sur-veyed. However, I set a new course, ten degrees round to the south of the old one, to clear Portland Bill by a safe six miles.

For the sea off Portland Bill is a famously dreadful spot. Reading about it had made me so scared of going anywhere near it that I'd waited for perfect weather and a neap tide before daring to creep round its outskirts. It had chewed up and swallowed warships, cargo boats, trawlers, yachts, whose submerged wrecks were marked on the chart by an insect swarm of double-dagger signs. Portland Race belongs with the legendary horrors of mythology: it is much bigger, is much more powerful and has claimed many more lives than the piddling whirlpool of Charybdis.

There is no mystery about it. The Race is simply a prod-uct of an unfortunate collision of geographical circum-stances.

On a map, Portland Bill is a pendulous dewdrop hanging from Dorset's nose. It is a three-mile island of quarried limestone, connected to the mainland by a low and narrow beach of piled shingle. The eddies created by this curious

obstruction to the tidal stream cause a continuous southward swirl of current on both sides of the Bill. This current
drives at right angles straight into the main flow of the
stream which goes east on the flood and west on the ebb.
Such a meeting of opposed bodies of water would cause
confusion anywhere, but off the Bill the effect is violently
exacerbated by a broad, shallow ledge of shingle, coral,
stone and broken shells. The tide, finding itself abruptly
balked in midstream, pours over the uneven bottom of the
ledge at tremendous speed, like water from a hose whose
end has been squeezed between forefinger and thumb.
When it is further inflamed by a contrary wind, the sea on
the ledge turns to boiling milk. Water stands on its end in
foaming pillars. It seethes and hisses and growls. It can
reach out and grab any boat ass enough to be in sight of it.

The *Admiralty Pilot* notes:

> Though the greatest observed spring rate of the
> stream off the Bill is 7.2 knots, at a position of 1.3
> miles 160° from the lighthouse, yet stronger streams,
> possibly up to as much as 10 knots, may be found in
> the immediate vicinity of, but not necessarily in, the
> race.

There are people who will not immediately quake in their
boots at the idea of the sea traveling at 7.2 or even at 10
knots; but a comfortable pace for a bicycle is a wild and
dangerous speed for a body of ocean water. Seven to 10
knots is as fast as a mountain torrent. If a southwesterly tidal
stream of 7.2 knots flowed through the Straits of Dover, a
lunatic in a life jacket could walk into the sea on Dover
beach, let his arms and legs hang limp, and be cast out,
albeit senseless, on the rocks of Cap Gris Nez just two hours
later. It would be an eventful two hours, of blocklike waves,
whirlpools, boils and loud surf; but it would not begin to
rival the terrors of Portland Race, since it would lack both
the uneven ledge and the violent impact of one tidal stream
crashing into another.

The speed of the sea off Portland Bill is in the Olympic

class. A 7-knot tide is so thunderously fast that only a lunatic would choose to get mixed up with it. But tides of 3 or 4 knots crop up all round the British coast. Wherever a headland sticks out into the stream, or the sea is funneled into a channel, impeded by sandbanks or lent extra weight by a river, the tide quickens. The sea moves at 4 knots in the Dover Straits (and much faster off the entrance to Dover's artificial harbor), at 3.5 knots off the bulge of East Anglia, at 4.5 knots in the Bristol Channel and in the North Channel between Scotland and Ulster. The figures may look innocent, but the streams themselves are savage; great masses of spooling water which pour over the seafloor and break jaggedly into the wind. There's nothing you can do with these magnificent and unruly tides except submit to them. If the wind's in the right quarter, you can hitch a bumpy ride on their backs; otherwise you stay in port, waiting for the moon to shift out of line with the sun and the tides to weaken.

Nine miles off Portland Bill, the drifting land on the beam began to slow as the boat nosed into the mainstream. There was an odd serrated edge to half the horizon, and the sea in the distance, viewed through binoculars, was peppered with scurf. A few minutes later I could hear the Race in the wind—not a dramatic noise, but the wheezy breathing of a sleeping bronchitic. I meant to keep it that way, and added five more southerly degrees to my course, just in case. It took an age to move the twin lighthouses on the Bill from my bow to my stern as the boat slowly elbowed its way against the dying ebb.

I was giddy with exhilaration at having got past the Race, a hazard which I had been dreading for days. From now on it was downhill all the way, with an eastgoing tide and the open cockpit full of sunshine. I toasted my luck in whisky and admired the view—a sea of bottle-green corduroy with the boat's wake stretching behind like a steadily unfastening zip.

I was too busy playing with metaphors to notice that the literal sea, which was not corduroy at all, had another occupant besides *Gosfield Maid*. The Cherbourg–Weymouth roll-on-roll-off ferry, originally observed as a dot the size of a distant sea gull, was a quarter of a mile off and bearing down on me at twenty knots. My fault entirely. Had not Commander King drummed it into me that *If to starboard red appear, it is your duty to keep clear?* The boat's wheel was locked to the autopilot, and it took a frantic fumble to release it. There was a long abusive whoop from the ferry's horn.

"Sorry! *Sorry!*"

The rudder grumbled in its chains and *Gosfield Maid* swung away from the bows of the ferry in dreamlike slow motion.

"I'm *awfully* sorry—"

The ship rolled past, as big as a hospital, its windows full of faces. On the sun deck a party of schoolgirls stood pointing down and laughing. It hadn't occurred to me before that I was quite such an obvious figure of fun.

Regardez là-bas! Le petit homme dans le petit bateau!

I waved. The girls clutched each other, enjoying the absurdity of getting an answering response from the animal in its cage. A helical twist of orange peel fell short of the cockpit and disappeared astern. Food for the monkey. The laughing girls were swept away to England while I tumbled harmlessly in the ferry's wake. They'd find plenty more to giggle over where they were going.

I spent the next hour and a half obligingly living up to the girls' opinion of me as a perfect fool. In all my apprehensive reading-up of Portland Race, I hadn't taken in the fact that there was another, modestly famous race on the next block. St. Alban's Head also produced a collision of streams on a shallow ledge. The pilot book had a paragraph about it, and the overfalls were shown on the chart as a cluster of little whorls and wriggly lines. The thing was extremely well advertised, but I failed to read the advance publicity and wandered carelessly into the middle of St. Alban's Race.

I took the zigzag tracks of white for a school of porpoises at play. They came threading through the water under the bow, making the sky tilt and the boat slither sideways down the face of a wave. They seemed unusually boisterous for porpoises. A gobbet of foam splashed on the roof and dribbled down the wheelhouse windows. The wheel, after another dash to free it from the autopilot, felt as if it were turning on thin air one moment and in thick glue the next. There was no pattern to the waves: they came in packs, bouncing up and down with their tongues hanging out. Nor was there much force in them. The tidal streams were weak, and there wasn't enough wind to seriously frustrate them. The race gave the boat a few irritable shakes and tweaks, removed my deck brush as a forfeit, and disgorged us.

It was a stupid, cocksure, quite unnecessary encounter. Given the good weather and the lazy tides, there would have been some point in deliberately steering *Gosfield Maid* into the race to see how the boat handled in a confused sea. There wasn't a grain of real danger in these conditions. But to blunder into a tide race by a silly oversight was something to be ashamed of. After an obsessively cautious, heart-in-mouth courtship I had started to take the sea for granted.

"The sea's no place for the Walter Mittys of this world," said the Captain of Dartmouth.

"The sea's a job. It's like accountancy—or writing books," Commander King said. "Treat it as a proper job and you'll be all right."

The next hour was penitential work. I tightened the shivering genoa sail on the winch. I took compass bearings on every identifiable bump of land and laid them out on the chart until *Gosfield Maid* was supported by a slowly extending cat's-cradle of pencil lines strung between Anvil Point, Warren Hill and the smudge of chalk on the western tip of the Isle of Wight. I pricked off each new distance with dividers against the latitude scale on the side of the chart. (One sea mile is a minute of latitude—a flexible measurement, since the miles get shorter and shorter as the earth flattens around the poles.) The flood tide was quickening, and the boat was moving at seven, then eight knots over the seafloor, unraveling the gray thread of land on the beam.

This low coast was short of marks. Its charted towns and villages—Christchurch, Highcliffe, New Milton, Milford-on-Sea—failed to show on the skyline. The best the binoculars could offer was the intermittent wink of bungalow windows above a crumbled earth-face at the edge of the water. No sign, anywhere, of 1959. Not a single scowling youth on the foreshore. Not even a twist of woodsmoke from an abandoned camp of the Oedipal guerrillas.

What I was looking for through the glasses was the string of parish halls and Women's Institutes which you could rent, for immoral purposes, for ten shillings for a Saturday night. Outside each hall was a tangle of piled bicycles; inside, the keen sweet stink of cigarettes and a storm of rock-and-roll.

The brand names of the cigarettes—Anchor, Strand, Weights, Woodys—had as homely a period ring to them now as Tiffany, Bugatti or Lalique. The rock-and-roll, at tinny full volume, came out of a Dansette gramophone, a year or two before anybody had learned to call the thing a record player.

Everyone was in uniform. Their toggled duffel coats were heaped on a trestle table. The sweaters of the boys hung in shapeless short skirts above their knees. The fastidious girls, all heels and hairdos, moved as if they had been blown in glass and were liable to a fatal fracture, while the boys shambled and slouched, their antique cigarettes pouched in the corners of their lips, their lids hanging low, their faces cast in the required pose of unillusioned *Weltschmerz*.

Even when they were in each other's arms, the boys and the girls were separated by the Atlantic Ocean. The girls knew exactly where they were—in Harold Macmillan's England, a bountiful country that would yield, if not next year, then the year after, engagement rings, white weddings, houses with gardens, fridges, spin-dryers, Mothercare smocks, holidays abroad (with a G.B. sticker on the boot of the Rover), lots of jobs for fun and pin money, a green and pleasant future. But the boys were a world elsewhere, in an imaginary America of bums and hoboes, crash-pads and one-night stands.

Right, you said, *Right*, when what you meant was "Yes," and the best sentences all finished with the word *man*. If you could manage to bring it off (a difficult trick if your voice was still tainted with the braying vowels of boarding school), the proper way of introducing any new remark was to shrug it in with a *Like . . .* , followed by a long exhalation of smoke through the nose, followed by the remark itself.

Like . . . you want to hitch to Bournemouth, man?

Right.

This dream America, discovered in the books of Jack Kerouac and the films of James Dean, was a land exclusively inhabited by rude sons striking their fathers dead. From now on, fathers were finished. God was down already, although the girls persisted in being sentimentally superstitious about him. Mr. Macmillan, waffling, with insufferable paternalism, about how we had never had it so good, was for the chop, along with all the rest of the old fools who ran England as if it were a gentleman's club in St. James's. That left only the daily warfare of the breakfast table, the late-night skirmish on the stairs, the old, pitiless and sullen wrangle between real father and real son—a conflict as stylized as a Noh play.

How many times do I have to tell you that I will not have you wearing that C.N.D. badge in this house?

Fuck off.

What did you say?

Nothing.

The sulky heroes of the American cinema stood their ground with contemptuous passivity. Hands sunk deep in the pockets of their jeans, lips curled in a sneer, they kicked at the dust with their boots and dispatched the father figures with a mean wriggle of their shoulders.

Have you been smoking in your room again?

Nah.

It smells like a French estaminet in there.

Yeah.

In the parish halls on Saturday nights, the James Deans and Neal Cassadys of the south coast lounged over a shared quarter-bottle of Scotch and waited for the girls to make the first move. Highcliffe, or New Milton, or Milford-on-Sea was just an illusory trick of the light. You were on the road, somewhere far out in that America of the spirit where Allen Ginsberg had seen the best minds of his generation destroyed, et cetera.

You're not dancing?

Nah.
Want to dance?
Yeah. Okay.

The boys slopped about the floor in their long sweaters, knees bent, shoulders hunched, like easygoing gorillas. The girls, who were so soft and bosomy from the waist up, were curiously slippery and reptilian from the waist down. Every time you came together, you could feel not flesh, but the elasticated roll-ons which they wore under their skirts. Safely girdled against American influences, they danced like spinning tops, talked brightly, and wouldn't even smoke.

Later, much later, after the girls had gone home in their fathers' cars, the bums and hoboes came into their own. They stood on the dark verges of the Hampshire roads, thumbing lifts. The A33 from Bournemouth to Southampton was Highway 5. Red taillights faded out over the hill, going south to L. A. and San Diego. Trucks cruised through the long cloisterd avenue of black pines.

Can I score a Woody off you, man?
Sure thing.

Sooner or later, the driver of a Hillman Minx or a Ford Popular would come to a stop, seeing a pair of schoolboys out too late for their parents' peace of mind. He'd reach across from the driver's seat and the door of a Chevy sedan would open.

Where ya goin', fella?
I dunno. Purdy far.

If only I could actually see into the bungalow windows now, I'd probably manage to spot a fellow hobo or two there—fathers of sons and daughters older than themselves. Did they stay up till all hours, waiting to "read the riot act" and sniff their children's breath for booze, or, shakey with apprehension, ask to see their children's forearms for signs of something worse? Tramping past their houses in *Gosfield Maid*, it seemed to me that I had taken the whole game a great deal more seriously than it was ever intended to be played. Like, I was still on the road.

The past and the present were too all of a piece to be true. In the low sun the tongues of foam on the wave crests were as thick and yellow as gouts of clotted cream. Ahead, the Needles were standing proud of the chalk cliff behind them, looking more like stumpy thimbles than needles. Feet planted wide on the wheelhouse floor, I swayed pleasantly in time to the boat's rhythmical lurching in a slow and easy sea. A Buddy Holly number.

> Tha-ere you go and baby,
> He-ere am I-I,
> Well, you left me he-ere so I could sit and cry-y . . .

A 45 in a torn white paper sleeve. Holly's voice, throbbing with glottal echoes, came more clearly over the waves than it had ever done out of the Dansette, jumping the spark gap of twenty-something years.

> Well, golly gee, what have you done to me?
> I guess it doesn't matter any more . . .

No, indeed. Rocking and rolling, trying to get a bearing on the Needles lighthouse in front and on 1959 behind, I thought, I've thrown away my nights and wasted all my days over You-
>   u-
>   u-
>   oo, and brought the boat's head round a point to starboard.

Lymington, where I berthed, was in the money: it both was and wasn't the town I knew, and it was hard to recover my land legs as the streets rose and sank in a sick-making swell. On home ground one moment, in bottomless water the next, I floundered up Quay Hill and out into the High Street.

The Lymington I remembered was handsome, spinsterly and dull. It was just the kind of bourgeois burg in the deep sticks that a self-respecting angel-headed hipster was honor-bound to light out from at the first possible opportunity, preferably riding on a boxcar roof. Its rosy brickwork and bowfronted shops were Georgian and Queen Anne; its dominant voices were refined and Edwardian.

They played a game called goff on the links, and larnched their boats down at the quay. The forsythia in their exquisitely tended gardens bloomed yaller for them in the early spring, when they were quite orfen to be seen taking cups of cawfee on their wrought-iron bal-*coneys*. I was occasionally introduced to their granddaughters, who were, without exception, fraffly nice gairls. The Lymingtonians handled words like envelope, fanfare and garage as foreign upstarts, and corrected my pronunciation of them by saying them again in French. Ongve*lopp*. Fong*farr*. Gah-*raj*. Their manners—at least whenever they encountered the bums and hoboes—were distinctly frorsty.

Born in the 1880s and '90s, the retired gentry set the tone of the place and did their best to maintain Lymington as a museum in which their own ways of speech and feeling were reverently conserved. Their conservatism, in every sense of the word, was ardent. The key to their character lay in their beautifully preserved shoes—brogues, handmade in 1923 or thereabouts, which had been so waxed and buffed that their polish lay in a deep lucent film on a spiderweb of tiny cracks like the glaze on a Ming vase. Their tweeds, apparently of much the same vintage, were fluted and patched with leather at the elbows, cuffs and knees. The skin of their faces, most of which had seen long service in the tropics, had the same crazed, antique finish as the leather of their shoes.

They were so spry, so sure of the way in which they ran their world, that I was gloomily convinced that they had the gift of eternal life. In the year 2000, they'd still be changing their books at Boots' Lending Library and gruffing the time of day in the bar of the Royal Lymington Yacht Club, the retired rear-admirals jostling for precedence over the retired air vice-marshals. They'd look after themselves exactly as they looked after their shoes. Their loving thrift was justified only by the assumption that they'd live forever, saving, investing, turning their collars and reknitting their old jerseys, as perpetually self-renewing as winter trees.

As soon as I stepped ashore, I knew they were dead. The
windows of Lymington's quayside restaurants were bright,
slaphappy collages of credit cards. They wouldn't have
stood for *that*. Eating out was something that you grumbled
over having to do, once or twice a year, at an hotel, where
you spent a contented half-hour reading the bill at the end
and making noises of irritable disbelief. Nor would they
have tolerated the nautical boutiques with their displays of
high-fashion storm gear and the port and starboard lanterns
which were meant to grace not a boat but an inglenook
fireplace or the cocktail bar in the (shiver my timbers!)
lounge.

But all this was nothing compared with what had happened to the salt marshes, a wide southward sweep of banks
of springy glasswort, where herons creaked into the air on
rusty wings and long-legged curlews went prying in the mud
for lugworms. From the Royal Lymington Yacht Club, the
official HQ of the gentry, you could sit at the big telescope
on its brass tripod and combine some unobstructed orni-
thology with a few choice remarks about how Major Dash-
Pouncet had just managed to gybe his old Bristol pilot cutter
off Jack-in-the-Basket.

In the Club, the word "development" was pronounced in
the same tone that one used for the word "war." Chaps were
taken aside. The whisper went round. Cabals were formed
in scented drawing rooms. The gentry were capable of
every strategy and subterfuge known to the ingenious military mind when it came to protecting the town from incur-
sions on its comfortable old architecture and brimming,
looking-glass Nature.

Yet somehow, sometime between 1959 and 1982, Lymington had been sacked by the barbarians of the new. The
marshes had been quarried out to make marinas. Where the
herons used to fish was now a solid mile of car parks, catwalks and floating jetties. The clink and jangle of steel
rigging against alloy masts rang out over Lymington like the
bells of a demented herd of alpine cows. The boats themselves, wedged into their slots like bits of a gigantic Lego
kit, appeared to be identical. Shark-nosed and white, they
wore their slit-eyed windows of smoked Perspex like an

army of mobsters in shades. They loafed sulkily in their
berths, their white plastic fenders sighing a little as they
grazed the jetty.

The gentry had seen the coming of fiberglass yachts, and
knew it was a fad that wouldn't last. "Tupperware," they
said, consigning the material from which the boat was made
to its proper station in the lower-lower-middle class. The
gentry's own boats were made of wood, with unwieldy gaffs
hanging from their masts like gallows trees. They treated
them as they treated their shoes. In floppy sun hats and old
trousers, they sanded and varnished their brightwork, re-
whipped the ends of their cherished manila ropes, stitched
their sails, and found themselves so happily engrossed in
their life's calling of conservation that half a summer of
manual labor would go by before they'd risk an afternoon's
voyage across to the Isle of Wight.

The boats in the marinas needed no such maintenance.
Many of them never left their jetties and were used only
occasionally as weekend chalets. Some were left unvisited
by their owners from one year's end to the next. These big
plastic toys spent nearly all their time lying idle, spoiling
the view and frightening the birds with the incessant tintin-
nabulation of their halyards.

There were, so I was told, about 1,300 yachts on the
Lymington River. At, say, £18,000 a throw, that would
mean a total value of nearly £25 million. The berthing fees
alone would come to about a million pounds a year. And all
this money was invested in a newfangled toffeelike sub-
stance made of resin and glass fiber called GRP. This unal-
luring acronym officially stands for glass-reinforced plastic;
looking at and listening to the vandalized salt marshes of
Lymington, I thought it might more appropriately stand for
gloatingly rich possession, and be pronounced to match, as
a tonsillitic rumble in the throat, *Gurrrrp*.

I had arrived in Lymington as a bum; I was now indignantly on the side of the fogies. The frippery of the place!
The gewgaws! The waste! The destruction! The money! If
any of the old guard did still survive, they must be boiling,
puce-faced, from behind high windows. This was worse

than "the hippies," worse than the infamous Beaulieu so-called Jazz Festival, worse than the crackpot Wykehamist, Gaitskell, worse than—there was no other word for it, it was worse than worse, it was *the worst*.

It took a little while to remove the pepper-and-salt mustache from my upper lip, undo the threadbare regimental tie and cool down into being a bum again. I was in no position to rail against the craze for owning boats, and the Lymington marinas were simply the inevitable consequence of a lot of people sharing my own dream of making an escape from an overcrowded country in a private ark. They were a perfectly fair reminder that the dream was not an innocent one: it violated the landscape and the wild things that lived there; it created its own kind of industrial pollution; as with so many dreams, there was an ugly twist to the idyll.

Yet it still seemed odd that this should have happened to Lymington, of all places. In the late 1950s when Britain had money to spare, no town could have been more genteelly frugal. Now, in the middle of Britain's worst slump for half a century, the town was awash in hard cash.

Lymington wasn't in the sticks anymore. In 1959 it had been a three-hour drive from London along a road on which the traffic fretted and squeezed through a dozen big villages and small towns. On Quay Hill, London was hardly more than a rumor, and the London people who did come down for the weekends, like the Rapps in their gun-metal Aston Martin, were exotic foreigners. But the motorways which had been built in the 1960s and 1970s had shrunk England to a country less than half the size of the one in which I grew up. Lymington was now an hour and a half away from Hyde Park Corner, and not much more than two hours from the cities of the Midlands like Coventry and Birmingham. Its keynote was struck not by its live-in gentry, but by the weekenders, the guys with the real gravy.

The marinas represented just a small tithe of the profits still to be made in Mrs. Thatcher's England. Behind each mean-eyed boat there lay the rich pickings of the real estate business, the money markets, the motor trade, North Sea

Oil, silicone chippery or the legerdemain of tax accountancy.

I ate at the Stanwell House, a hotel I remembered for its constrained and dowdy hush and its prevailing smell of overboiled greens. It had been a favorite of my grandmother's, who used to moor Fritz, her miniature dachshund, a neurotic dandy in his lime-green knitted winter coat, to the table leg with a round turn and two half-hitches, and bribe him with scraps to stop him from warbling like an off-key flute. Fritz would not have been welcome in the dining room now. People were scoffing chicken-liver pâté with walnuts and knocking back Château Langoa-Barton at £22.50 a bottle. They were not hushed. Their boisterous gold-card voices rang out over the tables, and they talked in the new slang of space and computers.

"We have lift-off on the Swanley deal . . ."

"I find the Volvo pretty user-friendly . . ."

I recognized their faces. They had the family features of Stepmar Securities Offshore (I.O.M.) Ltd. It took me a few moments longer to realize that had I been spotted at my table by a surviving retired rear-admiral, I would myself have been put down unhesitatingly as a Stepmar clone. It was my sort of people—sloppy-shouldered townees with loud voices and plastic money—who had lowered Lymington's tone and driven the herons away from the marshes.

I walked the two miles out of Lymington to the parsonage. The gorse was in flower on the common, where a leggy, fair-haired girl was up aboard a cantering pony. So Diana Double-Barrel, in hard hat and jodphurs, did still survive; but I couldn't remember whether the pony was called Achilles or Ajax. Ajax, I rather thought.

The parsonage hedge had been severely pruned and no longer rolled and billowed like the sea. The house's leaded windows showed clearly through the holly branches: new paint, new guttering, new curtains, new people. Staring in, I found my stare returned by a pale and sexless face behind the glass of my own room. I made a pantomime of following the flight of an imaginary bird—from the parsonage lawn, up over the Crowthers' roof, and into the stand of pines

behind. The face was still watching. I turned and went on
down the road, a marked man.

At St. Mark's, the name of a new clergyman had been
painted on the parish notice board by the lych-gate, but I
recognized nearly all the names on the slabs of the fresh
graves. In the porch I ducked my head and absentmindedly
took on the pious hunch of someone entering a church. But
the door was locked against vandals.

I found my parents less than twenty miles away, in the red-
light district of Southampton. The directions I'd been given
for reaching them in their new quarters were entertaining
to follow. You had to turn right at the tattooist's, right again
at the Indian grocery and off-premises license, then left
along the terrace where the prostitutes hung out their shin-
gles. My parents' house was on the first corner.

The terrace was built of blue-tinged Edwardian brick, and
the faces of its houses were aggressively English. The bulbous ornamental stuccowork around their doors and windows had once very nearly entitled them to be called villas.
They had the wholesome snobbery of Mr. Pooter, the dim
clerk in *Diary of a Nobody*, and there still clung to them the
stuffy, cozy, anxiously superior air of the bowler hat, the
Bicyclists' Association and the meat tea.

The original Pooters, who'd been proud to pay off their
mortgages at five bob a week, would have been baffled by
the appearance of the street now—by the turbaned Sikhs
on the corner, by the small brown boys who scuffled deco-
rously on the pavement, and, most of all, by the notices in
the windows. Where there should have been aspidistras on
gothic stands, there now hung pink striplights with black
transfer lettering, irregularly spaced and positioned:

F RE NCH MO DEL   JA QU I MISS TRESS

The blush-pink lights were just the right color for this
quiet and suburban combat zone; they promised mild

naughtiness rather than serious red-light depravity, a spot
of slap and tickle, not the heavy stuff with ropes and rubber.
Even so, it was an odd street on which to find oneself
looking for one's parents.

Their corner house was much the biggest on the terrace.
My father had bought it from an Indian landlord who had
run it, so he said, as a warren of student lodgings. It looked
to me as if it might make a handsome brothel. There wasn't
a twig of hedge round it: in their retirement from the
Church, my parents had chosen to advance full-frontally
on the secular world, and their new house was a sort of
parsonage-in-reverse, deliberately picked for its exposed
position in this louche and gamey quarter of the city.

I kissed my mother on the doorstep. "What an amazing
place to discover you in."

"*We* like it. It's got so much *character*, don't you think?"

The lingering notes of Swiss finishing school in my mother's voice were accentuated by the way in which, on turning
sixty, she had somehow managed to regain the bobbed and
boyish figure of the girl in the 1930s photographs. I wasn't
altogether surprised to hear that only that morning she'd
been propositioned by a cruising motorist on her way home
from the shops.

"I was rather bucked, actually. He was extremely polite
about it when I said no."

My father appeared in the doorway behind her. "Hullo,
old boy." But the *old boy* was the only surviving component
of the father I remembered. The beard which he'd started
in the 1970s had grown out into a luxuriant tangle of ginger,
jet and silver. Bespectacled, six-foot-two, with a long straggle of hair round his collar, he looked improbably like Lyt-
ton Strachey in one of his more etoilated and bony
postures. He wore a C.N.D. badge on his lapel, and his
pipe, like mine, was couched in the left-hand corner of his
mouth. Squaring up to each other with lopsided, smoker's
smiles, we bobbed and weaved like image and essence in a
looking glass. Father and son, definitely. But an outsider
might have found it difficult to tell who was which and
which was who.

Five minutes later, carrying a whisky bottle, he passed behind the chair where I was sitting in the drawing room. I sensed him slowing, then going suddenly astern.

"You've gone a bit thin on top," he said.

"Yes," I said. "It sort of happened all at once, over the winter."

"Gave me a bit of a shock, seeing it like that," my father said.

"Me too." I thought: *I* wouldn't much like to wake up and find myself the father of a bald son. His own hair, like his beard, was gratuitously abundant. No longer barbered to Church or Army regulations, it flowed and rippled on his skull, profuse and rivery.

"Well—that's your mother's family for you, I'm afraid," he said, slopping Scotch into glasses. "Your Uncle Peter was bald as a coot at twenty-five."

"I know. It's always been one of my chief failings, that I don't take more after you."

"Cheers," my father said.

Alfie, my parents' elderly dog, lay like a bundled rug in front of the popping gas fire, his eyes watering. On the mantelpiece, a large whorled ammonite was parked on top of a sheaf of bills.

"I went hunting for fossils when I was in Lyme Regis. They've all gone. They've been selling them off as tourist souvenirs."

"You heard that Christian Pitt died?"

"Yes, I did"; but I was looking at Cousin Emma seated at her writing desk, holding a quill pen. The window behind her gave on to a haha and a park with sheep grazing in the avenue of young elms. Her frame had been damaged in the move; bits of gilt had broken away, leaving chips and grazes of raw plaster. She looked as if she might have just been bought in a job lot at an auction.

For in their transfer from the parsonage the Ancestors had suddenly lost all their old power to hex. They used to follow one around the house with their offended eyes; a board of unapproachable trustees who could be seen to wince every time one touched a piece of their precious furniture or waded into the mashed potatoes with their crested forks. In the world of Miss Tress and the Pakistanis, they had become merely quaint. They might have been anyone's distant relatives. They certainly didn't look related to *us*.

My father showed me what he was working on now. In the old days it had always been some promising new cadet branch of the family; more honest Somerset yeoman farmers, Staffordshire tradesmen, army officers, minor gentry. Not any more. He was digging up the ancestors who would have gone to any lengths to avoid having their portraits painted—our criminal past. Reading between the lines of the shipping records of Guernsey and Southampton, he was piecing together an account of how our Channel Island connections had engaged in smuggling, privateering and the slave trade. We were respectable no longer. Rapine, plunder, fiddling the books and dealing under the counter ran in our blood. I saw the whole thing as a delicious smack in the eye for General Sir Edward and Cousin Emma.

My father was preparing a twenty-thousand-word paper on the subject for a scholarly journal of local history. He had shoe boxes of index cards listing dates of sailings, rigs, tonnages, harbor dues, prizes, cargoes. Little twelve-ton luggers, which had slipped out of port under cover of night in filthy weather in the 1760s, had succeeded in escaping the attention of the revenue men only to find themselves caught in the act by my assiduous father.

"This is going to land me in hot water," he said happily. "The good people of Guernsey like to think that they never ever dealt in slaves. I'm afraid I've got news for them." He settled his whisky glass on top of a precipitous stack of old copies of *New Society*, stretched his long legs out over half the width of the room, and talked of family villainies.

There were two men in my father's chair. One was my contemporary; a cheerful plain-clothes, bearded, radical debunker. I could only see the other, a far older man, if I squinted hard. His gaunt cassock fell in shiny folds around his knees; his lips were tight-reined, his shaven chin was pumice-gray, and his forehead was rippled in a permanent frown. While my father talked I tried and failed to get the two men to coalesce into one person, but they wouldn't go.

In 1959 my father would no more have voted Labour than he would have denounced God from his pulpit in St. Mark's. Now there was a red Labour Party poster taped to the drawing-room window. The Aldermaston marches had always been the symbolic High Ground over which we fought in the breakfast-table war.

"Do you honestly think," my father said from twenty miles away and a millennium ago, "that the British Government—or any other ruddy government, for that matter—is going to take serious note of the views of a rabble of spotty adolescents?"

Now it was my father who marched while I paid lip service to the cause but stayed away because I couldn't face the crowds, the officious marshals with their bullhorns, the day lost to work.

Both my parents were busy in their new life. My mother was teaching English to the Hindustani-speaking wife and daughters of the grocer on the corner. My father, though he had retired form his parish, still held office as Rural Dean of the city and was battling against the "diehards" of the diocesan "establishment." He was at present in "a bit of hot water" because he was disposing of a redundant Anglican church in Southampton to the Sikhs, who needed a temple. This had given him a nasty twenty-four hours in the national press, whose reporters had portrayed my father as a trendy vicar bent on selling off England's national heritage to a bunch of pagan immigrants.

He went on demonstrations, against the Bomb, against government cuts in the social services. He conducted funerals, on a free-lance basis, at the local crematorium. He tracked down new blackguardly relatives in the archives. In their spare time he and my mother were plotting an epic holiday through the pages of an atlas: they were going to go camping and bird-watching in the socialist republics of Bulgaria, Romania, Hungary and Czechoslovakia.

Extraordinary. But it was not really so extraordinary: my father was only keeping in tune with his Church and his

times. He was certainly a very different character from the
man I'd known in the 1950s; but the character of the
Church of England had changed just as dramatically in
the same twenty-five-year span.

In my childhood, the Church had been as grayly, fundamentally English in its texture as limestone country, fog, or
boiled beef and cabbage. Originally it had been an ingenious construction, put together by apostate intellectuals and
lawyers toadying to the interests of the Crown. Its mixture
of conscientious Protestantism and bureaucratic convenience had settled through the centuries like sediment ac-
cumulating at the bottom of a pond. All its power lay in its
invincible sluggishness. The dank smell of must, mildew
and old bones which clung to its buildings had worked its
way into the antique and desiccated finery of its clergy—
the soutanes, birettas, surplices, stoles, copes and chasubles
which used to fill a trunk in the parsonage box room. There
was the same smell in the men's voices, in the way they
pronounced the word "God" with a distinctively Anglican,
urbane, bored sigh, so that it came out as "Gard," as if the
Creator were a somewhat tiresome retired Major with
whom they were on nodding terms. Even in the 1950s,
these men were able to behave as if their Church were the
fulcrum around which English life revolved. After each
World War, their congregations dwindled further, but it
was the growing millions of conspicuous absentees who
were thought eccentric, not the Church. The C. of E. had
weathered lots of passing fads before; it would survive the
influence of Television and the habit of lying abed on Sunday mornings just as it had survived the assaults on it of
Cromwell, Wesley, Darwin. Its sheer sluggishness helped
to guarantee its eventual well-being; it was too torpid to
change, or even to diminish in its importance. It was on a
level with the monarchy: England wouldn't be England
without it.

I can still hear their complacent, piping voices coming
from behind the drawing-room door. "Ah, yes, poor soul."
"Hmmmmmmmmmmm . . ." "Yars." "Old Mrs. Tickeridge,
you know." "Yars—case for the moral-welfare worker,

rarlly." Their vicarages and rectories were, like ours, secluded from the world by such a quantity of shrubbery that
all alien ideas simply got lost, like golf balls, in the protective tangle of green.

Their congregations went on getting smaller. The old,
piping clergymen died, but too few young men turned up
to take their places. The cardboard thermometers which
stood outside almost every church, registering the progress
of the roof appeal, got stuck at a few hundred pounds. The
roofs fell in, the thermometers wilted in the rain and the
figures (painted on them by vicar's wives from one end of
the country to the other) turned into indecipherable
splodges of color.

The Church might just conceivably have withstood all of
this. What it couldn't take was the effective demolition of
its traditional parishes. The very word parish conjures up
the sort of place you might see on a biscuit tin or the box
of a jigsaw puzzle, with a green, a pump, a duckpond, a
rosy-cheeked postmistress, a general grocer, a butcher, a
pub and, right in the center of things, St. Barnabas or St.
Mark's or St. Aidan's. Just out of the picture, beyond the
cottage gardens with their hollyhocks and hardy annuals,
the Vicarage stood, twice as big and twice as important as
the doctor's house up the road.

It wasn't quite like that in the 1950s, but there was still a
sufficient resemblance to the picture to keep up the illusion
of the Church's claim to stand at the heart of English village
life, as well as the larger illusion that England was a country
based on the village, not on the city. But the cities were
gobbling up the villages on their outskirts. New roads
meant that villagers could nip into and out of the towns for
their shopping and amusements, while townees could invade
the villages as overnight and weekend residents. The bakery, the butcher's, the haberdasher-cum-ironmonger's went
broke, and their premises were converted into cottages for
outsiders. The pastureland behind the church was sold off
and became a maze of crescents of prefabricated houses
with Costa del Sol balconettes and carports. By 1970, no
one, not even the vicar, could persist in seeing the parish as

the small, self-contained microcosm of England. It wasn't small, it wasn't self-contained—and by 1982 its rosy-cheeked postmistress would be running the Video Club from the Post Office and doing a nice trade in snuff movies and lacy erotica at £1.00 a night with Sundays free.

Then there were the new parishes. In 1966 my father moved from a village which was just still a village to a gigantic building site on the edge of Southampton where twenty thousand people were stacked in concrete towers, filed there by the city council for future reference. It was a lonely, ugly, bald, impoverished and godless place. There was no center or direction in it. Its broad roads spoiled a fertile valley with their idle, nowhere-to-nowhere, sprawling loops, like the handwriting of a retarded child. There were two chemist's shops, where women queued at the counters with prescriptions for heavy sedatives. My father went on his pastoral rounds by way of spray-gunned elevators, a bewildered shepherd in search of a lost flock. One year, I counted his sheep for myself. Of twenty thousand parishioners, thirty-six, or it may have been thirty-seven, people turned up for church on Christmas Day. They looked old, pale and shell-shocked.

So did my father, and so did the Church at large. There was a lacerating irony even in its name now. Whatever else it may have been the Church of, it was not the Church of *England* anymore. It was almost as far out on the margins of modern English life as the Poetry Society or Rastafarianism —and it was on the margins that the Church regrouped.

No longer a national church (except in the fond daydreams of the most unobservantly pious), the C. of E. settled for being a sect. It was a very big sect indeed, with cells of dissenters spread throughout the world. It had money, influence, palaces, meeting places. It was organized on the lines of a huge corporation. The Archbishop of Canterbury looked foolish and irrelevant when he spoke for England, but he still represented an enormous, if scattered, constituency. If you tried to view it as the focal point of English life, the Church was pitifully enfeebled; but as a lobby of Christian feeling and opinion it was intimidatingly powerful.

Quite suddenly, in the middle of the 1970s, the Church of England became a church of troublesome priests and troublesome bishops. For the first time since the Restoration, a constitutional rift was beginning to open up between Church and State. Clerical commissions produced critical reports of Government policies on housing, social welfare, defense, wage control and the white-supremacist regimes in Africa. In the 1950s the smart cliché about the Church of England was that it was the Conservative Party at prayer; now the Church was attacking a Conservative Government with at least as much effect as the official parliamentary opposition. At the beginning of the Falklands expedition, priests had refused to bless guns and battleships; in churches, prayers were being said for the Argentinian as well as for the British forces, and the phrase "just settlement" was being widely substituted for the word "victory."

My father was part of this revolution and had been transformed by it. I had seen him as a High Anglican ritualist— the last man in an empty church, raising the Host to the sparrows in the rafters, with the candles blowing out and the hassocks growing mold in the pews. In fact he had emerged as a dissenter, a hot-water man, in a Church which had itself been reinvigorated by getting into hot water.

That evening Mrs. Thatcher appeared on the nine-o'clock news. Her lips were pursed in a tight bud of resolve; her upstanding sheaf of hair looked as if it were sustained not so much by blow-drying as by the force of personal electricity. She was talking in her Britannia voice.

My mother glanced up at the picture for a moment and said, "That woman"; then, "I do wish somebody would bump her off."

"Oh, come on, really," I said, and set to lecturing my mother on the democratic process. It was one of those infuriatingly reasonable lectures, grimly parental in tone and full of on-the-one-hand-this and on-the-other-that. Listening to myself, I heard the wittering accent of a 1950s cleric in full cry, but couldn't stop. My father stared over the top of his half-moon spectacles at the plummy curate who had invaded his drawing room. We seemed somehow to be all the wrong way round.

"I was just speaking figuratively," my mother said.

"Well, figuratively speaking, I suppose *I* wish somebody would bump her off too. With a ballot box."

"That was what I meant," my mother said.

I slept thinly in a narrow bed, a son's bed. The lights of slow-moving cars cruising the streets for prostitutes intermittently lit the room. My parents' strange new world of Sikhs, sailors, call girls, piracy and protest was altogether too adventurous to sleep through.

In the morning my father showed me the walled garden at the back of the house, where a vine was nailed up to the brickwork. It was the last week in April, and one had to look carefully to spot the curlicues of green which were breaking free of the sagging bundle of dry sticks.

"We should get a few gallons of wine from it this year, if we have any summer at all. Next year, though . . ." He spread his arms in a gesture which conjured a curtain of greenery around the yard, with sunlight filtering through the leaves and the grapes hanging overhead in opaline clusters, big as bull's-eyes—a vision of renewal, plenty, convivial pleasure. The young vine at the end of the garden was an infinitely happier symbol than the spiky parsonage hedge.

It is a mistake to let a priest go on a boat. Maritime lore has it that priests bring bad luck, because their chief purpose on board ship is to perform burials at sea. So if you do have a priest on hand, leave him ashore.

I argued that my priest was at least semi-retired, and therefore only half a threat to the voyage. One has to take risks sometimes. My parents and I sailed from Lymington in *Gosfield Maid*.

It was a foolish thing to do, as I realized within minutes of leaving the quay. In front of the popping gas fire in Southampton, whisky in hand, I had been a bit too eloquent about both the hazards and the enchantments of my own new life. Much had been made of the natural magic of navigation, of tides and tide races, of heavy weather when the sea scowled ferociously at the boat, of the trancelike passages of reflective solitude. As the level sank in the bottle, I changed from the son my parents knew to someone who combined all the essential properties of Joshua Slocum, Captain MacWhirr and a Guernsey slaver.

Prepared for a slice of heroic adventure, they found themselves in the middle of a floating vicarage garden fête. The sun shone. The salt in the air glittered like tinsel. In the enclosed water of the Solent, the stiffish southerly wind did no more than prettily tousle the sea. Though I had made an important fuss of laying compass courses on the chart and calculating tidal streams, there was no navigation, since everyone could see exactly where everywhere was. There was no solitude, either. There was hardly any room at all in which to move.

White yachts went sobbing and strumming past our bows and stern, their crews decked out in primrose vinyl and braided captains' hats. The whole Solent was a crazy-paving of interlaced wakes as I did my best to thread us through the pack of charging motor cruisers, fishing parties, ferries, dinghies, yachts. The entrance to the Beaulieu River was hidden behind a bright fleet of sailboards. A big container ship, leaving Southampton Water, scattered the small fry ahead of it like a pike in a pond.

"Racing!" shouted a furious Saturday admiral from his cockpit. "We're racing!"

"*He* seems cross," my mother said.

I hauled *Gosfield Maid* round in a shamble of flapping sails and gave way to the Isle of Wight, which steamed briskly off to starboard. This was not how I had planned things. My idea, sketched out long ago, had been that I would pilot my parents across the lonely face of the sea in a neat reversal of roles; the son would turn father, with all a father's air of calm and baffling expertise in the world.

The trouble was, I didn't know the ropes. Learning to manage the boat singlehanded, I hadn't bothered to take in their names. In any case, I was vain about not going in for the sort of salty talk which the amateur sailors liked to sprinkle over their prose in *Yachting Monthly* and their con-

versation in yacht club bars. Let them keep their vangs and
kicking straps and stays'l halyards—I meant to live in ordinary daily English. What I hadn't reckoned on was that this
made me perfectly unable to communicate the simplest instruction to my anxious-to-help father, who had done a bit
of sailing in his time.

"No, not that rope. The other one. The one next to it—
the one that's tied to that cleat thing."

"The topping lift," my father said, producing a surprise
trump. The points of his beard glinted in the sun. In his
white cricket sweater, gray flannels and sneakers, still as
long and lean as he had been in his twenties, he looked
comfortably in command of the occasion. The passing
yachtsmen would have nailed me as the unhandy passenger
on this outing.

"So this is what you call research?" My father grinned,
showing teeth that were as much in need as mine of restor-
ative work. His grin took in the swarm of pleasure craft, the
little waves, the high, holiday sky, the smell of suntan oil
in the air, the water skier in her scarlet wet suit who was
zipping by on the beam.

It certainly didn't look much like a voyage of discovery,
this weaving passage through the weekend crowds, with my
father now at the wheel and my mother getting up a picnic
in the galley. It was only too obvious what I was really up
to. In my mother's phrase, I was "going boating." The water
skier ran a needlessly fast circle round Gosfield Maid and made
off toward Cowes.

"Anyone for pâté?" my mother said.

"We could lie hove-to . . . perhaps?" my father said,
smoke from his pipe mingling with smoke from mine. "Back
the jib and tighten up the mainsail . . .?" The deferential
question marks in his voice almost, but not quite, concealed
the fact that these were captain's orders. We backed the jib,
we tightened the mainsail, and the boat fossicked about on
the water while we lunched in the open cockpit.

"It's not usually like this," I said.

"No, it must get very rough sometimes," my mother said
encouragingly. "But she's a lovely little boat."

I saw my entire voyage being wrapped up in a tarpaulin
and buried at sea.

We floated through the afternoon, a family among all the
other families who were playing about with their expensive
toys. Off Spit Sand Fort I tried to save the day with a
solemn disquisition on the changing sociology of boat own-
ership, the emergence of a new leisure class, the conspicuous excess of fat in this southern quarter of Mrs. Thatcher's
England. But the argument was rather spoiled by the sudden
intrusion of a madman in a brand-new Princess motor
cruiser with a flying bridge and tarpon deck, which he was
using as a ballistic missle against *Gosfield Maid*.

"If to starboard red appear, it is *your* duty to keep clear!"
I yelled as he roared past our paintwork. He banked, waved
and shot away to carve up someone else.

"We're a bit worried about getting into Hungary, with
Daddy being a priest . . ."

"It may be a wise move to get a new passport. With just
'Retired' in it. What do you think, old boy?"

These were the voices of serious adventure and exploration. I'd always seen myself as the man most likely to disappear under armed guard at some frontier post with barbed
wire and machine-gun emplacements, but now it was my
father who was going to get the interrogation and a spell in
the slammer.

"You're not planning to go in with contraband bibles and
prayer books, are you?"

"No, just bird guides."

"Wear your C.N.D. badge," I said, wondering whether
my father would catch the echo from a quarter of a century
back. "They're very keen on C.N.D. badges, but you have
to spend a lot of time explaining that you mind their bombs
just as much as you mind ours."

At the approach to Chichester Harbour I took over the
wheel. Here, at least, there was need of some fine pilotage.
I brought the Nab Tower behind us into line at 184° and
headed for the beacon on the bar at 004°. The course was
clearly enough marked by the evening stream of returning
sailing dinghies, but I was determined to cling to every last

bit of expertise that I could lay my hands on. There was a gratifying lumpiness in the sea as it shallowed over the sand, and the boat lurched just enough to rattle the plates in the galley and dislodge the odd book from the shelves. *Leave the beacon half a cable to port . . . watch the shoal of broken water to starboard . . .*

"You always used to do that when you were a little boy, when you were concentrating," my mother said.

"Do what?" The incoming tide was sweeping us through the buoyed channel; a tufted sand dune whizzed past the window to starboard, looking as yellow as butter in the low, cold sun.

"Stick your tongue out between your lips. Like you're doing now."

Recalled to infancy, I moored the boat at the end of a jetty in a hideous marina. Fenders out, ropes tight, we were exactly two and a half miles short of 1951.

My father was a theological student at the college attached to Chichester Cathedral. During his training we lived in a rented house six miles away, at Aldwick. He was still addressed as "Major" then, a title which must have seemed an odd one for the boyish figure bicycling between his young family and his lectures, with his Artillery beret pulled down over his ears and his college scarf flying.

I hired a car from a garage in Chichester and we drove off in pursuit of that distant cyclist. The landscape was confusing. The narrow gritted lanes were roads now; they'd lost their tricky bends and their high hedges. The Sussex villages had run together into a dribble of brick and cinderblock. But we found our house easily enough: 12 Nyetimber Lane, Aldwick, Sussex, England, The World, The Universe, Space. We snooped about the grounds of the college and were stopped by a priestling young enough to be my son.

"I say, can I help?"

"Just looking round," my father said. "I used to be a student here myself."

"Really?" the boy's surprise was understandable. My father's beard sprouted from the hood of his blue plastic
parka; the soles of his sneakers were beginning to come
apart from the uppers. He did not look like anyone's conventional notion of a canon of the Church of England. As a
version of the boy's own future, he looked distinctly alarm-
ing.

"Oh . . ." the boy said. "Well, I suppose you'll know
pretty well . . . where everything is . . .?"

"Yes, thanks."

"Goody." The boy beamed vacantly, curatelike, and
ground a lingering heel in the gravel before making his
escape.

"That had him foxed," my father said. "Have you got any
baccy on you, by any chance?"

There was a particular memory which I wanted to track
down—my father's first sermon.

"Not a hope," my father said. "I haven't a clue where that
was. I certainly can't remember the sermon."

"I can. It was on Scott's last expedition. Captain Oates
walking out of the tent into the snow. Greater love hath no
man than this. All that."

"Oh, lord. *Was* it?"

"It was Festival of Britain year. Captain Oates represented
the spirit of British self-sacrifice . . ."

"It sounds *Thatcherite*," my mother said.

"Oh, it was."

"You're teasing."

"No, I'm not. It's absolutely clear in my head, as sharp as
a photograph."

It was, too. A patch of icy sky showed through the chapel
rafters. It was a 3:30 winter Evensong on a November Sunday. Half a dozen camphor-smelling ladies had turned up
to hear about Captain Oates. My father wore his father's
surplice. His voice was surprisingly shy as it echoed in the
whitewashed stone arches, failing to find its proper size.

"Dearly beloved brethren, the Scripture moveth us in
sundry places . . ."

I was determined to find this sundry place. It stood in a

railed enclosure of chalky turf, with a stand of bare trees a few yards from the door. At 4:20, when the service was over, it was dusk and the trees were mysteriously reclothed with foliage. With a sudden churr of wings, all the leaves turned simultaneously into an enormous flock of starlings. They made the dark sky black overhead for a minute or so, then settled again, gossiping noisily in the branches.

Now you know what a plague of locusts looks like, my father said.

"Don't you remember the starlings?"

"What starlings?"

"The starlings outside the chapel, after Captain Oates."

"Wait a moment," my mother said, "something's coming back."

"Half-past three. November 1951. Sometime in Advent. A chapel running parallel with a lane. Iron railings. Trees. Starlings. Scott's last expedition. Somewhere in Sussex."

"You're sure this isn't one of your fictions?" my father said.

"Absolutely positive."

"Yes," he said, "I think I—half-remember it."

"I do," my mother said. "Definitely. Yes. Jonathan's right, dear. It was the starlings that did it. It was a very drafty little church."

"There was a gaping hole in the roof."

"It was this side of Chichester, I'm sure."

We searched the Ordnance Survey map in the car. It was richly dotted with small crosses by the sides of minor roads, and we made a long, looping tour of the ecclesiastical architecture of West Sussex, up lanes that went nowhere, cutting through new housing developments and industrial parks, skirting trailer sites, wheat fields, vegetable gardens, recreation grounds. Somewhere near Runcton, or Oving, or Mundham, or Bersted, or—there was no shortage of candidates. The churches and chapels stood in woody tangles of spring green, their graveyards waist-deep in grass and thistle. The ink had run on the notices which were pinned to their doors, but one could still make out that Communion was celebrated here on the second Sunday of every month. Most were locked. The few that were open smelled of dereliction, with streaks of birdlime down their aisles, bats in their belfries and the *New English Bible* which had been left on the lectern gone prematurely antique with the damp.

None felt right. "I'm all at sea on this one," my father said, and it was true: between the Festival of Britain and the year of the Falklands War, there had been so much heavy weather, thick fog, leeway lost and tidal streams left uncalculated that it was impossible to work out where we were.

"Isn't *this* it?" my mother said at a chapel like a tumbledown cottage, dwarfed by its yew tree and surrounded by tombstones. "I'm sure it is. Look—there's where we saw the starlings."

"No. There weren't any graves. It was much more exposed. It was at quite a different angle to the road."

"Perhaps they've changed the road," my mother said.

"I expect it's gone, anyway," my father said.

"It must have been standing since about 1300," I said. "They can't have pulled it down."

I was thinking of our old ancestor hunts on summer holidays—the way you had to peel the moss off the stone as if you were skinning a rabbit. The dead made themselves so accessible then; we'd collect half a dozen new relatives in an afternoon, their names, addresses, dates, occupations, even, sometimes, the diseases from which they'd died. No such luck now.

"Why don't we call it a day?" my father said, glooming under the yew tree in his parka. "I must say, it doesn't sound as if it was any great shakes as a sermon—"

"It was a fantastic sermon. You had me on the edge of my seat."

"*Captain Oates.* I still don't remember it, you know."

That night we watched the ten-o'clock news on television in the boat. The latest on the Falklands front was that Vera Lynn—the "Forces' Sweetheart," from a thousand military concerts and wartime radio broadcasts—had come out of her long retirement to sing what the newscaster described

as "a new patriotic song," all proceeds to the Falklands Fund.
Peter de Savary had put up the money, André Previn had
done the music; the song was presented as a major contribution by the Home Front to the morale and welfare of Our
Boys in the South Atlantic.

A lot of dust had gathered on Miss Lynn's voice since I'd
last heard it, warbling sweetly about bluebirds *ohover* the
white cliffs of *Dohover*, but its dustiness was like the
scratchy burr of a 78 played on a horn gramophone; it made
it more evocative, not less; it brought back memories of the
gallant little ships, the blackout, whale-meat steaks and
London-can-take-it.

The song was called "I Love This Land," and it hinged on
the refrain:

> It will stay this way for e-e-ver,
> Which is why I love this land!

On each reprise, the couplet sounded slightly more drivel-
ing than it had the last time round. You had only to look at
Vera Lynn at sixty-five to see that it enshrined a wonderful,
vainglorious untruth. But there was a dotty kind of truth in
it too. It stated—more nakedly than anyone had dared to
do so far—the terms of the daydream in which England was
living in 1982.

CHAPTER 5

THE MERRYING
OF ENGLAND

I left Chichester Harbour on a still, dank
Thursday. After two days of gales, the 0630
shipping forecast promised winds Variable, Force 3 or Less.
The inked needle drooped low on the drum of the barograph, but it had remained steady overnight on 998 millibars, and the depression over southern England had come
to a standstill and was said to be filling.

I parked a flask of coffee and a bowl of Trail Mix on the
wheelhouse shelf and rumbled off on the falling tide, leaving a wake of spun glass in the water behind. The reedy
mudbanks opened into a broad mall of moored yachts,
every one rooted to its dull reflection. Padlocked for the
week, the yachts were being used by cormorants as fishing
platforms. The birds stood fixed on the crosstrees in prehis-
toric silhouette against the misty gray of the sky, looking a
great deal more secure in their commands than the absentee
owners of these craft. They kept watch on the tarnished
water without moving a muscle.

The sea at the mouth of the harbor was as sluggish as oil.

It sucked languidly at the sand on the channel's edge. Dead ahead, where the tide ran fast, its surface was engraved with ornamental loops and scrolls. It parted, viscously, round the bows of *Gosfield Maid*, bulged up her sides and shattered in her wake.

The Solent was blessedly empty of sails today. The furred outline of the Isle of Wight looked as far away as France. I should, perhaps, have paid more serious attention than I did to the anvil-shaped cloud which stood over the island, as sharp in its outline as an ink stain on a tablecloth. It was a cloud from which a god might choose to descend in order to get up to some mischief in the world in a ceiling by Tiepolo. But the forecast was Variable, 3 or Less, and I headed complacently out to sea.

To the east, a chain of rocky ledges ran out for several miles from Selsey Bill. There was a lane through the rocks, close inshore, in the Looe Channel, but the tide sprinted through it, and I would have to claw my way up against the ebb stream. It seemed a better idea to take the long way round, going ten miles out to the Owers lightship, then setting a northeast course for Newhaven. In any case, I was tired of hugging the shore. A day's hike around the Owers, even if it all had to be done under engine, would restore some of the space and solitude of the journey which I'd lost on the Solent: the horizon would be bigger, the perspective less foreshortened; I'd be out of territorial waters and back in the serious business of being alone at sea.

At ten, there was just enough of a breeze blowing out of the northeast to make it worthwhile to get the sails up. At eleven, *Gosfield Maid* began to yield and bend to the gusts, showing her flanks as the whitecaps slapped noisily around the bilges. At half-past eleven, there was a message from the Coastguard on the VHF: Southeasterly, Gale 8, Imminent. The docile depression had shaken off its forecast lethargy. It was deepening fast and haring away in the general direction of Biscay. The Coastguard's warning seemed a bit superfluous now: the sea was breaking out in lumps all round the boat and rags of foam, torn off the wave tops, were plastering themselves against the wheelhouse window.

Buckled into the safety harness, I went out to get the mainsail down. The twenty feet of narrow deck between the cockpit and the mast turned into a trepid journey on hands and knees. The sea kept on climbing to my level, then plummeting sharply out of sight. It was preferable to avoid watching it. Halfway to the mast, I remembered how I'd once had to get home like this, as a student of eighteen. The best part of a bottle of gin, drunk rapidly from a beer mug, will produce a facsimile of the effects of a Gale Force 8 on the deck of a small boat.

I trapped a bucketful of cold seawater between my jersey and my bare chest, spat salt and wriggled along, taking the seamed teak foot by slippery foot. At least it was smooth. On the morning after my previous passage like this, I'd awakened to find both knees black with clotted blood.

The freed sail came thunderclapping down the mast. Lashing it up to its boom, I was beaten about the head and face with wings of flapping polyester while the masthead went off on an aimless ramble round the sky, and I clung on, wet through but possessed by a sort of manic elation as I bullied the sail into submission. On the slow crawl back to the wheelhouse, I was laughing out loud. None of this experience belonged to me. It felt sublimely ridiculous to be squirming about on one's tummy in such an unexpected roughhouse brawl.

Back inside, it was necessary to move like a spaceman in a capsule, clumsily swimming from point to point through an atmosphere whose center of gravity was shifting so continuously that one was made effectively weightless. Picking my moment, I swam down the companionway into the saloon to change my sodden jersey. The business of changing took several minutes of lurching trials and errors. Finding my face briefly close to the barograph, I noticed that the needle too was defying gravity. Since leaving Chichester Harbour it had sketched a steep scarp face on the paper, rising seven or eight millibars in less than three hours.

A situation in which there are absolutely no decisions to make is a cause of high spirits in itself—and there were no decisions to make now. I couldn't go back to Chichester. It was too far, and the bar at the entrance would be uncrossable. Littlehampton, the nearest port, twelve miles to the north, also had a bar, and there was a firmly deterrent note about it in the pilot: "Entrance dangerous in strong SE winds." Shoreham earned the same warning. There was nothing at all to do except settle down and enjoy my gale.

It was a fine explosive mixture of air and water, and *Gosfield Maid* jounced about in it as easily as a corked bottle. John, the trawler owner in Lyme Regis, had looked over her ship-sized oak frames and the long curve of the deck toward her massive bows and said, "She's a real boat, not like they flimsy yachts—she'll look after you." For the first time since I'd set out, the boat was looking after me. Her hull had been built originally for service as a fishing boat in the North Sea off Scotland, and this modest Channel gale was well within her range. She fitted herself into the commotion of the sea, every pitch and roll a strategic adjustment to the changing shape of the water. Her timbers creaked and flexed as she arranged the waves around herself like pillows on a bed.

In the veering wind there was at first no pattern to the water. It heaped up in slabs and collapsed on itself in a loutish show of undirected energy. The shoreline had disappeared. There was just miles of stirred and twisted sea, a mass of meringues. Then, as the hunting wind found its proper strength and direction, the sea began to march in line. Ahead, the waves looked shapeless, each one an indecipherable configuration of ridges and planes; but as they rolled astern, flipping the wheelhouse skyward and making the propellor howl as it came clear of the water for a split second, they revealed themselves as an orderly procession. Behind the boat, the sea was lined with dark troughs; they stretched away out of sight, as closely ruled as harp strings.

Facing the waves, they looked disproportionately small compared with the rearing flights of the boat's bows as she rode into the continuous wash of foam that dribbled down their faces. They became lordly only when they took their leave of her, giving the odd impression that the sea ahead was far calmer than the sea behind.

For some time I'd caught intermittent glimpses of a cargo ship apparently at anchor. Random bits of it—masts, bows, bridge—would show over the waves for a moment, then get engulfed again. It was, I supposed, waiting for the tide to rise enough for it to get into Littlehampton or Shoreham. It was blotted out by a rain squall, and I lost it for good in the premature blue dusk which followed the rain.

Then, half an hour later, there was another dark squall in the sky, somewhere out to starboard. The squall turned matt black, a new twist in a day full of meteorological curiosities. It was sixty yards off and steaming straight for me when the squall resolved into the coaster, its riveted plates bleeding rust, the twin anchor ports on its bows looking like a bull's flared nostrils. I passed ahead of the thing by a boat's length. Neither of us had seen the other in the murk; and it was the coaster which had right of way.

This incident quite failed to dent the mood of placid detachment which had settled on me in the gale. A miss is as good as a mile, I thought, and went on watching waves. It was exactly as if I were very drunk indeed, with the drunkard's sublime immunity to the hazards of the world. It was not until the wind eased, the sky cleared, the force went out of the sea and the water became suddenly sloppy and innocuous that I came out of the trance.

It was dark now. There were a lot of puddled lights to the north, three or four miles off. Since they all seemed to be winking, it was impossible to tell which were navigation lights and which were neon signs or flashing *Star Wars* machines. Elbowing my way inshore, I picked out a long illuminated promenade and a couple of onion domes at the root of a pier. I had, apparently, discovered Brighton.

Newhaven was another nine miles on. Too far. After the last few days, I'd sworn that I'd avoid marinas for the rest of the trip, and I rounded the pierhead of Brighton marina with a feeling of resentful disappointment. There had been real splendor in the sea outside; but inside the jaws of the marina, the splendor shriveled. What had I been up to all day? *Going boating.*

Below, the saloon looked as if it had been burgled. The

books on the floor had got on intimate terms with a broken
jar of marmalade. The casing of the transistor radio had
smashed, and the radio was spilling its innards. Someone
had been throwing crockery around the place. I sat in the
middle of this depressing mess and tried to pour a slug of
Scotch into a tumbler. It wouldn't go. The neck of the
bottle wavered, hit the glass, drew back. Whisky splashed
over the floor and into the pages of *William the Conqueror* by
P. G. Wodehouse. I tried again, and poured some whisky
into the ashtray on the table. I gave up and sucked the stuff
straight out of the bottle, shaking with all the fright I'd
failed to feel at sea.

Land-sick, clinging to the railing and planting my feet in a
clumsy waltz step, I was making a rough passage of Brighton
promenade, where a torchlight procession was overtaking
me. There was a whoop-whooping tremolo echo on the PA
system which was booming announcements over the sea.
    "The Par-par-par Tridge-tridge-Green . . . Bom-bom-
bom-bonfire-fire-fire . . . So-so-so-societee-ee-ee!"
    The bonfire societies of Sussex went marching past with
their bedraggled floats, whose bright poster colors had run
in the rain and whose lath-and-tarpaper work had been
knocked out of shape by the gale. The torchlights were
electric and powered by car batteries aboard the floats.
They shone on a bewildering assortment of Ancient Britons,
Puritans in tall hats, Aztecs, clowns, Red Indians, Elizabethan courtiers and Victorians in frock coats. Each float in
the procession was trying to mount an appropriate musical
entertainment, but the combined effect of lutes, bongo
drums, saxophones, electric guitars, bagpipe chanters,
penny whistles, Jews' harps, mandolins and bugles was not
good. I yearned for earmuffs and aspirin.
    As the procession and I reached the center of town, we
ran into a cacophony of another kind. The poor weather
had kept a lot of people away, but there were still a hundred
spectators or so, standing in huddles on the pavements, and
for every huddle there was another language—a warble of

Japanese under a lamppost, a snatch of Cockney on the steps of a hotel, a bit of Idaho, a bit of Rouen, a bit of Frankfurt, a bit of Melbourne, a bit of everything. Cameras flashed in the crowd like buoys at sea. A float of rather damp and cold-looking Regency dandies rounded the corner of Old Steyne and made for the floodlit confection of the Royal Pavilion with its fretted facade and gleaming minarets and turban domes.

The bonfire societies could not have hit on a better spot for their parade of make-believe. It was just what modern Brighton had been designed for. When George IV ordered John Nash to revamp his pavilion, he demanded a mixture of the "Chinese" and "Hindu" styles to liven things up around his favorite bathing beach. What he actually got was perceived as a weird seaside mock-up of the Kremlin. *The Guide to Watering Places*, published in 1825, two years after Nash had finished work on the Royal Pavilion, is clearly flummoxed:

> The whole form and appearance of this splendid building has recently experienced a complete and entire change. Considerable additions have been lately made to the former edifice, and the style of the architecture has been altered so as to imitate the Kremlin of Moscow. This change has at least given novelty to the appearance of the whole, as it exhibits a specimen of the Eastern style, hitherto unknown in Great Britain.

Chinese, Hindoo, Russki, Roundhead, Punk—they were all one on the caterwauling floats. I ducked out of the cavalcade and took shelter in a restaurant which had a single table left after nearly all the rest had been jammed together to accommodate a coachload of roaring German tourists. I looked out the window beside me: the torches and glad rags of the bonfire societies formed a crazy piebald frieze as they flounced and jigged their way across the glass, their music drowned by German jokes and German laughter.

Nowhere outside Africa, I thought, were the tribespeople

so willing to dress up in "traditional" costumes and caper for the entertainment of their visitors. The season was just beginning now; by June and July, it would be hard to stop at an English village without running into tabarded medieval knights in armor preparing for a joust, carfuls of Cavaliers about to refight some old battle in the Civil War, Elizabethans hogging themselves at a Banquet, or prancing Morrismen in bells. The thing had become a national industry. Year by year, England was being made more picturesquely merrie.

These bucolic theatricals were a very new fad. Even the Morris dancers, whose claim to stretch back through the mists of time was strongest, were new. Their dances and costumes had been researched and revived by Cecil Sharp, the folklorist, in the 1890s. A federation of Morris clubs had been set up in the 1920s. But it wasn't until the late 1950s that the movement really got underway. Now every village worth its salt had a Morris "side" to go with its cricket team, and the dancers themselves were firmly of the belief that they were the inheritors of an unbroken British tradition.

As industries go, the merrying business was a steal. It was like chain letters or picking money off trees. It brought in the yen and the marks and the dollars, but no wages bill was involved. People made their costumes at home and fought, danced and paraded for the love of it. Until a few years ago, Amateur Dramatics had meant a scatter of relatives and friends of the performers sitting on hard chairs in the village hall through an excruciatingly long evening of J. B. Priestley. Now a Saturday junket on the green could draw coachfuls of prosperous foreigners who actually *wanted* to watch. Forget *Time and the Conways*—bring on the knights and the Morrismen!

On the way home to the boat, I passed a pair of Puritans snogging energetically in a bus shelter. A little farther on, I heard a Victorian in a tailcoat and stovepipe hat inquiring of an Ancient Briton in woad, "Where was that fuckin' pub we was in last year, then?"

The next morning I made a couple of telephone calls from the marina office, then spent a hasty hour tidying the saloon and polishing the brasswork on the wheel. I found a hiding place for my notebook in a drawer in the forecabin, under a pile of socks.

At noon, I spotted my visitor a hundred yards away across the catwalks. Focusing on him with the binoculars, I saw he was wearing an elegant miniature pair of binoculars himself. In his Papa Doc tinted spectacles and an L. L. Bean duck hunter's camouflage shirt, with a little brown backpack hoisted on his shoulders, Paul Theroux was on his travels.

"Hi—how you doing?"

Ten years before, Paul and I had been friends and allies, but the friendship had since somewhat soured and thinned. Nor had either of us been best pleased when each had discovered that the other was planning a journey, and a book, about the British coast. It was too close a coincidence for comfort. Paul was working his way round clockwise, by train and on foot, while I was going counterclockwise by sea. At Brighton, the two plots intersected briefly and uneasily aboard *Gosfield Maid.*

It took Paul less than five minutes to sum up the boat. He hunted through the saloon, inspecting pictures, books, the charcoal stove, the gimbaled oil lamps, the new, lavender-smelling gleam of the woodwork.

"Yeah," he said, "it's kind of . . . *tubby* . . . and . . . *bookish.*"

The phrase rattled me. I rather thought that somewhere I had written it down myself.

"You making a lot of notes?"

"No," I lied. "I seem too busy with things like weather and navigation to notice anything on land. What about you?"

"No," Paul lied. "There's nothing to write about, is there? I don't know whether there's a book in this at all. I may turn out to have just spent the summer walking. Still, it keeps you fit—"

He came up into the wheelhouse, where he looked over the open pages of the log. They were innocent of any small talk except for details of courses steered, winds, compass bearings, barometric pressures and a crinkly, tongue-shaped spill of red wine.

"What's that?"

"The depth-sounder."

"Okay."

Wary, protective of our separate books, we dealt with each other at strained arm's length. For a moment, I saw us as Britain and Argentina meeting on neutral ground in Peru.

"Lunch?"

"Yeah," Paul looked at his watch. "But I've got to be getting along this afternoon."

"Where are you heading?"

"Oh . . ." Paul was evidently wondering whether this was going to give too much away, and deciding that it wasn't. "Bognor Regis. Know Bognor?"

"We lived just outside, when I was nine, ten. When my father was at theological college at Chichester."

"Ah huh," he didn't pursue the matter of Bognor.

We took the miniature railway from the marina to the pier. Passing the nudist beach, Paul made a rapid note in his book, which he quickly tucked away. I thought, I'd better take a closer look at the nudist beach on my way back, I may have missed something apart from the obvious goose-pimples and sagging bums.

At the pier, we pushed our way through the lazy crowd; two men at work, impeded by idlers. As we waited for the traffic to give us an opening on the promenade, a lean and dingy man in a flapping thrift-shop overcoat detached himself from the crowd. He had a camera and a monkey, and there was a helplessly eager look in his eye as he made a beeline for Paul in his hiking gear. After hours of searching, at last he'd found an American Tourist; he was shoveling his monkey onto Paul's shoulder and fiddling with the controls on his camera.

"Take your picture, sir?"

The monkey was scrawny and gray, the size of a rat. It was clinging to Paul's hair and grinning with fright.

"Get that monkey off my back," Paul said. It was a clipped and military instruction. The man responded with a monkey grin and raised the viewfinder to his eye. "Get that monkey off my back! Will you get that goddamn monkey off my back?" Paul raised his hand to pull the creature out of his hair; the man leaped forward, grabbed his monkey and cuddled it resentfully. Paul shook out his shoulders and strode off through the traffic. I caught up with him a minute later.

". . . sonofabitch," Paul was saying.

"Poor guy—you were the first American tourist he'd seen all morning," I said, and immediately wished I'd kept my mouth shut.

We lunched at Wheeler's. It was, to begin with at least, stiff going. Guarding our hands close to our chests, we played a sort of conversational *misère*, each aiming to lose the trick by finessing a story out of the other. How was Lymington? Oh, dull. Very dull. Nothing worth seeing there. And Margate? Gangs of skinheads and bikers—much what you'd expect, you know.

The condition of England was too prickly a subject for either of us to manage. America was a little easier. We talked of Paul's last holiday on Cape Cod, when he'd tried to talk his teenage sons into enrolling for two weeks in the local high school.

"They wouldn't play along," Paul said, pleased at their resilience. " 'Who wants to be a guinea pig for your research?' they said. They gave me a lecture on *ethics*. They weren't going to sweat along in high school just so they could figure in a goddamn *story*."

"The young frighten hell out of me," I said. "Their principles always seem so much higher than mine ever were."

"Yeah," Paul said; "they don't open other people's letters." He concentrated on the busywork of scissoring the flesh away from the bone of his Dover sole.

Suddenly, apropos of nothing, he came to life—my old friend. He was describing a hill in Massachusetts, just outside Boston, where he'd gone tobogganing as a child. "It was an *alp*, you know? You could slide a mile down it, with the snow sizzling by your ears." The winter before, he'd driven his sons, Marcel and Louis, to this famous place. "All the way, in the car, I was building it up—'You wait till we get there—' I was more excited than the boys were. 'Aw, shut up, Dad.' 'Paul always exaggerates—' You know, all that stuff. Then we got there. You know what? It was like *this*." He laid his forearm flat on the table between his glass of mineral water and my half-bottle of Muscadet. "It wasn't even a *hill*. It was *nothing*."

"You're describing my voyage," I said. "I went back to the village outside Lymington where—" but the Italian waiter got in the way of the story. When next left to ourselves, we took refuge in a formal little seminar on a home-revisited story by V. S. Pritchett.

We separated on the Old Steyne, Paul on the Bognor trail, I to catch the toy railway to my boat. He turned and called, "Watch out for the Goodwin Sands! They're *really* dangerous. I've seen them. They're all over wrecks."

"I've got the charts," I shouted back, lamely, unwilling to allow the last word to Paul's maddening American know-how.

When the train stopped at the nudist beach, and a group of overweight people in their late middle age got off for a spell of health and efficiency under the overcast sky, I scrutinized the beach, the signboard on its edge, the pallid nudists. What the hell had Paul seen there?

His book, *The Kingdom by the Sea*, came out a year later, in 1983. I read it avidly and with mounting anxiety. It had only one seriously flat patch, I thought—his account of our meeting in Brighton. There wasn't a single start of recognition for me in his two pages: what he described was not at all what I remembered. But then, memory, as Paul had demonstrated with his forearm lying flat on the table at Wheeler's, is a great maker of fictions.

I sailed for Rye in a pacific offshore wind which was doing no more than crimp and tease the sea. In the immediate vicinity of the boat, the sunshine was hard and bright, the small, neat waves were razor-edged and the water was a bold powder-blue. It looked as if one should be able to see for miles and miles; yet headlands which were marked on the chart as quite near at hand kept on vanishing cleanly away behind me into an empty sky. I counted off the scalloped chalk busts of the Seven Sisters as they strolled past on the port beam, and made them nine.

The boat was sailing herself. There was nothing to do except count cliffs, brood over the compass card as it shivered in its bowl and keep an eye out for vagrant trawlers on the shoals. There was time to sit out on the patio of the cockpit, smoke a pipe, potter about making elevenses and read the papers that I'd bought before leaving the marina.

After three weeks of phony war and fizzled peace initiatives, the Falklands expedition was at last coming to some sort of climax. Today, May 1, the maritime exclusion zone which had been drawn round the islands, two hundred miles offshore, came into force. The first ships from the Task Force were expected to enter it later in the day.

The *Sun* was squealing with infantile excitement at the prospect of the atrocities to come:

> STICK THIS UP YOUR JUNTA!
> A *Sun* missile for Galtieri's gauchos!
>   The first missile to hit Galtieri's gauchos will come with love from the *Sun*.
>   And just in case he doesn't get the message, the weapon will have painted on its side "Up Yours, Galtieri!" and will be signed by Tony Snow—our man aboard H.M.S. *Invincible*.

I doubted whether the newspaper's grisly enthusiasm for the war was shared by many of its readers. Whenever I put my own ear to the wall, I heard a good deal of vociferous support for the Task Force expressed by members of the tweedy and choleric classes; but the people whom I met on quaysides and in pubs seemed surprisingly indifferent to the adventure. There were some easygoing "Argie" jokes, as when a man excused himself from the circle at the bar to go to the lavatory, saying that he was going "to make some Argie beer and sandwiches." A few minutes later in the same pub, the latest dispatch from the Task Force came up on television; the proprietor immediately changed channels to a darts match, with paunchy gorillas chucking innocent missiles at treble-twenties. The *Sun* headlines—INTO BATTLE! FULL AHEAD FOR WAR! DEADLINE TONIGHT. HIGH NOON! YANKS A MILLION!—contrived to suggest that all over Britain men and women were going wild with patriotic fervor, but I saw very few signs of it in the seaside towns where *Gosfield Maid* took up lodgings.

The entrance to Rye Harbour is a hidden door in a monotonous low coastline of hillocks, dunes and tufty trees. You need to have blind faith in your compass to find it, and it only shows at just the moment when you've decided that the chart is telling you lies, that Rye Harbour doesn't exist, and that you are within two hundred yards of shipwreck in the breakers on a deserted beach. You squeeze through an aperture in the sand no wider than a country lane, and find yourself, Alice-like, in a looking-glass land full of water; marshy, silvered, painfully brilliant on the eye.

Beyond the timber wharf, with its screaming chainsaws and its oily stink of pine dust, the surface of the glass was littered with the hulks of fishing boats and barges, their rib cages doubled in reflection. Rye itself was two miles off—a dense pyramid of red roofs, towers and castle battlements, rising improbably out of the wide lake made by the flooding tide. It glowed too richly for England; it was too pretty, too all-of-a-piece. English towns do not, under normal circumstances, float on pure light and ripple brightly in the sky. Rye did, and I steered for it cautiously, not wishing to run aground inside an optical illusion.

The buoyed channel led in a series of knight's moves round the lake, with Rye traveling from west to east and back again across the horizon. Then the boat was suddenly deep in beds of wallflowers, garden gnomes, toy windmills, bird tables and window boxes. I found an elderly man in a sun hat reclining in his Barcalounger on the starboard bow. "You want to keep more over that way for the channel," he said. Grazing his hardy annuals, I brought the boat's head round, steered clear of someone's dog, cruised through the middle of someone else's picnic lunch, and brought up under the eaves of the oasthouses on Strand Quay.

That a visitor was jumping aboard, collecting ropes and making *Gosfield Maid* fast to the bollards on the wall didn't surprise me a bit; it seemed an inevitable part of the general domestic chumminess of Rye, where boats and houses were locked in such an intimate tangle that everyone was living in everyone else's pocket. My visitor was making himself at home in the saloon. He was tangled and loose-jointed, with a stack of fair hair over a lucid face like an oriel window. He was standing at his full height in the cabin, and there were several separate stories of him.

"Your headroom! It's a palace, isn't it? You should see mine—"

In jeans, broken moccasins and faded denim workshirt, he didn't look like a yachtsman, and he seemed too slender and lightly muscled to have earned the cracks and calluses on his hands. His voice was urban, his skin was open-air and pink.

Over the next two days, the different bits of Nick O'Brien assembled themselves. Fifteen months before, he'd been selling carpets in a flooring center in Croydon, where he lived with his wife in a terraced house. The job was boring and the marriage was cracking up. When his wife left him, Nick sold his car and his stereo system, rented his house, bought a boat, left the flooring center and became a water gypsy. He told me about his last meeting with the area manager of the carpet company.

" 'There's three million unemployed,' he said. 'What d'you think you're going to do?' 'Sail,' I said. 'Sail away. I'm buying a boat.' 'You'll be back,' he said. You could see it on his face—you know . . . poor sod, like his wife's hopped it and now he's going off his trolly. 'What do you know about *sailing*?' he said. 'Not a lot,' I said. 'But I can learn, can't I?' He sort of sighed, like he was dealing with a right loony. 'See you in time for the autumn sale,' he said, 'when it starts getting cold,' and gave me my cards. I thought then and there, I'm never going back, not if it kills me."

Nick's domestic economy was a model of belt-tightening

frugality. The rent from his house, after he had paid the insurance and the real estate agent's commission, brought him £1,100 a year. It was enough, he said. He ate no meat, caught his own fish, collected his own vegetables from the seashore. Wherever possible, he laid up at anchor in estuaries where no harbor dues were payable; Rye was the first port he'd entered in six months where a charge was levied, and he'd slipped in in the small hours, hoping to escape the notice of the harbormaster. For entertainment he listened to BBC Radio 4 and plodded assiduously round free art galleries and museums. He was happy.

"I've got something in my life now that none of my friends have got. None of them."

"What's that?"

"Direction."

Freedom, yes—but *direction?* For more than a year, Nick O'Brien had been going off in all directions like a jumping jack. Last spring, he'd taught himself to sail and navigate around the east coast of England. In the early summer, he'd bought a plastic sextant, secondhand, practiced with it for a week, and set off across the North Sea. He'd wandered round the edges of Holland, West Germany, Denmark, Sweden. In the autumn, instead of returning to the flooring center, he'd sailed back to the Thames and put up for the winter in the creeks around the Swale and Medway. Now he was striking out, in the most leisurely way possible, for France, Spain, Portugal, maybe Africa, he thought.

"Winter in Africa. That sounds all right, doesn't it?"

We took a bottle of claret from *Gosfield Maid's* cellar in the bilges and climbed across to Nick's boat, *Sussex Rowan.* It was a fiberglass sloop, tiny for such a full-time life: a few inches over 20 feet long. It looked like a minature floating junkyard, hung about with car tires, its deck loaded with plastic sacks, paint cans and fish crates. A supermarket trolly was lashed to the mast, and a rusty funnel stuck up through the foredeck.

In contrast to its disreputable exterior, the inside of the boat was like a tidy dolls' house. The whole of the forecabin was occupied by a wood-burning stove of a kind that might once have heated a Victorian boarding school. In the saloon there was a double bed, fastidiously tucked and turned, to port, with a gas cooker, a sink and a closet-sized john to starboard. On the central table, some fresh wildflowers stood in a jam jar.

"It's . . . like the fetal life," Nick said. "I must have had a pretty good time in the womb, I reckon."

Even sitting down, I had to duck my head. I looked over Nick's library on the shelf by the bed. There were field guides to plants and birds, two vegetarian cookbooks, *Food For Free*, a nautical almanac, Admiralty sight-reduction tables. The Literature section held a single book—Herman Hesse's *Steppenwolf*.

He showed me his charts. There were just two of them. One was falling to bits and showed the whole of the North Sea and some of the Baltic, from the Dover Straits to Oslo; the other, in relatively mint condition, covered the entire English Channel from Dover to Brest.

"You use these for navigation? They're on an impossibly small scale."

"Yes, but look at all the water on them. Then there are the little charts in the almanac for getting into places—it's all you need, really."

It made me worry for his safety. "Would you like some of mine—the ones I've used already, from here to Land's End?"

"No, thanks. I'd get confused if I changed scale now. Anyway, there's nowhere I could put them."

I thought I understood his reluctance. His two charts miniaturized the continent of Europe down to roughly the same scale on which he'd miniaturized his life. They were just right for Nick O'Brien, though I would no more have used them to sail by than I'd have used the maps in the endpapers of my diary.

"I suppose you'll need one more to get to Africa—"

"There's an Admiralty chart for the whole of the North Atlantic," Nick said.

At low tide, we walked together across the salt marshes to the sea. Nick was full of his newly acquired natural history. He named the wading curlews and turnstones, the snipe ricocheting up ahead of us, the lapwings with their pigtail crests. He found a thick bed of tuberous marsh samphire and stopped to harvest it.

"It's brilliant in sandwiches," he said. "See that stuff where you're standing? Scurvy grass. It's solid with vitamin C. They used to make sailors eat it, poor buggers—it tastes revolting."

"What's that bird there?"

"Greenshank. This time last year, you know, the only birds I ever knew were sparrows. When I walked out of the job, I didn't know *anything*. For me, it's been like going to a university. Every day I'm learning. There's only one thing wrong for me now. I wish there was a girl to share it all with. It's the only thing I miss—"

"You think your life's big enough to *share?*" It looked to me as if the addition of a girl, even a very small girl indeed, to the minuscule world of *Sussex Rowan* would sink it instantly.

There had been a girl once, in the winter, Nick said. She'd moved into the boat when it was moored in Faversham creek. "It didn't last, unfortunately."

"How long?"

"Five days."

The temperature outside the boat had been ten degrees below freezing-point. The mud around them froze as the tide ebbed. Nick's friend had balked at washing herself and her clothes in icy seawater as he did. Yet he still seemed puzzled as to why she'd left.

"I don't think she really liked boats," he said, hands deep in his pockets, frowning at the sky. "What I need is someone who really likes boats."

On the walk back to Rye, I talked about my own voyage. With Nick O'Brien, it was a voyage again, not simply a bad case of going boating.

"I can teach you basic astro," he said. "You could learn to use a sextant in a couple of hours. There's nothing to it. It's a nice feeling—knowing you can find exactly where you are when you're miles out of sight of land. It makes you independent, like. Just you and the sun . . ."

"I'd like that—"

"You won't be able to stop this, you know. You'll keep on going. I can tell. When you've learned how to live like a seagull, it's not a thing you can just give up like that. I wouldn't trade it. Nor will you. I bet you anything—"

By eleven the next morning a circle of tourist coaches surrounded Rye on its hill like a defensive laager of voortrekker wagons. For Rye was famous. It wasn't famous in the way that most towns are, for making and doing things—Axminster for carpets, Cambridge for degrees, Melton Mowbray for pork pies, Nottingham for lace. Rye was famous for doing nothing. "Deserted by the sea . . . miraculously preserved from the developers . . . Rye is arguably the most enchanting town in the British Isles," said the brochure which Nick O'Brien collected from the tourist kiosk because, like most things in Nick's life, it was free.

We poked about through the streets, a pair of ignorant sight-seers in our own country. The polished cobbles were lapped in a pink surf of fallen cherry blossom; the half-timbered Tudor houses were up to their ears in honeysuckle and tea roses. Remembering Eliot on Kipling ("The first condition of understanding a foreign country is to smell it"), I sniffed at Rye, but it gave nothing away; it was as if someone had sprayed the town from end to end with a floral-scented underarm deodorant in order to give it the dehumanized loveliness of a glossy color photograph.

It was oddly hushed too. Doves purred and hiccuped in their dovecotes overhead, and the voices of the other visitors echoed overloudly under the sagging gables, like people talking in church. Wherever one looked, one saw another Cyclops—a slowly turning head culminating in the lidless mauve eye of a Yashica or a Nikon. Rye was going on record. There must now be at least a hundred holiday snaps, preserved in albums across the globe, in which Nick O'Brien and I figure as trespassers on the composition.

"Who are those people there?"

"Nobody. They were in the way."

I had meant to buy provisions for *Gosfield Maid*, but though the Mint was lined with shopfronts, there were no remotely useful things for sale. There were plenty of antiques and curios; there were "galleries" stuffed with anemic water-colors of oasthouses, fishing boats and gingerbread thatched hovels; there were "potteries" with untempting displays of folk earthenware in their windows—urns, vases and tankards all tricked out in a warty toad-skin glaze. It was true that you could buy souvenir tea towels and plastic pinafores with pictures of Rye on them, but there wasn't an egg, or a half-pound of butter, or a pint of milk to be seen.

Even getting a cup of coffee was a problem. The place was solid with cafés, but I winced at the prospect of establishments with names like Ye Olde Tucke Shoppe and Simon the Pieman and hunted in vain for some grubby snack bar which would at least acknowledge that it shared the same century as Nick and I.

"This was exactly what used to drive Edward Burra to his wit's ends."

"Edward who?"

Edward Burra was not mentioned in Nick's free guide. Although he was Rye's best-known native son, he and the town were apparently still at loggerheads even after his death. In letters he always gave his address as "Wry." Burra had no taste for the quaint and picturesque; his paintings glory in, and pine for, the raw, noisy, sexy twentieth-century world from which Rye had turned its genteel face. Leaving the family house on the pretext that he was going out for ten minutes to post a letter, he decamped to Forty-second Street, where he roistered happily with male whores from Harlem and bothered to write home only after he'd been gone a year. Yet Burra needed Rye in much the same way that Flaubert needed his provincial bourgeoisie and Marx his capitalists: exasperation with the place invigorated Burra's work just as powerfully as if he'd loved it. He did come back. When he inherited his house on the corner of Church Square, he covered the windows with brown paper to exclude the intolerably pretty view. Painting by the light of a bare electric bulb, he was off in a private heaven of strippers, drunks, gangsters and lounging black boys with diamond-splinter eyes and watermelon smiles, while Rye went on being wry beyond the brown paper screen.

The area around Burra's house was heavily infested with artists at their easels, all of them registering the same received image, of mellow brick and old timber, jasmine and hollyhocks. The paintings themselves were fussy, lifeless things, with dicky perspectives and clouds of porridge floating in their skies. But their straw-hatted executioners had more in common with Burra than either they or Burra would probably have cared to admit. Like him, they'd blotted out the tiresome England in which they actually lived, because they preferred to paint, like him, by artificial light. Their rustic, thatched old-world utopia was not so very far in spirit from the version of pastoral which Burra made out of the gay dives off Times Square.

Rye itself was not so much a town now as a work of sentimental art—a depiction of life, not life in its own right. It was crude art, too, starved of paradox and contingent detail. In every brushstroke there was the same remorseless charm. "REBUILT 1420," boasted the plaque on the honeysuckled Mermaid Inn, ryely self-preening. At 12:15 the Quarter Boys, a pair of gilded cherubs armed with gongsticks, went into action on the clock tower of St. Mary's Church. Nick O'Brien scrutinized them closely, wrinkling his eyes against the sun.

"They're made of GRP," he said.

"Are you sure?"

"You can see the lines of the mold. That's fiberglass, that is, no question."

They'd fooled me, but on second look I saw they couldn't possibly have been either carved of wood or more than a few years old. Having caught Rye out red-handed in the possession of a pair of GRP cherubim, I wasn't going to be so easily taken in again. I regarded it with a policeman's mistrustful eye and saw fiberglass cherry blossom, fiberglass cobblestones, toppling facades of fiberglass Tudor, all protected from the sea by a dinky fiberglass castle.

At the bottom of Mermaid Street, I found my suspicions gratifyingly confirmed. Housed in a disused timber ware-

house there was the Rye Town Model, a perfect scale replica of the place, beam for beam and eave for eave, with a
son et lumière show to clue the visitor in on the town's history.
It was an enthralling piece of artifice in its way, though I
was wrong about the materials used in its construction: the
houses were made of polystyrene, the cobbled streets of
enameled tapioca.

It was also redundant, for Rye itself was a model town:
this was a model of a model, a picture within a picture, the
second step of an infinite regression. At the end you'd need
a spectroscope to examine what was happening, and all
you'd see would be zillions of tiny subatomic tourists
swarming out of tiny subatomic buses and congealing round
a particle of half-timbered antimatter.

Rye had found that there was a profit to be made out of its
own dereliction. The town had been in decline for so long
that the picturesque business of slowly crumbling on its hill
had become its only form of conspicuous activity. It was
crumbling when Defoe visited it in the 1720s, and had
crumbled a bit more when Henry James, living in Lamb
House, wrote in 1901 of the "small romance of Rye" with
"its old browns that turn to red and old reds which turn to
purple." "These tones of evening," James wrote, "are now
pretty much all that Rye has left to give."

Rye had spun its evening out to such a length that dawn
was now showing on its horizon. In 1982, there was a little
light industry on the unvisited fringes of the town, a little
commercial fishing, a little shipping going in and out of its
harbor—and for the first time in several hundred years Rye
was in business on a grand scale. Its very failure as a town
had emerged as a marketable commodity for which there
was an apparently unlimited international demand. Stagna-
tion and decay, smartly painted and packaged, were selling
like hot cakes.

Looking at the Rye Town Model, I thought how horribly
well it might be made to work as a representation of Britain
at large. Britain too was in a state of industrial decline. Its

manufacturing machinery was antique. The country's best hope lay, according to the government, in making a rapid shift from "high tech" through "low tech" to no tech at all. Making things in Britain was too expensive and cumbersome a process now. The "service industry" was the coming thing.

Seen in this light, Rye was a solution of sorts to a national problem; it was in the vanguard of industry. Rye was nothing but services, with jobs for waiters, salesclerks, ticket sellers, P.R. men, holiday home leasers, hoteliers, coach drivers, tour guides. Its manufactures were most prominently represented by pottery which might as easily have been thrown in a camp of Ancient Britons and by derivative little watercolors clipped into spray-gilt plastic frames. Not much tech there.

The Rye Town Model showed how you could turn almost anything that didn't work into a museum piece. Its most startling application came up during the miners' strike of 1984, in a parliamentary debate on pit closures. One Conservative member saw no problem: it was easy, he said— just close the unproductive pits and reopen them as museums. Redundant miners could be retrained as tour guides and conduct coach parties down the shafts, through the tunnels and round the exhausted coal faces. It struck me as a weird vision. The miners, presumably, would have their faces artfully blacked with greasepaint, wear Davy lamps and carry canaries around in cages. Intrigued by the Swiftian simplicity of this proposal, I rang the National Coal Board to ask them if they were taking it seriously.

The press officer was huffy. There was, he said, nothing at all original in that idea; the N.C.B. had been doing it for years. There were four closed pits now functioning as "living museums"—two in South Wales, one in Stoke-on-Trent and one in Northumberland. Yes, certainly they were planning more.

His irritably matter-of-fact tone (of course the Coal Board is involved in the tourist industry—didn't you know *that*?) pointed up a truth about tourism which the British were doing their best to ignore. Depending on their point of view, they saw the tourists either as disfiguring scar tissue

on an otherwise healthy body or as a happy extra, like
marzipan and icing on a cake. The tourists were neither of
these things. They were as central, as organic to our period
as the steel and cotton mills of the eighteenth century. Like
the mills, they were beginning to change everyone's pattern
of life and alter the basic fabric of the country.

In 1982, nearly thirteen million foreign tourists de-
scended on Britain, and their numbers were climbing by a
steady million a year. There were nineteen million house-
holds in the country, so by 1989 one might expect to see a
foreign tourist for every single dwelling in the land. There
would be no council flat without a quiet American, no suburban semi without a shutter-happy Japanese. Streams of
buses would shunt them from Anne Hathaway's Cottage to
ruined car factories in Dagenham and Oxford, to defunct
coal mines, closed-down universities, deserted high-rise
buildings . . . as far as I could see, there was no logical end
to the possible merrying of England on the Rye Town
model.

This marketing of a whole country as a historical facade
is being ingeniously managed by the P.R. industry. The
posters issued by the British Tourist Authority neatly state
the terms of sale. For every major client there is a different
Britain on offer. The poster designed for Saudi Arabia and
the Gulf states shows what looks like a vastly intricate
mosque, and it took me several seconds to work out that it
is actually a picture of Brighton's Royal Pavilion. Below this
there are two twinned images: one of a Daimler illegally
parked in Knightsbridge outside Harrods, the other of a
woman bargaining with a smiling shopkeeper over a counter
laden with goodies. In Arabic, Britain is a Moslem country
with a famously well-stocked souk.

A poster designed for exhibition in Europe and the
United States takes an altogether different line. Beneath an
improbably cloudless sky, a dozen friendly Britons, young
and old, are taking refreshment on the greensward outside
a thatched and timbered pub. They hold tankards of mild
ale, and are simultaneously playing skittles and helping
themselves to generous slices from a great cartwheel of

cheese. A space has been left in the front of the picture for the tourist to perch on the dry-stone wall and join in this rustic fun.

Both posters make an important splash of what the Tourist Authority calls "Britain's scenery." The word is deadly accurate. The green and rolling hills, the packhorse bridges spanning silver brooks, are theatrical decorations, painted hangings to charm the eye. When people step out from behind the scenery, they are by definition actors, performing a play for the tourists' entertainment. *Britain* goes into italic type because it is the title of a jovial masque. The *dramatis personae* of *Britain* are types and humors—figures like the genial Mine Host, the Old Salt, the Apple-Cheeked Old Lady At The Village Shop, the Country Squire and a complete fairy-story set of Princes, Queens, Princesses, Duchesses and Dukes.

It is, as Plato argued when he banned the profession from his Republic, a dangerous thing to treat people as actors because they tend to lose any secure sense of their own authenticity. The British had noticed this clearly enough in other people's countries, had seen the Costa Brava, Majorca, the Cyclades all "hopelessly spoiled" by mass tourism, with sweet old fishermen and colorful *taverna* keepers transformed, almost overnight, into fast-talking sharpies and masters of the quick buck. They were slower to see that Britain itself was spoiled in exactly the same way by exactly the same process.

It showed on people's faces—the cold glaze of boredom at the prospect of dealing with yet another bloody stranger.

"Excuse me, but can you tell me which way—"

"I'm not an information bureau, mate."

The English were now walking through their parts with frank resentment. They were tired to death of being polite, of smiling while their pictures were taken, of answering damn-fool questions, of being peered at and poked and condescended to in their roles as Friendly Natives. They were friendly no longer. In these pretty towns on the south coast, they carried rudeness to the point of open challenge. They took their revenge on the tourists by marking up their bills and serving them with a dismissive I'm-as-good-as-you-are slamming down of plates on tables.

"Can I have the bill, please?"

"When I'm ready."

They advertised their snappishness at being so intruded on by strangers with a forest of surly, prohibitive notices, erected at every opportunity, in gardens, shops, pubs, fields, parks. No Children, No Pets, No Picnics, No Credit, No Photographs, No Beachwear, No Coaches, No Loitering, No Bare Feet, No Games, No Transistors, No Fishing, No Change Given, *No Dice!*

A few hundred yards from Strand Quay I found a pub to which no tourists were ever drawn. It stood on the edge of the 1950s housing development where the working class of Rye lived in convenient exile from their old, unsanitary and now hugely valuable cottages in the center of town. It didn't have a single oak beam, or a horse brass, or a yard of ale. A Space Invaders machine chattered to itself in a corner. The dart board, enclosed in an old tractor tire, was leaking its stuffing like a crippled sofa. At the bar three elderly men were mooning silently over their beer. They looked up as I opened the door, then looked quickly back inside their glasses. I was a trespasser.

"Bloody tourists," I said, trying to ingratiate myself with the company. "You can't move up there for the tourists."

"Ur."

"I thought I was in Tokyo."

"Ur." Then, warily, "What *you* here for, then?"

"Business," I said determinedly. "I work with boats."

"Ur."

There was a silence of several minutes before the man sitting nearest to me finally turned his narrow face aside from his glass. He was wearing a very old suit and a set of very new teeth. "Them buggers," he said. "Japs. It's all bloody Japs now. And French. We got French up there. Froggie bastards. And Eyeties and Yanks. All the fuckin' nations. They've even got Russians up there—*Russians!*"

"Someone must be making a packet," I said.

"Not me, worse luck. Not me."

"I bet there's a few rich buggers creaming it off in Rye."

"Ur."

On the next pint he unbuttoned. He'd just turned eighty. His name was Les. He was alone. His wife had died, he'd fallen out with his daughter. His father had died young of a fit of hiccups ("It were terrible—the noise").

"I were born fifty years too late," he said, and laughed, a miserable, wheezy, confidential, graveyard laugh.

He never went up the Mint or the High Street now, he said. He couldn't recognize the town as he had known it. "Them antiquey shops and tea shops—they're like yo-yos. Here today, gone tomorrow. I won't go there."

"What was there before the tourists came?"

"Butchers," he said warmly. "They had a lot of butchers up there. With these what-d'you-callums—these *carcasses*—hanging up on hooks. Whole sides of meat. Pigs. Cows. Mutton. You'd smell 'em a mile off, the butchers up there. *Yur.* There was blood on the floor of them, used to run out into the street, down the cobbles."

He was remembering Rye as it had once been with his nose. There were the wood and coal yards . . . the gasworks (he dwelt fondly on the gasworks) . . . the steam trawlers tied up to the quay.

"It was all *Captain* then. Captain this, Captain that. There were Captain Smith . . . Captain Shore . . . they was all captains then."

It was a nostalgia for life itself, this reminiscent savoring of the farty smell of the gasworks, the taste of coal-fired steam, the reek of butchered flesh. "They bombed the gasworks in the bloody war," Les said, "and then the bloody tourists come."

I asked him if he remembered Mr. James in Lamb House. "Yur," he said. "He had a girl in to do his typing for him. In the Garden House there. I'd hear the typing when I were walking past. She were fast at it, too. All clickety click, you never heard her stop. They bloody bombed the Garden House in the war and all."

"And Mr. James himself?"

"He did books." It was evidently an activity that Les had

little time for—not a proper art like high-speed typing. "It's a pity old Burgess Noakes is dead, you could have had a proper talk with him."

"Who?"

"Burgess Noakes?" Les stared at me as if he'd revealed an astounding gap in my knowledge. "Burgess Noakes. He were Mr. James's batman. He was a wonderful bloke, Burgess Noakes was. Tell a story? He'd make you laugh. Went all over the bloody world. Seen every bloody thing. He went to *Umurrica*. Umurrica. New York . . . all them places, Burgess Noakes was there. He took Mr. James with him to Umurrica too."

Sitting out in the cockpit of *Sussex Rowan*, Nick O'Brien gave me a lesson in the use of the sextant. I practiced plucking the sun out of the sky and planting it on rooftops, since there was no true horizon on which to rest it. It was a neat conjuring trick, all done by mirrors, and I liked the illusion of being able to tamper freely with the structure of the universe. Up till now I had treated my own sextant as an amusing toy; under Nick's tuition, I sweated through the mathematics of position-finding, rooting out the sun's Greenwich Hour Angle and Declination from the tables in the almanac. After half an hour I reckoned that I could probably take a competent Noon Sight; at the end of two hours I was fuddled by the intricacies of Azimuth Angle Z and whether intercepts were Towards or Away.

"Noon Sights are all you ever really need anyway," Nick said.

I wasn't sure quite what I was practicing for, but it seemed a good idea to get the hang of basic astronavigation in case one day I might have to do a bunk and escape into serious blue water.

"Away."

"No, you've got it wrong. It's Towards."

"And you picked this up all by yourself?"

"Yes. It's pretty obvious stuff. You don't need O-levels for it."

Simple possession of the sextant felt like a ticket to somewhere. Maybe I'd find myself wintering in Africa along with Nick and the swallows. If you could lick "astro," you could dispose yourself about the globe more or less as you pleased, and sail off to those remaining dots on the charts that were too small to land planeloads of tourists on, too small for laws, taxes, manila envelopes with windows in them. The boxed sextant, wrapped in its oily cloth, its lenses slotted into their green velveteen compartments, was a far more practical and reassuring object than the revolvers that some people keep under their pillows in case of emergency.

Indeed, it looked as if the sextant might have to be used in anger very much earlier than I had planned. At three o'clock in the afternoon of May 2, Falklands time, the submarine H.M.S. *Conqueror* torpedoed the Argentinian cruiser the *General Belgrano*. The news broke in Britain the following day. The Argentinian ship had been forty miles southwest of the declared exclusion zone. The Ministry of Defence spokesman who came on television to recite all Falklands news in a woeful bass at slow dictation speed gave the bare facts, and failed completely to explain why this attack had been launched on a ship which was more than two hours' steaming time away from the cordon round the Falklands, which I had taken to be the only conceivably legitimate theater of war. *Why?*

The papers were no help. The *Express* had an honorable front page:

SUNK
FEARS FOR 700 ON ARGENTINE WARSHIP
DOOMED: the veteran cruiser *General Belgrano* which survived Pearl Harbour but was lost yesterday.

The *Sun's* front page was dishonorable even by its own standards:

GOTCHA!
OUR LADS SINK GUNBOAT AND HOLE CRUISER.
The Navy had the Argies on their knees last night after a devastating double punch.

WALLOP! They torpedoed the 14,000-ton
Argentine cruiser *General Belgrano* and left it a useless
wreck.
WALLOP! Task force helicopters sank one Argentine
patrol boat and severely damaged another . . .

The Times ran two editorials on the sinking in its editions of
May 4 and May 5. They were significantly different in tone.
On the 4th, the paper was hesitant and regretful:

There can . . . be no rejoicing at the feat of British
arms this weekend. It had to be done, it may have to
be done again. Relief—but only relief—can
accompany any such unpleasant task successfully
accomplished with the minimum loss of life on both
sides . . .

"Minimum" seemed an odd word to use under the circumstances, but in other respects *The Times* accurately reflected
the concern and the queasiness felt by many people in Britain as they heard the news. On May 5, though, the paper
was taking a much stiffer line:

The sinking of the *General Belgrano* was justified
because the warship was not in its position close to
the exclusion zone either by accident or by
innocence. Its previous behaviour had shown it to
have hostile intentions . . .

Yes, but "close to" was still forty miles away from "inside."
Of course war is not cricket, but why bother to make rules
when you are prepared to break them within twenty-four
hours of their coming into force? Why had the British Cabinet agreed to the request of Sir Terence Lewin, the Chief
of the Defence Staff, to permit the sinking of the *Belgrano*
well outside its own declared threshold of war? It is frightening to be a citizen of a country whose government begins
to act as if it were no longer constrained by ordinary reason.
In international waters, forty miles outside the exclusion

zone, three hundred and sixty-eight sailors had been killed, some drowned, some burned. Their deaths seemed wanton.

Up till this moment, Mrs. Thatcher's government had been backed by many governments around the world whose sympathy with her cause was founded in ordinary reason. The Argentinian invasion of the Falklands was a transparent violation of international law. The Falklanders themselves were generally seen as a peaceable and defenseless people who were being trampled underfoot by the occupying army of a neofascist power. Before the sinking of the *Belgrano*, Britain's response to the invasion had sometimes been thought excessive but never entirely unreasonable.

Things had changed now. Alexander Haig, the American Secretary of State, who had broadly supported Mrs. Thatcher in the weeks before (YANKS A MILLION! AT LAST! REAGAN'S BACKING BRITAIN!), told a Congressional committee that the sinking of the *Belgrano* had "contributed to continuing the dispute." Italy and Ireland both voted to lift their sanctions against Argentina. In the United Nations, Britain suddenly found herself very nearly friendless.

This roar of international disapproval, intended to dispirit, succeeded in doing quite the reverse. It worked like a dose of sea air on the government and on the British press. Standing alone in the world was what the British liked to believe that they did best. It brought out the Dunkirk Spirit, which was now being busily rebottled as the Falklands Spirit. It reminded them that they were a beleaguered island people, and reinforced their pride in the heroic solitude of their geography. It brought out, in the British Isles at large, all the crabbiness, the xenophobia, the determination to take the rest of the world down a peg, the hunch-shouldered go-it-alone-ism of the Manx—and of the Falklanders themselves.

They . . . Them. Eight miles off Dungeness, with the coast of continental Europe showing as a thread of tinsel on the horizon to the east, the British looked to me like a very peculiar bunch of foreigners, definitely third persons and

not first. *Sussex Rowan* and *Gosfield Maid* had separated at the
Rye Fairway buoy: Nick O'Brien was going west, to a place
in Sussex that he'd heard of which didn't have a harbormaster and didn't levy dues; I was heading for the Thames and
London. I'd promised that I'd be there in two days' time,
but . . . It would be so easy to quit Britain now. The French
shore looked hardly farther away than the English one. I
had a passport and a yellow Q flag to hoist on the mizzenmast—a shift of course from 050° to 140°, and I could be
dining this evening in Boulogne, the standard hidey-hole
for English black sheep, from Victorian bankrupts to Lord
Lucan look-alikes. *Gosfield Maid* would have the wind behind
her. . . . A plate of grilled langoustines at *La Matelote*—and
after that, the exile's life of day-old papers, the BBC World
Service, letters from home and two rubbers of bridge with
Mrs. Meiklejohn and the rest of the ex-pats.

But I had *"Dinner, Linda, 8:15"* written in my diary, there
was a pile of unanswered mail waiting in my flat, and I was
in the magnetic field of England's dense and leaden bulk. I
was stuck with my orbit. I could no more alter course for
France than I could strike out for Polynesia.

I sheltered overnight (though "sheltered" was not really
the word for it) in Dover Harbour, a square mile of sea,
loosely corralled with breakwaters. The boat rolled, the
anchor chain growled and muttered in its locker; I slept
thinly through a continous program of bad dreams. In the
early sun, Vera Lynn's white cliffs were maculated with
grime; drained of color under a ragged fringe of green, they
looked much as I felt—not in good shape at all.

I took the back way round the Goodwin Sands, where
the water was river-calm, protected by the line of shoals to
seaward. Paul Theroux's interest in my possible wreckage
on the Goodwins was a landsman's fancy. People on land
think of the sea as a void, an emptiness, haunted by myth-
ological hazards. The sea marks the end of things. It is
where life stops and the unknown begins. It is a necessary,
comforting fiction to conceive of the sea as the residence of
gods and monsters—Aeolus, the Sirens, Scylla, Charybdis,
the Goodwins, the Bermuda Triangle. In fact the sea is just

an alternative known world. Its topography is as intricate as that of the land, its place names as particular and evocative, its maps and signposts rather more reliable. I made for the Downs, where I breakfasted, rattled through the Gull Stream on a two-knot tide, rounded North Foreland and crossed the boundary between the cold green quartzy water of the Dover Straits and the weak tea, flecked with scum, of the Thames Estuary. The meeting of the two waters was precisely marked by a long diagonal string of lazy eddies. A trail of sea garbage had fetched up along this line: busted fish crates, discarded floats, detergent bottles. Distended plastic bags floated just beneath the surface like a shoal of sickly plaice. On one eddy, a torn car seat was placidly swiveling on its own, as if its occupant had just popped in for a quick dip. A troop of noisy gulls patrolled the frontier, watching out for tasty bits of contraband sewage and long-dead fish and squabbling over the rich, plowed water left behind by *Gosfield Maid*.

It was not so much an estuary as a broad sea gulf, thirty miles from jaw to jaw, with the ebb tide turning it to an expanding archipelago as whaleback islands of mud and sand began to ease themselves out into the hazy sunshine. I'd seen the mouth of the Thames from aircraft before—a delta of smooth and gleaming flats, with wrinkled fans of water spilling out from the tiny brooks which divided the islands. Making the most of my last drink, waiting for the sudden dimming of the cabin lights as the engine note changed from a steady purr to the rattletrap growl of a badly loaded washing machine, for the double ping that went with the seat-belt sign and the call to extinguish "all smok-ing materials," I had been too anxious on other accounts to take any serious interest in the Thames. Now that I was actually on it, I wished that I'd concentrated a little harder on the view from the plane window; it would have been like looking down from the top floor on a lot of people blunder-ing about inside Hampton Court Maze.

Lines of buoys stretched out everywhere, and some of the separate channels were so close to each other that it would be easy to wander out of one and into another, and collide with a sandbank on the way. It was like going blind-fold, feeling one's way from buoy to buoy, marking each one off on the chart as it slid past the boat, setting the compass course for the next, groping along with the needle on the depth-sounder bouncing puckishly from 1 fathom to 3 and back to 1 again.

This thin, pale water didn't look like sea, nor did the land around it look like land. It was wide-open, flat and boggy, only by a few degrees less liquid in consistency than the stuff which was officially designated as water on the chart. It seemed that the basic entropy of eastern England, its river and its sea, was unusually volatile. Heat the whole lot up a little in a tropic summer, or freeze them in a severe winter, and everything would swap places, with oil tankers cruis-ing placidly through the Kentish swamplands and cricketers hitting sixes down the Edinburgh Channel. Or perhaps they'd simply all combine into primal sludge, a frog heaven with insufficient water to set a walnut shell afloat for long.

Even flattered by the sun, it was a landscape of spectacu-lar desolation, its empty sweeps of brown and gray occa-sionally broken by strange, angular pieces of Meccano work. A herd of hammer-headed cranes appeared to have found a watering hole on the northern shore. Pylons marched in line across the marshes. The top-heavy concrete towers of a power station were free-floating in sky. The estuary itself—so far as one could see what *was* the estuary itself—was dotted about with forts built on tall stilts, left over from old wars. Seen from a distance, they took on a momentary period charm, as old-fashioned plate cameras mounted on their tripods. Off the Isle of Grain—which, in this realm of ambiguous distinctions between sea and soil, was not, of course, an island at all, merely a boggy promon-tory—the rusty deckworks of the S.S. *Richard Montgomery* stuck out at a jaunty angle from its graveyard of thick slime. The wreck was ringed around with warning buoys and Keep Off notices. It had been an American supply ship during World War II, with a cargo of ammunition and high explo-sives. When it went down, it was thought too dangerous to risk trying to salvage the cargo, and it was still intact forty years on. There were rumors that it could blow up at any moment, going off with a bang that would take most of the people of Sheerness and Wallend with it. Once a year it provoked the same Parliamentary question and received the same dusty Parliamentary answer, that it was safest left where it was. But in Sheerness, people race for their cellars whenever a car backfires. Passing it at close quarters, I lowered the engine revs of *Gosfield Maid*, keen not to become the man who made the vibrations that blew a hefty chunk of urban Kent to muddy smithereens.

Yet these charmless and forbidding marshes had been the making of London as a world city. London was tucked deep inland, more than sixty miles from the mouth of the delta. It squatted in its lair like one of Freud's anal-retentive personalities, hoarding itself to itself, protected from the sea by a boggy plain of what looked and smelled like its own excrement. There was nothing to impede the wind across this flatland, and London's ships could sail from the sea into the city without once losing the wind. Intruders, though, could be picked off one by one as the river narrowed. London was perfectly immune to siege by an enemy fleet. It was, uniquely among national capitals, both England's snuggest port and England's most central market town. Prising my way toward it against the running tide, past sandbank after sandbank and up swatchway after swatchway, I wasn't sure whether I was approaching the city as a friend or an enemy, but it was clear that had I been in a Viking longboat I would have abandoned the raid long ago.

I'd steeled myself to maneuver through a great crowd of shipping, but there was a dead, dull Sunday-afternoon air on the estuary. Every so often a slab-sided bulk container would come sliding out from behind the marshes, but there weren't enough of them to make a crowd, and they didn't look much like ships. Tall as office buildings, long as boulevards, they pushed down Sea Reach, showing their enormous gross tonnage in the rude way in which they shoved the water aside with their blunt fronts. They certainly didn't add much light or color to the day.

I was too late to find the Thames as I remembered it—a great concourse of waterborne traffic, the flat surrounding landscape exotically forested with masts, flags, derricks, funnels, spars, bridgehouses. The container ships had killed all that twenty years ago. In the early 1960s, about 1,800 ships used to sail in and out of the Port of London every week. The average cargo ship then was a 5,000-tonner, and the London docks were packed with them. Their loading and unloading kept 35,000 dockers in work. Places like Bermondsey, Wapping and the Isle of Dogs were rich in ship-business, their streets rank with cargo smells, their pubs jammed to the doors. At twenty, I thought Wapping one of the most dangerous and exciting spots on earth.

Then the container ships came. Five and more times bigger than the old cargo boats, they couldn't fit into the docks, so they berthed at a string of new wharfside "terminals" downriver. Their roll-on, roll-off system of loading required very few dockers. By the 1980s, instead of 1,800 ships a week, there were 240; instead of the 35,000 men working in the docks there were 2,000; instead of 66 million tons of cargo a year, there were 45 million. The decline in overall trade was undramatic, but there were so many jobs gone, ships gone, docks filled-in, that the loss of life, in every sense of that phrase, was on a scale one might expect of a medium sized war.

The land, such as it was, stole imperceptibly in on either side round *Gosfield Maid*; blackened timber stakes and piles, scallop-shaped clifflets of gleaming mud. Past Mucking Creek, the Thames abruptly turned into a recognizable river, confined and disciplined by walls, fences, jetties, piers. Its color and texture changed too. Glossy with oil, darkened with blue clay, the water resembled a rich and meaty consommé. I had been barely holding my own against the river before, but as the flood tide got under way the boat began to pick up speed through Tilbury and Gravesend, Dartford and Rainham, a long industrial ribbon of ships, trucks and cranes, with the hands-in-pockets crew of solitary men on wharves doing nothing except watch the soupy water spool under their feet, bulging against the piles and streaming out in feather patterns as it went swelling on inland. You could spend whole days doing that, as I knew. It made you feel giddy and soft-headed and induced fine daydreams. Watching water move is a much sweeter and less unpredictable way of altering the mind than inhaling the smoke of marijuana.

There was one unexpected splash of beauty, in the Thames Barrier at Woolwich. Its silver cowls, ranged across the river like the helmets of giant knights, seemed like a freak instance of our century actually enriching the landscape instead of impoverishing it. The flood barrier itself would save London from drowning. Its massive hydraulics, its guillotines of rust-red steel, its shining and armorial piers made the entry to the city into something like a Roman triumph. The Thames barrier, as *Gosfield Maid* slid through Span C, promised something very big and very glorious around the next bend.

Indeed the next bend yielded the formal brief prettiness of Greenwich, then, after that, the wasteland. Brick dust blew across the river from the ruins of the Surrey Docks, which showed as miles of corrugated iron and slag piles, with earthmovers standing idle on tips of spoil, and toppling pyramids of crushed cars letting in cracks of sky through their wrecked innards. This was a weekday afternoon, still within working hours, but there wasn't a human being in sight. It looked as if the great work of destruction had been set in train years ago, then suddenly abandoned on a whim. A large blue notice at the entrance to what had once been a dock announced that a "WATERSPORTS COMPLEX" was to be built here, but the paint had peeled and the lettering rendered almost completely illegible by a rash of little scabs left on it by vagrant air-gun pellets.

By another lock, someone brave had set up a tiny farm with one cow, two sheep, a pig, a goat and some hens fenced in behind an improvised stockade of chicken wire and rusty bedsteads. The broken high wall behind the farm had been overpainted with a wildy optimistic mural of blue sky, green fields, oak trees, flowers, a rustic gate. The farm project was meant to give young children an introduction to nature: in this miserable acreage of scrap which was Rotherhithe, it looked like an act of doomed saintliness.

In Bermondsey, the spice warehouses were being torn down. Their backs were gone, but big iron hooks still hung from the pulleys which were cantilevered out from under their eaves, and there was a stubborn residual scent of cinnamon in the air, like a stain. On a lone atoll of redevelopment, where some yellow brickwork was rising behind scaffolding on a wharf, the natives had left prominent messages for the visitors: SOD OFF L.D.D.C. (this addressed to the London Docklands Development Corporation); THESE ARE OUR BACK GARDENS NOT YOURS; WE WANT HOUSES FOR LOCAL PEOPLE, NOT PALACES FOR PLAYBOYS.

There was very little traffic on the river now. The few barges and lighters were well outnumbered by the glassed-in excursion boats taking tourists to Greenwich and back, their P.A. systems booming. I heard *Gosfield Maid* pointed out as "one of the many yachts now to be seen sailing on the London River."

On the north bank, the warehouses were doing rather better out of the decade than the blitzed shambles on the other side. Gutted and repointed, their sooty brickwork scoured by pressure hoses, they were being converted into flats and offices, with salads of real estate agents' signs advertising luxury river-view penthouses to any millionaires who happened to be passing. One sign said STUDIO APARTMENTS FROM £85,000. For a bed-sit, even for a bed-sit with a view, the price seemed steep, particularly considering what the view was actually *of*—a little water and an infinity of dust, rubble, chain-link fencing and heaps of junked cars like so many squashed blowflies. £85,000? For *that*?

Below Tower Bridge, half a dozen yachts had gathered round the entrance to St. Katherine's Dock, waiting for high tide and the opening of the lock gates. Two were flying German ensigns, one was Dutch, and the foreign visitors were volubly approving all they saw—the evening light on the water, the handsome drawbridge, the fulsome stone battlements of the Tower behind it. Elated and shaky with the adventure of their two- and three-day passages across the North Sea, they'd arrived at a destination worthy of the excitement that they'd had in reaching it. In twenty minutes, now ten, now five, London would open to them like a treasure chest. I kept out of the talk on the jetty, the questions, the consulting of watches. I envied them their city. It sounded, even in languages I couldn't understand, like a marvelous place, but it didn't sound at all like the London I could see.

The lock gates opened, and we rafted into a pool over-hung with faces and cameras. I searched the faces and found my own friend there, conspicuous as the only person in the crowd who was not dressed in bright pastel holiday gear. When I waved, she didn't see, but I was answered by smiles and waves from several families of polite Japanese.

Alone among the London docks, St. Katherine's had—not so much survived as been mysteriously transmogrified. *Gosfield Maid*, with two on board now, motored into a sort of marine stage set, full of restored Thames barges, their red sails furled on their spars, historic steamships, yachts and motor cruisers. At the center of things, a white-painted clapboard pub called the Charles Dickens struck the requisite note of spanking new old-world. The warehouses had been quarried out into a pedestrian shopping mall of oil-lamp-lit boutiques. We squeaked past the gilded figurehead of a barge, and pleased though I was to see my friend, I thought, this looks like a wasted journey, to have sailed a hundred and twenty-five sea miles only to arrive back at the Rye Town Model.

She drove at a terrifying speed. Lighted hoardings flashed by over our heads, far too fast for me to read what they said. Giant packs of cigarettes, bottles of beer, airplanes, faces—the images sped past, but I had no time to grasp whose images they were. Nor did I remember Linda as a demon driver. Crouched low in my seat, with the safety harness buckled tight around my chest, I wondered what on earth had happened to her character in my absence.

"Please slow down—"

"I'm only doing thirty."

"You can't be."

"Look at the clock."

"I suppose it's me. Six knots is my top speed."

I tried to adjust back to a city that felt like a fireworks display of rockets and whizzbangs. It was too fast, too bright, too loud to take in. We shot through an underpass and came out at the other end like a bullet.

"You know about the *Sheffield?*" Linda said.

"*Sheffield?* No—"

"The Argentinians have sunk it with an Exocet."

"Were many people killed?"

"I don't think so. Twenty—something like that. Not like the *Belgrano.*"

"I suppose it might sober Thatcher up. Do you hear people talking about the war much?"

"Not much. It's just something else that's on the TV."

"Is anyone for it?"

"No one I know. I suspect my mother might be for it. At least, she reads the *Daily Telegraph*. I suppose that must mean she's for it."

"*My* mother's dead set against it. She talks as if she was trying to get up a military coup against the government."

"I wouldn't put much hope in a coup organized by your mother."

The flat appeared to belong to a stranger, a warren of unaired and dusty rooms, too big and bare to be at home in. The pile of mail was full of the usual threats to distrain my goods, sever my electricity supply and cut my telephone off at the root. Life on the third floor seemed perilously high. The plane tree in the street outside was thick with green. Its leaves brushed my windows and darkened the living room. When I'd been here last, the tree had been bare, the room full of winter sun.

It was at night that London seemed strangest. I'd grown used to a sky of cold ultramarine in which you could pick out the Great Bear and find Polaris without thinking. The sky over North Kensington was starless, a sickly electric orange in which even the moon was hard to find. Deep into the small hours this synthetic sky glowed through the bedroom curtains, and I'd come awake, expecting to find it already afternoon.

Once I yelled my way out of a nightmare. This was a useful but embarrassing trick. Trapped in nightmares as a child, I'd tried to scream and managed only a dry choked rattle in the throat which brought no one in the dream to my rescue; then I learned to break the barrier, waking myself with a whoop that began far back inside the dream and lived noisily on into the room where I found myself sitting up in bed and hollering. I never knew exactly how loud these screams actually were. They happened only when I slept alone.

On my third night back in the city, I woke appalled at having drawn attention to myself in such a shaming way. *Had* the neighbors heard? It had sounded to me like a very loud scream indeed. I listened, in the weird orange light that passed for darkness. Not a sound. Then there was. It was a low, bubbling cry of fright, repeated twice. I went to the window, but no one was out there. The gardens were still, the windows of the houses at the back were all unlit. Silence. When the cry, or rather gurgle, came next time, I pinpointed it to a curtained window with a raised sash, thirty yards away.

At 0335, the explanation struck me as perfectly obvious: this was a London nightmare, transmitted like a virus from sleeping stranger to sleeping stranger, working its way slowly round and down from the northern heights of Hampstead and Highgate, through Brondesbury, Kilburn, Kensal Rise, sidling off to Westbourne Park and drifting along Ladbroke Grove to Notting Hill. Each screamer was handing the dream on intact to its next victim—and the dream was of London itself, a surreal city in which you tried to run, fell, called for help, and woke to hear the strangled sounds of all the other people who were trying to shout their way out of the labyrinth.

There was no weather in this city: there was rain, of course, and sometimes the sun shone, but there was no *weather*. You couldn't tell which direction the wind was coming from, or even if there was any wind at all. The branches of the plane tree jostled outside the window every time a bus went past; London air was kept in a continuous slow swirl by the passage of traffic through the streets. But the cycle of Atlantic depressions and ridges of high pressure, with the wind swinging round, southwest to northeast, northwest to south, seemed to pass clean over the top of London's head. I listened out of habit to the shipping forecasts, but they were like news from abroad. "Humber, Thames. Southwest 7 to Gale 8, perhaps Severe Gale 9 in Thames later. Rain later. Moderate becoming poor." But the leaves were hardly stirring in the plane tree, and the visibility, at least as far as the elevated M40 motorway to the south, was excellent and getting even better.

There was no weather, and no horizon. You couldn't move around the city by instinct, feeling your course by the way the shadows fell, measuring distance traveled by the transit of trees and hilltops, as countrymen and sailors do. You navigated by artificial landmarks, monument to monument, with no compass points: Eros to Winged Victory to Harrods, then right and left and right again.

In thirteen years of living in London, I'd learned to think of the artifice of the city as a kind of nature in its own right; but on this visit I was being thrown by novelties that should have been novel only to the most naive of crofters on a day trip from Skye. London seemed unmanageable, unimaginable. I had approached it by a classic foreigner's route— exactly the same route that was taken by the Irish emigrants in the 1840s and the European Jews in the 1880s—and London had rewarded me by summarily demoting me to the role of tourist.

So I resorted to the solution of the tourist: I took a daylong guided coach tour to see the sights of London, this baffling foreign city which I was supposed to know by heart.

We London greenhorns were a mixed bunch. Most of us

were Americans, some of us were Japanese. A mother and daughter from South Africa sat in the seat across the aisle from mine. There was a Swiss family, not called Robinson, and a cadaverous lone Venezuelan, making a two-day pit stop between Tel Aviv and New York.

As is the way with travelers, the physical mechanics of our journeys preoccupied us rather more than the places we were passing through. As the coach moved off, it was full of voices talking not about what we could see through the windows, but about the logistics of tomorrow's itinerary, who'd got the hotel key, what was the best rate of exchange.

"They're asking one sixty at the desk."

"You can get one fifty-three at the Cambio place around the corner."

"It's only one forty-*eight* at the bank—"

"We can go to Brighton at 9:32, gets there at 10:42. Then we got to get the 6:37 . . ."

"We can take a cab, Herman. To the hotel. You can always take a cab—"

It made me think of tides. High Water at London Bridge at 1404, add an hour for British Summer Time, so depart 1304, two hours before High Water, and make Sheerness on the ebb . . .

The loudspeakers were switched on and our guide introduced himself as John. A short man in rubber shoes and a creased and shiny city suit, he had bangs of gray hair pasted over a bare skull. There was a slightly desiccated scholasticism in his voice, and I took him for a prep-school master who'd run into a spot of bother.

"Does anyone want French? Est-ce que personne qui veut moi de parler en Français?" There were no takers. He looked relieved.

The running commentary was recited rather than spoken, and it had to be continuously adjusted to the changing speed of the bus. At red lights and sudden holdups in the traffic, it slowed to a dead march of isolated words; as we accelerated away it quickened to a polysyllabic stream, like a new fragment of *Finnegans Wake*.

"Now . . . approaching   us . . . on . . . the . . . *right*

. . . we see . . . the . . . National . . . Portrait . . . Gal-
lery . . . where . . . many famous . . . portraits are . . .
on . . . view . . . including several of . . . Lady Di. We
are now entering Trafalgar Square, with its statues of Lord
Nelson, George Washington, who never told a lie, and
George the Fourth, who spent his life telling lies. Fromten-
inthemorningonwards, youcanbuyaquartpotofcorntofeedthe
pigeonsfromastallinthesquare—"

We were told to look out for the coats of arms which
were emblazoned over the front doors of shops patronized
"by appointment" by members of the Royal Family. "On
your right you will see Lillywhites, famous for its sporting
goods. As you'll see from the Queen's arms just up there,
the Queen buys all her sporting goods here." Given a little
imagination, you could see her, head-scarfed, perspiring,
pushing through the plate-glass doors shouldering a pair of
skis.

Lulled by the commentary, it was easy enough to drift
into the picture-book city which we'd paid to see and
wanted to believe in. The essence of being a good tourist
lay in ignoring everything you actually saw and listening
instead to what the guide told you you should see. Obedi-
ently we found ourselves in streets that were crawling with
Royalty. We kept on almost spotting them in the shops,
behind the windows of the morning rooms of their clubs,
in the apartments of their palaces, and riding their horses
on Rotten Row. The Connaught was "the hotel where English aristocrats who live in the country stay when they
come up to Town to conduct their business." *No*, you had
to tell yourself as you looked out at the group of people on
the hotel steps waiting for the doorman to flag them a taxi,
they are *not* American tourists, they are the Earl and Count-
ess of Glossop, with the Honourable Jocelyn Glossop, Lady
Bastable and the Duke of Surrey. The oriental-looking man
is with them because he does their laundry.

Mayfair turned out to be "where the aristocrats of London
live. A three-room apartment in a brownstone of the kind
you see approaching you on the left would cost about £250,
or $400, a week to rent." The guide's prices, like much of

the rest of his information, were a long way wide of the mark, but they made this strange new world of brownstones in Mayfair cozily accessible. For $400 you could be an aristocrat for a week, strolling out from your apartment to blow a few bucks at roulette at the Clermont or take tea at the Ritz with Lady Di.

"Lady Di" was the heroine of our day's story. In the commentary she still retained her virginal title, even though we were due to visit St. Paul's, which had been billed as "the place where Lady Di and Prince Charles got married." Lady Di cropped up everywhere. She even appeared in the glass-pagoda bar-restaurant on the Serpentine which "was designed by Anthony Armstrong-Jones, the ex-husband of Princess Margaret, who is now Lady Di's aunt."

We only just missed her—in person—on Beauchamp Place. "Lady Di was in and out of all these boutiques when she was making up her trousseau, and she still pops back regularly to keep up with the latest fashions."

There was a five minute stop for a photocall on Westminster Bridge, where we had a snatch of "Earth hath not seen anything so fair . . ." by the Famous Lake Poet, William Wordsworth. I stayed in the coach, looking out on a wonderfully simplified city, London revealed as a cabinet of famous icons. The red buses and black taxicabs were icons; Big Ben was an icon. The Royals and aristocrats, who were so tantalizingly nearly visible to us, were the city's iconic residents, and if we couldn't reach out and actually touch them, that was a failure of faith on our part. Blessed are they that have not seen Lady Di and yet have believed.

It was low tide, and the river below us had shrunk down the walls of the Palace of Westminster, leaving the stonework brown and dripping. The wasteland of Bermondsey was less than three miles away to the east, but the Thames had tucked it tastefully out of sight behind a right-angled bend. I thought, if I were from Omaha, I'd go to Bermondsey, and Rotherhithe, and Brixton, and the wrong end of Ladbroke Grove. I'd take some pictures really worth the taking. I'd be a tourist in bad-dream country.

To be in time for the Changing of the Guard, we had to

do Westminster Abbey in fifteen minutes flat, with our five-foot guide rallying us around him by waving his "growie" umbrella high over his head. We piled at speed around the tombs of Queen Elizabeth I and Queen Mary, stamped across the tomb of Joseph Addison and raced to keep up with the airborne umbrella as it flew off in the direction of Poets' Corner. The Abbey was dotted about with signs on plinths saying "NO LECTURING/KEINE ERLÄUTERUNGEN," but by each sign there stood a lecturer, banging on about kings and queens, roodlofts and misericords, treating the plinth as a handy support and rendezvous. Robed vergers stood in hiding beside all the most uninteresting tombs while the tourist troops, led by their lecturing platoon commanders, ransacked the church for curiosities.

"Congratulations, everybody! Right on time!" said our guide over the speakers as the last bashful Japanese was packed on board the coach. "We are now proceeding to see the Changing of the Guard at Buckingham Palace."

We climbed all over the traffic island of the Victoria Memorial in search of the best vantage point from which to take our pictures. The band played. The bearskins looked like bearskins, the sentry boxes like sentry boxes, and the ritual drill as old as England. For our guide, the Changing of the Guard was the one break in the day when he could retire from his script and lounge in the wings. He turned his back on the pageantry, leaned against the railings, dabbed at his nose with a hanky and sneaked a fugitive look at his pink *Financial Times*. His twin bangs of wiry hair blew up in the breeze like a pair of rabbit's ears.

"How long have you been on this job?" I said.

He stared at me. Not a friendly gaze. "I see you've been taking a lot of notes," he said. "What's your game, then?"

"I've lived here for thirteen years. I've never seen things like the Changing of the Guard. I'm learning a lot from your commentary." All true.

He wasn't a disgraced schoolmaster. He'd been a book-keeper in the City. Hankering to get away from his high stool, he'd taken evening classes in how to be a London guide. He'd been at it now for twenty-one years. "Too long," he said.

"It must have been a bit different then."

"Yes, there weren't these packages in those days. They were more educated. More interested in history. Now you tell them anything historical, they're bored after five minutes."

Yankee Doodle Dandy went the band behind us. Hand in hand with the Changing of the Guard, there was the parallel ceremony of the Changing of the Cameras. So that everyone could be seen to have stood outside Buckingham Palace, all pictures had to be taken twice, with the photographer formally relinquishing the camera to his next of kin to do the honors. I offered to photograph the two South Africans together, and found my services in demand all over the Memorial. I snapped everybody and was snapped in return. A photograph was cast-iron proof. It would hold up as evidence that the picture book was real and that we were part of the story.

After the Changing of the Guard, Whitehall and Downing Street. The coach slowed so that we could snap the Prime Minister's residence through the windows. The two policemen at the barrier across the street grinned like maniacs as the camera lenses showed from behind the glass. They had important parts to play in the masque. At least one pair of Friendly London Bobbies is required for each performance, and our men hammed it up for us as if we were a party of visiting big-shot producers with contracts for star roles like the Highland Piper or the Yeoman Warder of the Tower in our pockets.

We lunched, disgustingly, at a ferro-concrete hotel of many stories around the back of Euston Station.

"What's this?"

"Risso's," the waiter said, chucking a pair of brown woolen mittens on my plate. They were filled with something soft, but whether it was fish, flesh or vegetable I couldn't fathom. Nor did I plumb too deeply.

The Swiss woman was lancing her rissoles like boils. She said: "London is not so clean a city, I think. We live in Geneva. Geneva is very clean."

The lone Venezuelan said, in careful and exact English: "I wish to disagree. London is very clean." He paused and, wishing, apparently, to temper his disagreement with the Swiss woman, added, "in comparison with Caracas."

At the table behind us, four Americans were engaged in a discussion about the relative merits of rival brands of diarrhea tablets. One said, "We brought over about a *gallon* of Pepto-Bismol. It's in our *room*—"

I thought, if I were from Omaha, I'd call diarrhea Lady Di's Revenge.

The tourists, who by this time had made me confess my nationality and citizenship, had a fund of sad stories about their reception in England. Urgent messages for them had been casually mislaid by the staff of their hotels, they'd found inexplicable charges on their bills, "Service" had been rudely demanded on top of a 15-percent standard service charge, their queries had been met with shrugging discourtesy. Yet none of them said they wished they hadn't come. England was living up to everybody's expectations of it— the sights, the ceremonial, the wonderful old homes, the Royal Family, the costumes, the traditions, the bad manners and the disagreeable food.

"I'm afraid we've turned into just another of those countries that have been swamped by strangers," I said. "There's very little curiosity or friendliness left."

"Oh, *no!*" said an American, as indignantly as if I'd been caught out setting fire to the flag. "You have so much to be *proud* of in your country. I don't understand you. I think Britain's *great.*"

On the way to St. Paul's and the route of Lady Di's wedding procession, the coach got stuck outside a particularly ripe example of 1960s English public housing. It was called Camelot Tower, and some architectural critic with a spray gun had added the words "IS SHIT" in letters six feet high after its name. We gazed politely at the graffito. The traffic was locked solid. This was a serious test of a tour guide's skill.

"If you look now to your left, you'll see a council *tower block.* There are some people in London who are too poor to pay an economic rent, and the government provides apartments for these people in blocks like this. People living here pay whatever they feel they can afford—just a few pounds—for their apartments, and the government makes up the rest of the money out of taxes."

It had never occurred to me before, but I could see what our guide meant: council flats were, well, really, kind of . . . *sweet*.

It was three o'clock by the time we made St. Paul's, and I was halfway up the steps, following the umbrella, when my nerve snapped. The prospect of more lectures, more tombs, the very carpet on which Lady Di had set her precious feet, let alone the Tower ravens and the Crown Jewels, opened ahead of me like a course of dental surgery. As I saw the last of our party disappear into the gloom of the cathedral nave for their first lecture, the afternoon ballooned with sudden light and warmth. *Fiesta!* I could walk where I wanted, see what I chose, I was free of the lifeless and pedantic gabble of the bulkhead speakers in the coach. I did what people tend to do with freedom, and ran for the nearest hole in the ground.

Rattling through the tunnel of the Central Line, I looked out furtively, affectionately, at my fellow passengers. Some had their eyes closed, some toyed with papers, some looked abstractedly upward as if they were doing sums in their heads. Walls of black moss streamed past inches from the windows; looped cables, toolboxes. Each time the doors sighed open at a lighted station they let in a gust of subterranean wind. It tasted metallic, of burned carbons and newsprint—a warm, industrial mistral, as particular to the city as Big Ben or red buses, quite different from the rotting-vegetable odor of the New York subway or the reek of Gauloises in the Paris Métro. Everyone aboard the carriage had mastered the trick of looking as if he or she were alone in an empty room. Everyone was traveling under sealed orders to a separate destination. In a fleeting conceit, I saw us all as members of the Underground, moving in secret through Occupied London, and for the first time on the trip, the city felt like home again.

It was two months later, with *Gosfield Maid* parked in a cove on the Scottish west coast, that I ran into Harvey Swanson, the kilted and sporraned Minneapolitan tourist.

Running fast out of time and weather, I had taken a shortcut through Scotland, sailing down the Caledonian Canal from the Moray Firth through Loch Ness to Fort William. It was a leaden, windless afternoon when the lock gates at the bottom of the staircase opened on Loch Linnhe, a crooked gullet of sea, fifty miles long, which advances deep into the Highlands from the open Atlantic. Though the water was still and the air dank around the boat, there was a lot of high-altitude activity overhead, with the sky clearing and Ben Nevis growing rapidly in size behind my back. Every time I checked it, it appeared to have added another five or six hundred cubits to its stature. As the sky emptied of gray, it disclosed high streaks and puffs of cloud, ribbed like jet-trails, traveling at improbably high speed over the mountain tops, while on the boat the mizzen sail hung limp and wet, without enough wind to shake its creases out.

The forecast was bad: South, veering West, Gale 8 to Severe Gale 9. But Loch Linnhe was so deeply sheltered, so studded with protective bays and islands that it seemed sensible to keep on moving until the wind actually arrived. I was motoring placidly through the Corran Narrows, smelling woodsmoke on the shore, when the gale showed up with all the exaggerated bustle of the latecomer at a formal dinner which has been kept spoiling for him. It came funneling through the sea loch, turning the water white and darkening the trees on the hills and islands. *Gosfield Maid* bowed and shivered as the wind hit her, and the four-mile run to a safe cleft in the granite and pine near the mouth of Loch Leven was slow and splashy. It took only minutes for the jagged little whitecaps to build into a strong sea swell which plumed over the bows and made the frames and planking boom like a drum.

I ran close inshore under the trees, put both anchors down, and rejoiced in my luck. The place I'd found was beautiful, deserted and wonderfully snug, surrounded on three sides by rock, tamaris, heather and pinewoods. A big sea trout jumped near the boat and fell back into the water with a smack. The breaking wavelets in the cove were brown and thick with peat. The gale could go on blowing for a week as far as I was concerned; it was a luxury to be marooned here, with fresh run sea trout for the taking, the companionable chatter of the trees in the wind, the wild view astern of torn water and sunlit purple mountains. I sat contentedly up in the wheelhouse, sketching and drinking whisky, while the gale got into its full stride.

It blew all night, through the whole of the next day and into the day after. As it veered, it discovered chinks in the landscape and harried the cove. *Gosfield Maid* was snubbing and fretting at her chains, and I thought it wise to keep an anchor-watch, getting up every two hours and struggling forward through the wind to inspect the rocks and trees by torchlight to make sure they were still where I'd last left them. In the morning, the rain came in a magnificent storm, whiting-out the hills behind and making the water nearby look as if it had been deluged in confectioner's sugar. By afternoon, Loch Linnhe was arched and cloistered with rainbows and the hills had changed color, from purple to a livid Astroturf green.

There was no question of rowing ashore: this tremendous wind (which had lately been officially promoted from Severe Gale 9 to Storm 10), would easily mistake my inflatable dinghy for a toy balloon. I spent a whole day reading *Robinson Crusoe*, a book I'd been meaning to bone up on since I first left Fowey. Crusoe, the exemplary busy Protestant, set about the painstaking work of empire, colonizing and Christianizing his island, while I loafed in the wheelhouse, leading a lax, unshaven, Catholic, shirt-tails-out sort of life. The trout, which were now jumping all round the boat, trying to shake themselves free of their sea-lice, were safe from me: I'd lost my only mackerel lure to an underwater snag on the previous evening. I ate things out of tins at irregular intervals, failed to do the washing-up, forgot to listen to the news, and generally made a poor showing as a castaway.

Occasionally a car would pull in off the road, barely fifty yards off from the boat. People got out, took their pictures, and drove on to the next scenic spot along the route. The wind kept on coming in tornado squalls, which corkscrewed their way round the cove and brought the water to the boil, and as I went into my second day of forced exile from a world so near that I could almost touch it, I realized that I was quickly running out of rations. How long can one sustain life on two tins of mandarin oranges, half a stale loaf, three eggs, a steak-and-kidney pudding, a couple of packets of noodle soup and a tin of processed peas? I began to have fantasies about sending SOS messages to the motorists by heliograph.

The gale blew out in the late afternoon of the third day. I rowed the few yards ashore and dragged the dinghy up the beach. I was ferociously hungry, since I'd cast lots for breakfast and the short straw had fallen to the steak-and-kidney pudding, leaving only dried noodles and flakes of chicken for lunch.

While marooned, I'd spent a long time studying a wooden sign on the shore through the binoculars. It was three-quarters hidden by a tree, and I'd been unable to decide whether it was a Forestry Commission warning against starting fires or an announcement of the imminent presence of a hotel. It turned out as I'd hoped. HOTEL 1 MILE—NON-RESIDENTS WELCOME. I followed the arrow up a track that led round the top of the headland, squelching through pine needles under the dripping trees. It went on for a good deal longer than a mile. The first sign of civilization was a thicket of blowsy rhododendrons which had lost their petals in the gale. Then, in dim gray outline through the pines, there was a large hunk of late-period Scottish Baronial, with mullioned windows, clustered chimney pots and ivy. There were no notices anywhere, and no car park; there was what sounded like the Laird's Irish Wolfhound, and I prayed that the dog was kept chained.

My mistake was clear when I got to the porch inside the door. It was jammed solid with the usual clobber of country amusements—shooting sticks, umbrellas, gumboots, gar-

dening baskets, croquet mallets, balls of twine, chewed tennis balls, cartridge bags and rusty ice skates hung on hooks.
Through the inner door I could see a lot of people in kilts
and evening dress holding sherry glasses and baying at each
other across the hall.

I was making my apologies to a pair of green rubber
waders and backing out as inconspicuously as I could when
the inner door opened and a woman in a ball gown said,
"Why! How nice of you to come!"

"I'm awfully sorry—I thought you were the hotel."

"*Do* come in. You're just in time—"

"I'm not dressed properly—"

"Oh—you're just *fine!*"

It took a little while to register the fact that not only was
the woman's voice American, but so were all the voices of
the hearty kilted gentry.

"You mean this *is* the hotel?"

"Well, we just prefer to think of ourselves as a *home.*"

A glass of sherry appeared out of nowhere.

"This is my *husband*—I'm sorry, I didn't catch your
name?"

I was whirled round the hall and introduced to everybody
—MacPhersons and McFarlanes and Mackintoshes and
Campbells and Hendersons and McPhees and Kitzingers
and Swansons.

I had indeed gate-crashed an authentic Scottish country
houseparty, but it was a houseparty whose guests had been
selected, discreetly, through the advertising columns of *The
New Yorker.* It was inauthentic only in the nicest possible
ways. The food at dinner was an incomparable improvement on actuality. A serious stickler for realistic detail
would have insisted on burned mutton chops, black gravy
and cold mashed potato; we had roundels of pink beef,
delicately sauced, with half-moon side plates of *nouvelle cuisine* vegetables. The realist would have limited conversation
to waspish huffs and grunts; the talk here was loud, bright
and continuous. Dusty wines were fetched up from the cellar, more courses came.

I covertly inspected the inside of my wallet. With no

menu, no wine list, no hint of prices anywhere, it was impossible to guess how much all this was going to cost; impossible to ask, too, for fear of shattering the make-believe. It was simply not the sort of question you could put at an authentic Scottish country houseparty.

"You know our hosts are Mormons?" my neighbor said. "From New York State."

I should have guessed. Such an impeccable *mise-en-scène* could have been mounted only by an artist serenely detached from the world of his artifice. No genuine Scottish nobleman, trying to find a new way of paying for his leaky roof and collapsed fences, could possibly have pulled off a theatrical coup like this: it required the controlled and alienated vision of a pair of total abstainers from another culture altogether to create this event, which was both plausibly accurate and romantically gilded.

After dinner, we retired to the hall, where just the right brand of elderly female golden labrador dozed in front of just the right sort of warmthless log fire. The Mormons brought us port and brandy and cigars.

I was joined on the club fender by Harvey Swanson. Mr. Swanson had a spray of lace at his throat, a short green velvet jacket with silver buttons, a kilt and a toggled leather sporran. Somewhere in his wardrobe there must have been a tam-o'-shanter to match.

He and his wife had flown over from Minneapolis, and I caught in his voice that dry, gravelly sound of the Scandinavian northwest of the United States. *Swanson/Svensson*, I thought. Perhaps I was eyeing his fantastic costume with rather too obvious curiosity, since he apparently felt called on to explain it. "This is Gordon," he said. "Dress Gordon."

"It's terrific—"

"The Gordons are on my mother's side."

"Ah, I see."

Big, fair, bespectacled, in fine shape in his prosperous sixties, Mr. Swanson was having one hell of a time, he said. He'd gone fishing, he'd seen cabers tossed, he'd lunched in castles, searched Loch Ness for its monster, had taken about a thousand pictures and wasn't looking forward one bit to going home next week. This, he said, was really something else. He tugged at his spray of lace, which was tickling his chin.

"And you? Are you vacationing in Scotland too?"

I explained what I was doing—the voyage round Britain, the two-day gale, the boat at anchor in the cove, the walk through the pines and rhododendrons, my surprise and pleasure at finding myself in this scene of the play.

No one I had met so far had shown a fraction of Mr. Swanson's enthusiasm for my journey. He was bowled over by it. He slapped his bare knee in vicarious enjoyment—for as I described it, so it became Harvey Swanson's journey too. He called his wife over. "Shirley! Listen to this gentleman, will you? I want you to hear this."

Mr. Swanson wanted the measurements of the boat, the details of the rig, wanted to know how I cooked, where I slept, whether I had a shower on board, radar, satellite navigation, icebox, TV, fish locator, life raft, barbecue grill. "This I want to see," he said, and we made a date for him to visit with me at nine the next morning.

"And you're sailing, all on your own, into all these little harbors round the British coast?"

"Yes. That's the idea."

"And you just hang in there for as long as you like and then put out to sea again?"

"Right."

"You must be having some *adventures*."

"Well, you know—one or two."

"Some of the guys you must meet—like the old guys? They must be really something. And all those *places*—"

"Harvey likes to fish," Mrs. Swanson said. "He's a big fisherman. Me, I don't care for the water too much. I like to go by car."

"God, I envy you. *That* is what I call a real adventure. All those crazy characters . . ." He shook his head, flicked cigar ash out of his lace jabot. "That boat . . . This must be the trip of a lifetime for you, right?"

The more that Harvey Swanson talked, the guiltier I became. Mr. Swanson's voyage was a rhapsody in blue, punctuated by wonderful characters, wonderful old streets, lashings of thatch and half-timbering, folk tales and customs, the tossings of cabers, the jingle of Morrismen, the skirl of the pipes—it was a glorious summer excursion through wonderland, with a dash of heroic danger added, like Tabasco, to sharpen the cocktail. When I set it beside my voyage, mine lost on every point. It was glum and lackluster. It was reprehensibly short of the wonder and delight with which Mr. Swanson had generously endowed it. Yes, I said, yes; meaning sort of, and almost, and not quite. I did my best to save Mr. Swanson from realizing that by his lights, I was a sad-sack voyager, that the things I saw were not a patch on his bold and colorful visions.

It was only when I was rowing back to *Gosfield Maid*, with sea trout leaping by moonlight, that I cheered up. There *were* some crazy characters to be encountered on my voyage too. If you were looking for a memorable player in the Masque of Britain, could you do better than to find a Minneapolitan of Swedish extraction, wearing Dress Gordon and pretending to be a houseguest at a shooting party in a Scottish baronial lodge which was actually a hotel run by Mormons from Upper New York State?

CHAPTER 6

VOYAGE TO THE FAR NORTH

I t took a fortnight to restore my standing as a citizen and settle my differences with the authorities in London, then I was blessedly free to catch the morning ebb and set out on passage for The North.

The North! When I heard myself using the phrase at dinner in Notting Hill, it sounded uncomfortably grandiloquent; after all, the train from King's Cross to Paragon Station in Hull takes only two and a half hours—not quite the stuff of geographical epic. But I was conforming to the custom of the country. In the south of England, good manners demand that you speak of The North as if it were a fabulously distant realm. You should try to imply that places like Wigan, Leeds or Hull are well within the Arctic Circle and that they probably eat babies there.

People who live on small islands fall easily into this ostentatious way with the points of the compass. It is a famous specific against claustrophobia, and it endows the most tinpot places with marvelous sweeps of airy latitude and longitude.

The Manx were expert at it. In Port St. Mary, on the southern edge of the island, it was reckoned improper to go north of the fairy bridge without giving at least a day's advance notice of the journey. A shopping trip to Douglas, fourteen miles away, was something to be announced a week ahead. To go to Ramsey, farther north even than the great mountain of Snaefell, was justified only if you had relatives there, and then only on official festivals like Christmases and birthdays. A lot was made of the fact—if it was a fact—that tomatoes ripened in Port St. Mary a good nine days (make it ten) before their sun-starved cousins in Ramsey and Andreas; and tourists were encouraged to call the south of the island The Manx Riviera, a tag designed to suggest that the men of Ramsey went about in snow boots and fur hats with earflaps. On an island nine miles wide and thirty miles from top to bottom, this mythologized geography was a necessity: it gave Man depth and space, enlarged it with shadowy, unvisited regions, and rescued the Manx from stifling in their cramped quarters.

England was bigger than Man, but it wasn't so very much bigger. As nations go, it was a Lilliput—less than half the size of Italy, less than a quarter that of France. Quite small American states, like Florida and Iowa, were bigger than England. But it was larger by a few square miles than Tennessee. Any country which can only just top the acreage of Tennessee needs to lay claim to frozen wastes at one end and palm trees and parasols at the other—an imaginary terrain which matches up to its sense of dignity and importance in the world.

So Hull was a long, long way from London. I was advised to pack warm clothes for the journey. "Up there, you get the wind coming straight off the steppes of Russia." I was warned of midsummer nights of perpetual twilight in the high latitudes of England. Whenever I said "Hull," someone would chime in, pat on cue, with "From Hell, Hull and Halifax, good Lord preserve us" and look smugly witty.

Aboard *Gosfield Maid*, trudging along at four to six knots, it was at least possible to honor this legendary English distance between The South and The North. Harborbound for days on end by gales or warnings of gales, setting out on a morning and turning back after an hour of being rolled, slapped and tumbled, I made satisfactorily slow progress. It took three weeks to reach the Humber from the Thames— about the same time as most small boats take to cross the Atlantic. This made excellent sense: it put Hull at a distance of approximately 2,400 miles from Tower Bridge, which sounds just about right.

The character of the North Sea was bad but interesting. It was shallow, riddled with shifting bars and shoals. The sand in the water gave it a fierce crystalline glitter in the rare shafts of sunshine. There were patches of trouble even in calms, as the strong tide sluiced over the uneven bottom and the boat careened about in the slop. In any wind, the waves broke short and sharp, crowding on one another's backs. In gales, watched glumly from the safe vantage point of a drenched promenade, with *Gosfield Maid* lying in retirement behind a harbor wall, the North Sea shattered into surf like boiling yellow cat-sick. It threw up sand, and more sand, and more sand, converting roads into temporary beaches and the ends of fields into strips of desert.

It needed to be watched with more suspicion than any other domestic British sea. There were plenty of harbors along the coast, but almost none of them were approachable in anything more than a stiffish breeze. It afforded rich opportunities for going aground: miles offshore, well out of sight of land, it was ridged and pale as it foamed over the shoals. I sailed cautiously from buoy to buoy, ticking each one off on the chart as I passed it; I listened to every shipping forecast, and ran for shelter at any mention of a wind of Force 5 or worse. More often than not, the big winds never came, and I'd sit out on a pier end in Lowestoft or Yarmouth, watching lazy waves nuzzling the sand and wishing that I were out at sea and nearer to The North.

The tricky and volatile nature of the water was offset by the extreme modesty of the neighboring land. The flats of Essex, Suffolk, Norfolk and Lincolnshire rarely showed themselves at all by day. In fine weather, they formed a faint line, provisionally penciled in, between the cloud banks and the sea; but they usually came out only at night, as a ribbon of shore lights, suddenly, surprisingly, close at hand.

Although it was deepening into summer, the sails of pleasure craft grew steadily fewer. Trawlers worked around the offshore banks, oil-rig supply vessels were busy gophering between the ports and the rigs and gas platforms, which stood   out   on   the   horizon   in   capitals—

T   H   A   A   H   T   . . .

an eccentric way of spelling Money.

Somewhere off the hidden coast of Suffolk, a Dunlin flew in through the open window of the wheelhouse and took up a confidently self-possessed perch on the compass. Plump, long-legged, with a beak like a miniature scythe, it stood placidly watching me while I looked it up in the bird guide and checked its ID. I offered it cake crumbs, which it spurned. *Food*, said the bird guide: *Molluscs, crustaceans, worms, insects and their larvae.* No wonder. After fifteen minutes or so, the Dunlin grew bored with my company and flew off in the general direction of Lowestoft.

Farther north, there were puffins: gangs of disreputable dandies who took no care of their appearance and bobbed scruffily about on the top of the water, fighting and fishing by turns. As the sea began to empty of other craft, schools of dolphins homed in on *Gosfield Maid* and amused themselves with the boat, sometimes for an hour at a time. They skirled in the wake and came corkscrewing under the bows, showing good-humored snouts and serious eyes. Nor was it just the boat they wanted; it was my personal attention. If I stood out in the cockpit, they stayed in the wake; if I moved forward to the bows, the school came too. At night they put up a spectacular show—friendly torpedoes of phosphorescence, streaking brilliantly through the water, leaving zigzag tracks of light behind them in the sea.

In every account of long solitary voyages, from the Anglo-Saxon poem "The Seafarer" to the books of Francis Chichester and Jacques Moitessier, there is a ritual moment when the voyager makes friends with a gannet, or a pigeon, or a pilot fish or a dolphin. The occasion is both real and symbolic. It signals the departure of the sailor from human society and his magical assumption into the community of Nature. From here on in, he is at one with the birds and the fish, his tie with the land formally severed.

On the North Sea it was easy to understand the importance of that moment. The coast was a mere six or seven miles off, I'd only left the land a few hours before, and I'd return to it in a few hours' time; but the isolating power of the sea works with astonishing rapidity and strength. You can drop clean out of society in a day and find yourself at the center of a world where the concerns of society are of Martian remoteness compared with the grinning swoop of the bottle-nosed dolphin in your wake.

I heard, now, and tried to think about the news of British ships being sunk in the South Atlantic—*Ardent, Antelope, Coventry, Atlantic Conveyor*—and battles at Goose Green and Bluff Cove, but all bulletins from the Falklands seemed fictive and theoretical. The television in the saloon had taken to yielding only blare and fuzz lately, and its poor reception seemed to correspond with some failure of the circuitry in my own head. I listened avidly to the weather forecasts on the radio, but drifted off station when the same voice continued from the last report of barometric pressure to the first headline on the news. When I eventually tacked through the loitering bunch of big ships at anchor in the mouth of the Humber, I felt something close to what an astronaut in a satellite must feel when he re-enters the earth's atmosphere after three weeks in outer space.

It was exciting to be back here at last. I found the needle-point spire of Patrington Church, an old friend, and the stubby towers of Ottringham and Easington. The sky was huge and rinsed of color, the land below it flat, lonely, Mongolian in its level, sandy emptiness. A file of telegraph poles, a chicken farm, a collapsing barn of rusty corrugated iron were friendly human intrusions here. They had both the pathos and the assertiveness of homesteaders' gimcrack buildings on the Frontier. The brown river, so much more

weighty and substantial than the land around it, flooded
through, busy, broken, showing its fangs as it raced over
the flats and rampaged in the deeps with muddy rips and
whirlpools. *Humber* was a good name for it, with its echoes
of *umber* and *somber*—a shady, sullen, lowering, earthy,
gloomy river. It was hard to steer a clean course on it, and
I could hear things falling about downstairs as the Humber
got hold of the boat and gave it a few warning cuffs and
clouts. With a westerly wind blowing into a fast westgoing
tide, the river was in a very surly mood even by its own
blunt standards of good manners. *Gosfield Maid* rolled and
splashed upchannel, her decks awash in somber Humber
water, collecting gobbets of brown cotton candy in her
rigging as she went.

It was like trying to repair one's relationship with an old
family dog which has been stricken with amnesia. Down,
Humber, *down!* Stop *snarling!* Perhaps it was just the boat
that the river didn't recognize. For I was idiotically pleased
to see the Humber.

I'd lived for nearly five years on the river's edge. Mrs.
Jackson, my landlady, had warned me when I arrived on my
first afternoon as a freshman at the university, "They say
Hull's a sight easier to get to than it is to get away from.
There's many more as comes here than as what leaves by
Paragon Station. There's a lot as only leaves this city in
their coffins, love. How d'you like your tea? Sugar?"

I had hung on after graduation. I'd taught for a term in a
Hull secondary school. I'd started a doctorate, reading a
dozen novels a week, making desultory notes, playing
poker in the evenings, getting married and unmarried, and
generally kept myself in the way of the idle occupation that
passed for "doing research." The doctoral dissertation got as
far as a rather short first chapter—a chapter so good that it
seemed a shame to spoil it by making additions. In the easy
academic climate of the 1960s I left Hull, undoctored, un-
mastered even, to lecture at another university.

But it was in the vacations, and in term-time evenings,
that I fell in love with the city. I moonlighted from my
studies as a private-hire taxi driver and roamed the dark

streets in a radio-controlled Vauxhall Velox. We were a scruffy fleet whose official slogan was "No. 1 for Weddings, Funerals, Functions." It must have been under the heading of Functions that most of our business came our way: we smuggled duty-free cigarettes and whisky out of the docks in hidden compartments under the back seats. The cargo skippers who were our "fares" on these trips took care of the policemen at the dock gates. We went on all-night crawls of the pubs and clubs, the cars full of fishermen just home from a month on the Icelandic cod grounds. The clubs were smoky halls, full of trestle tables and rich with the smell of spilled Tetley's Ale, where Whispering Willie cuddled the microphone close to his lips and confided to it a stream of homely filth about mothers-in-law and outdoor lavs, then surrendered it to the platinum blonde who sang "Love Is a Many-Splendored Thing" and "Red Sails in the Sunset" in a curiously seamless blend of movie-American and flat-voweled Hull. We stopped by the Continental, a surviving music hall where arthritic unicyclists made painful circuits of the stage and jugglers dropped their batons into the laps of the audience. The star performers at these places were invariably billed by the compère as having come "all the way from Leeds," our local Vegas.

The function we were most often called on to perform, though, was to effect introductions. For two of my years in the city, I was Hull's Miss Lonelyhearts, bringing a little warmth and light into the lives of speechless deep-sea trawlermen from Iceland, Norway, Poland and Denmark. They would collapse into the seat beside me, radiant with schnapps, and produce their one essential word of English. "*Girrrl!*"

I'd been given The List along with my official license to ply for private hire within the city limits. It was soon more impressively adorned with footnotes than the single chapter of my dissertation—"*Fat blonde, won't have Icelanders, ring three times, then quick double-ring*"; "*Old, skinny, likes Danes, tips*"; "*Lah-di-dah, picky, £7—10—0.*"

All the girls were older than I was; many of them were much the same age as my mother. They were friendly, treating me as a colleague in their business and serving me cups of Nescafé in the front rooms of their furnished flats off the Beverley Road. When they had to pay the cab fare of their slumberous charges, they said, "How'd you like it, love, cash or kind?"

"Uh—cash, please, thank you."

"Well, you know where to come if you want a bit of the other, don't you, love? Ta-ta, dear."

"Ta-ta."

"Oh, and remember. He's got to be back on his ship by eight. Get a car round here for seven in the morning, will you, love?"

Even as I was delivering the latest glazed Icelander to the bed of one of these tolerant women, I found it hard to think of their trade as "prostitution." It was so flat and easygoing, so lacking in vicious glamour; it was a domestic service, like home nursing, as profoundly unsexy as the administering of bedpans and catheters.

I crisscrossed the city until it became a matter of pride never to need to ask for directions to any street, however short and tucked away. Taxi drivers share with gangsters and policemen an arcane urban knowledge which is deliberately kept hidden from the ordinary citizen. I knew where you could buy a bottle of whisky at 4 A.M., whom to go to for an abortion, which chemist still stocked Benzedrine long after the stuff had been officially outlawed; I knew one or two things that I mustn't write now, twenty years later, because they might still interest Hull's Chief Constable. Nor was this knowledge confined to the lawless underside of the city's life. I was part of the before-dawn stir in the fish docks, with the fog standing thick round the deck-houses of the trawlers, the "bobbers" piling crates of cod on the flagstones of the market, working under blurred and yellowed arc lights, the tea stalls, painted up in bright circus lettering, the strolling Owners, in vicuña coats and bowler hats, the trawler skippers, grand as kings, standing on bollards armed with whistles, raising a scratch crew for a voyage. My private-hire license was a sedentary man's ticket of entry to the strange, dangerous, smelly culture of The Fishing.

It was a world that was romantic even to those who lived inside it. Trying to teach English to fifteen-year-olds from Hessle, the trawlermen's suburb of the city, I had a tough time for my first week or two. My Anglican curate's voice gave girls fits of the giggles every time I spoke. Their satchel flaps were biroed, in enormous loving letters, with the names of John, Paul, Ringo and George. They were all looking forward to brief and flighty careers in Woolworth's and Birds Eye Foods. But every boy had a serious faraway look in his eye. He was "going to make a deckie learner"— to be an apprentice deckhand on one of the boats in the distant-water fleet.

Neither girls nor boys made much headway with the reading I set them. They failed to thrill to "Adlestrop" by Edward Thomas, were indifferent to the animal poems of Ted Hughes, stared blankly when I roared out Vachel Lindsay's ballad of Simon Legree, and picked their noses through the most exciting bits of my dramatized readings from *Great Expectations* and *Wuthering Heights*.

They liked writing, though. From the girls I commissioned stories based on a day in the life of John/Paul/Ringo/George, and received a pile of loopy epics in which the life of a pop star was presented as a round of unmitigated luxury and indulgence, soured only by the absence of the love of a good woman. From the boys, I asked for essays on the theme of "Where I'll Be This Time Next Year." The essays came in misspelled, mispunctuated, big letters jumbled up with small ones, blotted, food-stained, often illegible, but vivid and passionate in a way that none of the girls' efforts came anywhere near matching.

In the boys' writing, frozen decks soared and plunged in black waves high as houses. Nets, throbbing with fish, were winched in under floodlights. Wild formations of ice grew on every shred of rigging, and had to be hacked off to save the trawler from growing top-heavy and turning turtle. Just before the winchman's leg was amputated by a loop of flying chain, the deckie learner sprang to the rescue. Down in the saloon, Skip himself poured the boy's tot: "I knew thee for a good lad," he said. "Thee'll do right enough." Outside the wind roared and the waves, tall as houses before, were as

big as blocks of council flats, as the trawler wallowed home
to Hull and Mother.

Every sentence was salted with technical jargon. The
boys knew the raw material of their world better than
most novelists do. Their fathers and brothers were all in
The Fishing, and a few lucky ones were already "down
for a boat" as, elsewhere in England, one might be "down"
for Winchester or Eton. The ones who were down for "beamers" jeered at "sterners" as the softie's option, while the
"sterners" ridiculed "beamers" for being as risibly old-
fashioned as coracles.

This fishy culture had settled deep into the brickwork of
the city. When the wind blew from the south, one breathed
dead fish from miles away. Fish got into the drawer of socks
and shirts, permeated one's books, clung to the thin curtains
of the bed-sitter. On hot summer afternoons, the reek of
cod was so thick in the air that one could have bottled it
and sold it for fish manure. No stranger, stepping off the
train at Paragon, could possibly have been stupid enough
to ask what Hull "did." Hull went fishing.

Now, cruising up to it at midmorning on the river, I felt
a surge of high elation. The town had been hideously
bombed (people said "flattened") during World War II, but
from the water it still looked old—a weathered fringe of
domes, spires and warehouses, straddling the junction of
the enormous Humber and the piddling River Hull. I had
arranged by radiotelephone to be at the entrance to the
Albert Dock at 1215, close on High Water, and for the best
part of an hour I loafed slowly along the wharves, already
home, nodding familiarly at the Victoria Pier where one
used to catch the ferry to New Holland (you could drink all
day as long as you stayed aboard the boat), at painted
names like Rix and Marr and Parkes and Boyd, at Holy
Trinity Church, at the bird-shitty cupola of City Hall.

I had known that The Fishing was dead—had been dead
for nearly ten years now, killed by Britain's losing to Iceland
in the Cod Wars. But when the lock opened to let *Gosfield
Maid*, and only *Gosfield Maid*, inside the Albert Dock, I
wasn't equipped to take in the enormous empty hole which
the death of The Fishing had left behind.

"Where shall I go?" I called to the lockkeeper.

"Anywhere you like. Anywhere you see a ladder."

The Albert Dock was nearly a mile long and nearly two hundred yards wide. No one used its proper name. It was just the Fish Dock. You could walk from side to side and end to end across the decks of the boats—as I knew from having once had to lug, with the help of two amiable Danes, the sack of a twenty-stone Norwegian back to his quarters after a happy night on Hessle Road. It was a self-contained city of ships, with a city's non-stop lamplit clamor.

It was just water. From the open lock gate it yawned ahead, colors marbling on its oily surface. There wasn't even a herring gull in sight.

No, that was not quite true. Once my eyes had got adjusted to the shock, I found: to port, one trawler flying the blue cross of Norway and apparently unloading a catch; to starboard, a square-rigged sail-training vessel with a troop of kids swarming up in the yards, and another big trawler, a 200-footer, flying no ensign and bare of visible crew. That was it. In this huge dock, the four of us appeared to be here for the same reason that stage directors order a warble of birdsong to accentuate a long dramatic silence: we turned the emptiness of Albert Dock into a spectacle.

It looked unbelievably lonely, more than enough to make one sob for want of company. I tucked *Gosfield Maid* under the stern of the sail-training schooner, and my ropes were expertly taken in charge by two of Hull's many unemployed teenage boys. It occurred to me that these boys' mothers might have *George, Paul, Ringo* or *John* written inside the flaps of their old school satchels—a thought which brought on an unpleasant twinge of vertigo.

I said: "It's amazing. When I was last here this dock was packed solid with trawlers. It was . . . nearly twenty years ago."

To someone of sixteen, twenty years might as well be a hundred. The boys looked down at Rip Van Winkle. "Ay," one said indifferently, "The Fishing's long gone now, mister," as if he were speaking of the slave trade.

This was how wounds healed in a civilization. Almost as

soon as they were inflicted they became part of History—
the deadly pleasure indulged in by old men blathering on
with stories that make young men yawn. The Fishing now
was just part of gaffers' talk, and the boys steered clear of
me, fearing me as a carrier of further anesthetic reminis-
cences.

I walked the mile-long wharf. The flagstones were beginning to tilt and split, losing the battle to the creeping greenery of ground elder, thistle, willow herb and cow parsley.
Rusty hawsers and piles of old fishnets had been swallowed
by the vegetation. Ahead of me, a nervous rabbit nibbled
and scarpered, nibbled and scarpered, as if it weren't sure
whether the wharf was now a legitimate meadow for a rabbit
to browse in.

At the end of the dock there were the low, crooked lanes
where the riggers, chandlers and compass-makers had their
shops, where you could buy cheap jerseys, thermal socks,
gutting aprons, smocks and sea boots. All shut, all gone.
Their windows were frosted over with a cake of oily dust
and there were padlocks on every door.

Beyond the shops, the small fish dock had had its lock
gates removed. At low tide it was a hillocky swamp of soft
mud, its only occupants the hulks of bikes and junked washing machines.

There were very few people about. One or two ancients
were walking their dogs among the ruins—all men, no
women. I was watched from a cautious distance and could
feel that I was cutting a curious figure here. I had spent the
previous night in Grimsby, getting ready to return to Hull
in style. Bathed, shampooed, in a fresh denim suit and a
Leonard of Paris tie, topped with a floppy wide-brimmed
brown felt hat, I knew exactly who I must be in the old
men's eyes. I was The Fishing's first foreign tourist—a por-
tent, maybe. After me, the deluge. You could land coach-
loads where you used to land cod, and make a Rye-style
killing out of History and desolation. Even now there were
plans to turn the Humber dock into a yacht marina. Perhaps
. . . perhaps . . . Could Hull turn into the Lymington of
the North, with the riggers' shops as seafood restaurants,

the chandlers' as nautical boutiques? Clearly someone was hoping so.

I got the story of what had happened since I left in the pubs round English Street over the forgotten taste of Tetley's No 1 Bitter Ale. The old men had all the time in the world to talk. Nor were they bored with strangers, as people were in the South. Hull, as yet, was no tourist attraction, and it was easy to sidle along the bar and into the conversation. My lonely berth in the Fish Dock was almost as good a passport here as my private-hire driver's license had been twenty years before.

The story came out in rags and scraps, but pieced together it had the clear, inevitable arc of tragedy.

Britain had been bound to lose the Cod Wars. The few gunboats which were sent to protect Hull's deepwater fleet were no match for the Icelandic Navy; and in 1975 Iceland's claim to a two-hundred-mile fishing limit was ratified by the International Law of the Sea conference in Geneva.

Excluded from the North Atlantic, the trawler owners dreamed up a scheme of salvation. They could go south, base themselves on Port Stanley in the Falklands, and fish there. There were already a Soviet and a Polish fleet working the cod grounds of the South Atlantic; why not one from Hull? But the British government, from which loans were needed to fund this logical migration, was not enthusiastic.

"It were that Mr. Ridley," one man said. " 'There's plenty of fish here,' were what old Ridley said. 'Why d'you want to go all the way down to the fuckin' Falklands when we've got seas full of fish at our back door?' It's like all them people in the government. None of them ever understood The Fishing."

The Falklands project foundered. In Hull, everyone was at loggerheads with everyone else. The owners squabbled about the future with the masters. The mates and deckhands, who were paid on a share system with a percentage of the catch, saw themselves as proudly independent capitalists and despised the idea of forming or joining a union to protect their jobs. The great thousand-ton trawlers were sold off one by one.

Some went to Australia and New Zealand. Some were converted into oceanographic survey ships. Some became supply vessels for the North Sea oil rigs. Some were sold for scrap. With each boat's loss went fifteen or twenty jobs for the men on board her, and another seventy or eighty jobs on shore. When I'd last been in Hull, there had been one hundred and fifty registered ships working out of the Fish Dock; now there were none.

But what about the people? I asked. Where were the exuberant would-be deckie learners of 1964? What had happened to the men whom I used to take on epic pub-and-club crawls, for whom the end of a good evening was the contented discovery that you could no longer walk?

If they were lucky, they had seagoing jobs in the oil business, down in Yarmouth or up in Aberdeen. Some had taken to seine netting over the shoals in the North Sea, fishing out of Whitby, Bridlington, Lowestoft. Many were on the dole.

"History's not been very kind to Hull," said Jimmy Johnstone, who had retired after representing a fishing constituency in Parliament for thirty years. "It's just History we're up against here. You can't blame it on Mrs. Thatcher. It's just bad luck that the Law of the Sea conference went against us, that the Humber Bridge came too late . . . We've had a dollop of bad luck here, and it's made people sort of . . . doleful, you know? *Doleful*. It's an old-fashioned word, but then Hull's an old-fashioned town. But it's no worse than that—it's just *doleful*."

"We're still the world's capital of fish fingers," said another man at the bar.

"But where does the fish come from now?"

"Oh—well, some of it's landed at the Fish Dock off of Norwegian sterners, but mostly, nowadays, they truck it in by road."

Fish? By road? To Hull?

"And they're putting up that new hotel by Victoria Pier, where the ferry used to go from. It's going to be a grand place, that, when it's done."

"For tourists?"

"Ay, and what's wrong with that? We've got some good museums, in Hull. People who are interested in History— Germans, and Dutch people and that, they all like Hull."

It was true that Hull was doleful, but it was a long way from being morose. There was too much spiky pride in the city for that, too much skeptical good humor. If Hull was going to have to endure hard times, it was going to see them out with good graveyard jokes and a face cast in an unflinching, if lopsided, grin. It was taking the death of The Fishing in the same spirit in which it had taken the Blitz.

"You know the one about Grimsby trawler that got lost in fog?"

"No."

"He were fishing off Dogger Bank. Then fog comes down. His Decca's on the blink. He's not looking after his course. He drifts for three days before fog comes up. Skipper looks out of wheelhouse, shakes his head. 'Where we at?' says Mate. 'Search me,' says Skip, 'we could be any bloody where. There's a hell of a lot of bloody water out there, and not a bloody ship in sight.' 'Hang on,' says Mate, 'There's only one place I know like that. We're in luck. We're in Hull. In bloody Fish Dock!'"

They had torn down the terraces of back-to-backs around the Hessle Road with their warrens of communicating yards and lean-to privies. In their place were smart semidetached houses standing in their own gardens. Even here though, some of the culture of The Fishing still clung. The houses were painted up as spruce as ships, with varnished bulkheads and newly scrubbed decks. "There isn't a sailor in the world who can resist a paintbrush," Jimmy Johnstone said, and these council semis were sailors' houses, garnished and trim enough to put in bottles.

"You'll be hard put to find a bad egg among them," Johnstone said fondly of his ex-constituents. "It's the danger of The Fishing that does that. It's the same as miners—wherever you get danger, real danger, you won't get bad eggs."

Among the jaunty salesmen in the lobby of the Royal Station Hotel, I looked out for Philip Larkin and eventually found his long, pale face, like a fugitive white barn owl caught in unaccustomed daylight. He was evidently prepared for all eventualities this evening. Although the temperature outside was in the sixties, he wore a winter overcoat and knotted scarf, and carried a furled brolly. He was beaming shyly, shortsightedly, and not quite in my direction. I planted myself in the center of the beam.

"Ah, there you are. It was the hat that threw me."

"I always wear a hat now I'm going bald."

Larkin's own large skull was as hairless as a cheese.

"Yes, I used to go in for hats once too. I never found they did any *permanent* good."

At the bar, he asked for a gin-and-tonic. "Would you mind making that a double gin? Since I've gone so deaf, I don't seem to be able to *see* single gins anymore."

As we sat down he said, "I'm a great deal deafer than I was when I last saw you," but the tone in which this was said, and the expression which accompanied it, suggested that a marked improvement in his health had taken place.

Larkin was wired for sound, with a conspicuous pink appliance lodged in each ear. His hearing aids, his thick glasses, the doughy rolls of smooth white flesh on which his chin rested in repose all had the accentuated reality of theatrical props. It was as if he took a melancholy, ironic satisfaction in advertising to the world just how far his worst fears about himself had already been confirmed. He was only sixty, but he insisted, lugubriously, on making you see him as one of his own Old Fools:

. . . These are the first signs:
Not knowing how, not hearing who, the power
Of choosing gone. Their looks show that they're for
    it:
Ash hair, toad hands, prune faces dried into lines—
How can they ignore it?

Larkin didn't ignore it. He dwelt on it with a strange
and solemn humor. His prosthetic appendages were of a
piece with the words of his poems: they told the plain,
miserable truth—and dared you both to laugh and not to
laugh.

"We won't get much of a meal here," Larkin said. "They
used to serve quite a decent dinner, but I gather that they've
gone completely down the drain."

"Well, don't let's eat here then," I said firmly, dreading a
Larkinesque dinner in which every course would prove that
things were getting worse and worse.

"Oh, there's nowhere else much, is there?"

"I passed a Lebanese restaurant on the way. That looked
all right."

"A *Lebanese* restaurant? In *Hull?* Good heavens."

Larkin spoke in a reedy plainsong. The one-note musical
drive of his voice was, I suspected, a relic of the technique
he must once have used to cure a childhood stammer.

"What sort of food would one get in a Lebanese restaurant? Would it be . . . *mushy?"*

Fiercely defending my decision to escape the Royal Station Hotel, I said, "No—you can get kebabs and salads and
things like that."

"But I *like* mushy food. It's the only food I really enjoy
now."

"Oh. Well, there'll be hummus and tabbouleh and tara-
masalata—they're all extremely mushy."

"Oh," Larkin said, suddenly skittish. "Then let's go Lebanese."

He drove us to the restaurant as if the one-mile drive
were a hazardous adventure and Hull a city as foreign as
Beirut itself. Arms braced rigid against the steering wheel,
searching myopically for landmarks through the wind-
screen, Larkin squeezed cautiously down on the accelerator,
allowing his car just enough petrol to get under way, then
lifted his foot off, leaving the car to coast, more and more
slowly, until, when it had almost reached a complete standstill, he repeated the procedure. It occurred to me that this
curious and unrelaxing style might be some kind of fuel-

economy technique that Larkin had read up in a motoring magazine.

I said: "I think it's on—what is it? Lowgate?"

"Lowgate? Where's Lowgate?"

"I think you turn right here . . ."

"This is *very* rare for me," Larkin said. "I don't see much of Hull nowadays. I've managed to reduce my life to a triangle. There's the house on Newland Park—far too big for me. Then there's the library, of course. Then there's a shop I go to on that block in Cottingham Road. That's about it, really."

The triangle he described was roughly equilateral, with each side measuring about two hundred yards. He appeared to be inspecting this account of his existence and vetting it for accuracy.

"There is the station and the train to Oxford," he admitted.

"Do you spend much time in Oxford now?"

"No, not as much as I'd like."

We drifted to a stop beside the restaurant. Larkin got out, locked the car and said, "Oh, dear. This is no good. I'm on a yellow line."

"It's long after six o'clock. Yellow lines only apply in the daytime."

"I don't want to be towed away."

"You won't be. It's perfectly legal. Look at all the other cars—"

Larkin scanned the street. "In my experience, what other people get away with is a pretty ropey guide to what one can get away with oneself." He laughed, a snuffling honk. "Still, I suppose one has to live dangerously sometimes."

He made a happy pantomime of being foxed by the menu, investigating words like "falafel" as if they were bombs that I'd called him in to dispose of. "How do you say it?" he demanded loudly. "Like 'kerfuffle'? Ferluffle?" An oval bat of pita arrived on his plate.

"What on *earth* is that?"

"It's unleavened bread—"

The snuffling laughter started up again. "Bread? It doesn't look anything like bread to me."

But he tucked into the hummus. "This is rather good. It tastes like . . . Farex."

For a moment I saw how his kitchen might look in the house on Newland Park, its shelves lined with tins of baby food. Did Larkin live on minced chicken and apple puree and green-vegetable goo? Or was this all part of an elaborate charade on the theme of second childhood, played out in fish-faced deadpan? I wasn't sure whether I was Larkin's confidant or his stooge.

He had been kind to me when I was a student at Hull. I had discovered within a couple of weeks of my arrival that Philip Larkin, who was, as far as I was concerned, the university's only ornament, had worked out a thousand ways of escape from undergraduates who wanted to talk poetry to him. I wanted to talk poetry to him, and like everyone else I was politely rebuffed. I got myself elected to the council of the students' union and invented a Library Committee, whose only member was myself. The function of the Library Committee was to meet the University Librarian once a month ("Couldn't you make that once a term?") and discuss things like opening hours, fines and longer loans. On my first entry to his office, disguised as a Library Committee, Larkin had taken out his handkerchief and waved it, saying, "White flag." The formal business of each meeting was summarily dispatched by Larkin. ("Stay open an hour later? In the *winter* term? Oh, I couldn't do that. All my girls would get raped on their way home.") The conditions of his treaty with me were strict: poetry was out, but we could talk about novels and jazz. I treasured these visits, past the security arrangements of his two secretaries; they were the only tutorials for which I was punctual, and Larkin himself seemed to exact some gloomy enjoyment out of discovering how little I had actually read. My role as stooge then consisted of having attributed to me an encyclopedic, but quite useless, knowledge of the works of Jack Kerouac, William Burroughs, Jean Genet and Thomas Wolfe. ("Of course, I suppose *The Afternoon Men* would seem a bit flat to you after *Naked Lunch*.")

He had been forty then—my age now; he had seemed to me to belong to a world as august and remote as Tenny-

son's. Had I seen the word "shy" written of Larkin, I would
have thought it mad; his withdrawnness was a grand quality, not a product of unhappy embarrassment and reticence.
Now he was just shy, funny, sad, but still as hard to gauge.

Watching him over the hummus, I'd been dogged by the
last four lines of "Dockery and Son"—the lines that you can
frighten yourself with in the dark:

> Life is first boredom, then fear.
> Whether or not we use it, it goes,
> And leaves what something hidden from us chose,
> And age, and then the only end of age.

It seemed to me that Larkin's way of nailing the unbearable
truth and saying it out loud in poems had perhaps become
intolerable to him—that his "drought" might stem from
being unable to face what his next poem might unfold. I
quoted the lines back to him.

"Oh, I wrote that a long time ago. No, I wouldn't say
that now. No boredom left for me, I'm afraid. It's fear all
the way." He meant every word, and laughed, challenging
me to find it funny too. One had to be brave to laugh with
Larkin.

"I suppose there must be some people . . ." he looked at
the knot of lounging waiters in the almost-empty restaurant,
refugees from another stricken city; "I suppose there must
be some people who think life is first fun, then contentment. Wouldn't wash in a poem, though, would it? 'Life is
first fun, then contentment.' Doesn't sound at all right to
me."

"There's some fun, though."

"Yes. *Some* fun."

"Old Dick Francis books?"

"Mmm. And people who make you laugh. Do you have
people who really make you laugh? It's much the most important thing."

"Yes, one or two. Who makes you laugh?"

"Kingsley," Larkin said. "Kingsley *always* makes me
laugh."

"I only know Amis to nod to," I said.

"Kingsley made me laugh at Oxford and he still makes me laugh now. That's something, isn't it? I always look forward to seeing Kingsley."

"And Sidney Bechet?"

"I don't seem to be able to listen to records much, now I've gone so bloody deaf."

This seemed the hardest of Larkin's afflictions. When I'd last seen him, fun had meant Jazz. In "For Sidney Bechet" he had written, "On me your voice falls as they say love should,/Like an enormous yes."

I said, "I'd been hoping you could pin down a record I lost years ago. It was a woman singer, black, doing one of those songs which advertised restaurants. I thought probably Memphis, maybe New Orleans. All I can remember is the refrain: 'Between Eighteenth and Nineteenth on Chestnut Street.' "

" 'Between . . .'?"

" 'Between Eighteenth and Nineteenth on Chestnut Street.' The tune's vivid, but I've lost the words and the name of the singer."

"What date?"

"Middling '30s, I think: 1933 or '4?"

"Oh, no," Larkin said, "The '30s are long after my time."

We had reached the bitter coffee stage, and the waiters had started to flick unnecessarily over tablecloths with rolled napkins. We were the last diners.

"Did *Jill* and *A Girl in Winter* come as hard as the poems have done? Couldn't you commission yourself to write another novel?"

"I'd *adore* to write a novel. I *love* novels. I've started novels. Five of them, I think. Five lost novels. No, it's not the writing that's so difficult with novels, it's the plots. Keeping them up. I don't know. Kingsley always seems to manage to find stories in his life; I'm afraid that mine's not the sort that easily lends itself to stories. That's probably it."

It had rained hard sometime while we were eating, and the streets dazzled. Larkin said, "I'll drive you to your boat."

"There's no need, I can walk." I was frightened that Lar-

kin, with his apparently shaky grasp of the city in which
he'd lived for a quarter of a century, would get hopelessly
lost on his way home from the Fish Dock.

"But I want to see your boat. I've been looking forward to
it all evening."

"Really?"

"Oh, yes—I *have* to see your boat."

He drove, at a snail's pace, across streets as flat as mirrors.
At the dock gates, he worried about getting locked in.

"You're quite safe. They're rusted permanently open
now."

We rolled and wallowed over the uneven paving stones,
past disused sheds and vegetable piles of fishing junk. Rabbits bolted for cover ahead of the glaring car. The enormous
empty dock was lit by a meager line of tall sodium lamps,
and *Gosfield Maid*, with only the tops of her masts showing,
was moored in a pool of primrose light.

"Here."

Larkin locked up his car again. He approached the edge
of the wharf, carefully watching to see where each fresh
footstep went. He positioned himself a dizzy two feet short
of the brink and leaned forward, blinking through his specs.

"*That's* it?"

"That's it."

"Extraordinary. And"—he was beginning to honk—"*this*
is how you live now? In that?"

"Yes. It seems bigger when you're inside it."

"You *sleep* there?"

"There's a separate cabin, up in front. It's quite cozy."

"And read and write? *Quite* extraordinary. Oh, I *have* enjoyed this—"

His face was frank with pleasure, his laughter a high
whoop that echoed in the sheds. *Gosfield Maid* was a joke
worthy, even, of Kingsley Amis. I was delighted that it
made Larkin laugh.

"Good heavens," he was dabbing at his mouth with his
handkerchief. "It's like the old woman who lived in a *shoe*."

"Do come down—I've got tons to drink on board."

"How would I *get* down?"

"The ladder there."

Larkin looked down beyond his feet at the single rusty bar which showed above the wharfside. The rain had given it a slippery gleam.

"It looks a long way, but it's only seven or eight steps down. I can give you a hand—"

Larkin studied the proposition. There seemed to be a 50–50 chance that he was going to step gloriously out of character—and that it was going to fall to me to ensure that this audacious, purifying move didn't end in a catastrophic splash.

His head wagged in a slow, considered negative. "No, I couldn't cope with that—and I'd have to come *up*, too, wouldn't I? I think I've had enough excitement for one evening. Besides, I'm drunk." He took a last look, and a last laugh, at the boat and went back to his car.

"So where will you be off to next?"

"It depends on the weather. Bridlington, I rather thought."

"Bridlington. Ah, Bridlington. Yes. You know I once heard Louis Armstrong play in Bridlington?"

I watched him sailing sedately through the puddles on the wharf, the car's suspension swaying as it floated over the bumps, its taillights making the oily water glow blood-red. He was soon lost behind the sheds, and I kept my fingers crossed for him as he headed back to his safe triangle.

Larkin died three years later in 1985. Until his death, I hadn't grasped how much he was loved in England. People minded about his dying, and mourned him, in a way that seemed strange for a poet, however admired his work. He had kept himself profoundly to himself. His word-perfect, world-imperfect, poems were as rare to show as famous comets. He wrote of being alone, of private dereliction, of living without love—inconsolable poems, teased and haunted by the beauty, only just out of reach, beyond the window of the railway carriage or the solitary room. The separating glass of windows figures again and again in his work. Yet he showed how such a life (a life from which most people would shrink in panic) could be managed with, if not quite gaiety, at least great dignity and grace. His poems are heartbreakingly exact. If poems can teach one anything, Larkin's teach that there is no desolation so bleak that it cannot be made habitable by style. If we live inside a bad joke, it is up to us to learn, at best and worst, to tell it well.

Late in the evening of Monday 14th June, my fortieth birthday, the Prime Minister announced to the House of Commons that the Argentinian troops had surrendered in Port Stanley.

THE HOUR OF OUR TRIUMPH! said the *Express.* WHITE FLAGS OVER STANLEY! said the *Mail.* WE'VE WON! said the *Sun.*

At Ascot, and throughout the land, it was a time for quiet rejoicing on this most British of days; and WHOOPEE! IT'S PARTY TIME IN PLYMOUTH!

Nor was this all. Within the week, Princess Diana gave birth to her first child in a London hospital. IT'S A BOY! The *Express* billed the event THE CROWNING GLORY:

> What times we live in! The excitement surrounding a Royal birth. A famous victory in the Falklands. A nation which, according to all recent opinion polls, exults in a common aim.

I looked for signs of rejoicing on the wharves and in the streets around the Fish Dock, but if people were dancing in Hull, they must have been doing it very quietly, and indoors.

Gosfield Maid went on sailing north. Past Flamborough Head, six miles offshore, I came upon a floating cache of chip boxes, Pepsi cans and Yugoplastic beach balls, and knew exactly where I was. It was the nearest I had so far come to Polynesian navigation—finding your way by watching the seaweed and the color of the water. So there, beyond the haze, was the Butlin's camp at Filey.

In the private-hire taxi business, the summer trips to Butlin's had been happy outings, with big tips for the driver at the end of the day. We ferried fishing families from the Hessle Road out to the dauntingly fenced perimeter of what appeared to be Stalag Luft VII, and brought them back to Hull after their week or fortnight of knees-ups, singsongs and parades, in which girl Redcoats in bobby sox kept their platoons of tough North Atlantic sailors on their toes from seven in the morning until lights-out at eleven.

There was one particularly big and taciturn trawler skipper, a man who must have scared the wits out of his deckie learners.

"Go on, love, tell the driver what you won." His wife was sitting in the back of the car with their son. The enormous skipper sat beside me, his meatball face focused expressionlessly on the dials in the dashboard.

"Nay." He hunched his shoulders round himself and scowled at the gear stick.

"Go on, Dad," the boy said.

"Driver don't want to know nowt like that."

"Oh, he does. Don't you, driver?"

"Yes," I said. "What was it you won?"

A mile of flat fields went by.

"It were a competition," he grunted.

"And what were it the competition for?" his wife said, speaking with the exaggerated, up-and-down elocution of a teacher in a nursery school.

"It were . . ." He gazed out over the fields as if he were expecting to find ice floes there. He tried again. "It were . . . The Grandest Dad and His Lad." As the full splendor of the title unrolled inside the car, his face involuntarily spread into a smile of pure, pink pride.

"That's terrific."

" 'Twere nowt," he said, still happily, embarrassedly unmanned. "Any road, every bugger gets a prize at Butlin's."

" 'The Grandest Dad and His Lad,' " his wife said. "And

we've got the trophy in the suitcase. I could show it you when we get home . . ."

"I'd like that," I said.

"Oh, *give* over," the skipper said, trying, and not quite succeeding, to turn back into the North Atlantic Hulk.

I hoped that they still held the competition for the Grandest Dad and His Lad at Filey. The smell in the wheelhouse, of hot car leather, sunburn, fizzy lemonade and Woolworth's lily-of-the-valley, seemed to come from some age of mythical innocence, like the years before 1914.

North Yorkshire became a surprising line of chalk cliffs, far whiter than those of Dover. The stunted trees on their tops, hunchbacked and bent by the prevailing northeasterlies, looked like Japanese bonsai. Near the boat, gannets came rocketing straight down out of the sky, Olympic topboarders, leaving a pencil-thin column of white spray at the point where they pierced the sea.

I stopped over in Whitby Harbour, just long enough to snatch a night's sleep and climb to the ruined abbey on the headland. I tried lying in the open stone coffin which the monks had used as a chastening *memento mori*, but it was six inches too short for a twentieth-century man, and had changed from a ritual penance to a curious measure of human progress. *Which of you by taking thought can add one cubit unto his stature?* In six centuries we had managed just a third of a cubit, which seemed a pretty fair guide to how we'd got on in most other departments of life too.

Out of an afternoon of light winds and unbroken sunshine in a high blue sky, I sailed into the perpetual gray overcast of Blyth in Northumberland. Miles south of the town you could taste coal on your tongue, gritty and sweet. As the air steadily darkened around the boat, Blyth grew out of the sea ahead, a weird, elaborate and puzzlingly beautiful composition in monochrome. The center of the piece was the delicate black crosshatching of the timber staithes, where docks had been built out at angles into a wide, slow-moving, inky river. Wonky railway tracks on stilts ran high over the water, and black elephant-trunk coal chutes hung slackly over the ends of the wharves. Everything in Blyth was the color of coal: the sable stone terraces, the wood, the water, the faces of the men on the docksides. Blyth seagulls were dingy with coal dust. The cargo ship ahead of me on the river maneuvered in scissored black silhouette. Within minutes of getting my ropes looped round a pair of black bollards in South Harbour, I watched *Gosfield Maid* go chameleon, her white hull fading to gray as she was assimilated into the Blyth picture.

I had expected nothing special of Blyth, had thought of it only as a useful stopping point on the way to the Farne Islands and Scotland. But as soon as I was inside the harbor, I felt my spirits rise at finding a berth in this serious, dark, angular place. Almost at the very end of England, Blyth looked more reassuringly like Home than anywhere that I had sailed to so far. I warmed to the dumpy, coal-faced, Pictish man who sang "Oh, Geordie's lost his plinker!" as he helped me run out breastropes and springs to the wharf. Well-seasoned in my dislike of yacht clubs, with their yo-ho-ho voices and their enervatingly bright sportiness, I had a contented evening aboard the blackened old lightship which served as the floating clubhouse of the Royal Northumberland. When I woke the next morning with coal in my throat, I knew I was going to stay on in Blyth despite the gentle forecast and the silvering of filtered sunlight on the staithes.

The whole port was rumbling softly across the water. Long strings of coal wagons were shunting slowly across the trelliswork viaducts. As each wagon reached the mouth of the chute, it flipped sideways and the coal poured, in a continuous low growl, into the cargo hold of the waiting ship, fifty or sixty feet below. Even from a perch on top of the chute, it was hard to see what was going on down in the holds. The gangs of dockers were so completely black that the black cargo seemed to have taken on a sort of wriggly, animal life of its own. As the men leveled and spread the coal in the bottom of the ship, all one could clearly see was the wink and flash of their heart-shaped shovels as they caught the sun.

In the early 1960s, more coal had been shipped from

Blyth than from any other port in Europe. The trade had halved since then, from seven million tons a year to three, but it still made a rich noise, tumbling through the chutes, the wagons swaying and clanking over the water. All this shoveling, bumping, groaning and roaring was a vast improvement on the mincing tones of fiberglass quarter-boys, and I happily watched my own skin turn Sri Lankan, then pale Nubian, as I rubbernecked on the scenic fringe of the coal industry.

"What's wi' you, then, hinny?" An amiable coal-Negro with a thermos flask came out from behind the chute.

"Nothing. Just looking."

"Ye'll get awful mucky, sitting there like that—"

"It won't make much difference, I'm so mucky already—"

He stared at me for a moment and disappeared behind the chute. Like the Fish Dock in Hull, the coal staithes in Blyth had attracted their first tourist.

I took a shower on the Royal Northumberland's lightship and walked up into the town. After the noise of the docks, there was a palpable hush in the streets, which seemed too wide, too long, for the few people who were abroad in them. There was a gappy look to the newish shopping parade; display windows blinded with whitewash, the lettering above the shops full of blanks, like an uncompleted crossword. BO TIQ E. NEW GENT. WILK N ON. F OR ST. The tooth-pulling had been done in such a piecemeal way that it was hard to guess what Blyth's face might have looked like in the days when it had a full set of snappers.

There was one shop where things were humming, where, in this unnaturally quiet and empty town, I had to stand in line for fifteen minutes before I was served. It was a bakery, and it looked like no bakery that I'd ever seen in England. The loaves in the window had been laid out on a pyramid of glass trays, and they had been arranged as if they were as precious as antiques. All the window dressers' craft of suggestive enticement had been lavished on them; they peeked tantalizingly at one from behind the glass . . . loaves like plump thatched cottages, loaves molded in twists and spirals and hoops and disks like Frisbees. Something special had been done in their baking, and their teak-colored crusts, cunningly lit from below, looked varnished. The baker's window was designed to give one a glimpse of a life of luxurious abundance. Only in the northeast, with its long history of hard times, could anyone have made so much out of bread, the symbolic staple of life itself. Elsewhere in England, the symbolism had been drained of real meaning long ago, but not here in Blyth. The stuff in the window was the stuff you prayed for in the Lord's Prayer— the stuff that went with circuses in Latin, and with jugs of wine and Thou in Persian. Bread meant Plenty.

When my turn came, I pointed at the shelves. "What are those? And those?"

"Them's stotties, and them's fadge."

I took the cowardly, southerly way out and came away with a conventional small brown.

The dusty silence, the spaces between the people were the outward and visible signs of the fact that in the center of Blyth, one man in three was out of a job.

Unemployment had never shown itself quite like this before—had never been so quiet and unobtrusive in its manners. The number of people without work in Britain now (about three and a quarter million) was almost exactly the same as in the Great Depression in 1931–32. Roughly the same number, therefore (say seven million), were, in one way or another, "living on the dole."

Yet unemployment in the 1930s had yielded a shaming and memorable collection of dramatic images. Even in the heads of people far too young to remember the Depression, there is a stock of black-and-white or sepia photographs of hunger marches, dole queues, ragged men with their hands in their pockets loafing sadly at street corners, of Victorian terraces with strings of washing hanging between the windows and young men idling the day away in chairs outside their houses. The Depression was picturesque. For photographers and filmmakers from Walker Evans to Humphrey Jennings it was a magnificent subject, full of human color and evocative squalor. The pictures they made of it were powerful enough to frighten governments.

There was nothing very dramatic or picturesque about unemployment in Blyth in 1982. In the fifty years between recessions, English society had gone indoors. People no longer lived in warrens where the toilet was outside and the street was a communal living room. They couldn't stand about in conspicuous knots all day, since the streets had been taken over by cars. They were not affectingly ragged, since synthetic fibers had blurred the visible distinctions between the clothes of rich and poor.

Unemployment had been a public event; it was now a private misery, to be borne alone, behind the curtains. It was identifiable not by things you could photograph and write heartstring-tugging reports about, but by gaps and absences. It was in the sound of a single car backfiring in a street where there should have been a continuous surflike wash of traffic. It was in the shops that weren't there, in the eerie feeling that the population had shrunk inside its walls, leaving a surfeit of unoccupied air.

If you wanted an image of unemployment in the 1980s, you'd have to go inward—to a room, decently furnished in nylon upholstery, where a man and his wife sit in the middle of an afternoon watching one of last year's movies on the rented video machine. Compared with a Walker Evans picture of Alabama sharecroppers on the porch of their ruinous one-room shack, it is not much of an image. It wouldn't frighten anyone, or make one want to pass the hat. Yet the quantity of *depression* in the image is no less great—the waste of life, the solitude, the resignation to circumstances.

What is most poignantly absent from the image is the likelihood that either the man or the woman will leave their chairs to join all the other men and women who are watching videos in curtained rooms. As long as unemployment means something so docile, so unsocialized, so quietly embarrassed, it is a commodity that any government can afford to have a lot of. It's only when the video gets switched off and the people head for the street that it will turn into a problem of social order—when ministers and heads of state will reach for "extreme measures" to "deal" with it.

On the way home to the boat, I stopped at Ridley Park, ten trim acres of well-pruned trees and razored civic turf set between the docks and the council houses. On a raised level of lawn there was a bowling green, where a dozen old men in flat caps and unbuttoned waistcoats were lost in a game as ceremonially ordered as a service of Holy Communion. Pipes clenched in the corners of their mouths, they ambled nimbly up to the line and delivered the ball with a sudden final twist of the wrist. The balls took forever to arrive. They came curving in out of the coal-tinged sea fret toward the jack. *Plock.* The old men clapped. The next ball swung abruptly off-target, as if allergic, and landed up among the wallflowers; the next drifted to a stop, like Philip Larkin's car, ten yards short of the jack. The face of each man was serene. Three feet up from the rest of the world on their grassy stage, they were out of the argument. They looked like the happiest people in all of Blyth.

In the bar of the lightship that evening, I heard how the town was clinging to life by its fingertips. Everyone had heard rumors that the National Coal Board wanted to close Bates's Colliery because its seams were geologically difficult to mine. Twenty percent of the coal shipped from the docks came from the colliery. Of the men who still had jobs, one in four was directly employed by Bates's. But the pit was "uneconomic."

"If the N.C.B. does close it, what will it mean?" I said.

The Northumbrian businessman with whom I was talking shrugged. "Your guess is as good as mine. The end of Blyth, I suppose. But what does *that* mean?"

All through the summer of 1984, the news on television looked as if it were being beamed from somewhere far abroad. The sky was too blue for England and the events too bloody. In a rolling landscape of little hills, like the background of a Florentine painting, ranks of uniformed men crouched behind their glittering riot shields while another army, of people dressed in pastel holiday clothes, pelted them with rocks. Cavalry charges, on handsome chestnut horses, were mounted out of coppices of trees, and packs of Alsatian dogs were set loose by their handlers, to go snarling round the heels of the retreating rioters.

If this was really England, it looked at first as if it must be some kind of historical reconstruction put on by the Tourist Authority: the Roman legions in conflict with the Saxon hordes, perhaps. If the cameras tracked back, they might reveal an applauding crowd of onlookers, checking the illustrated program to see who was supposed to be on Hadrian's side and who on Athelwulf's. At the end of the day, everybody, combatants and tourists alike, might sit down to a traditional banquet of roast ox, syllabub and mead, with musicians plucking at harps and blowing haut-boys.

The National Coal Board had announced a major reorganization of the coal industry. The "uneconomic" pits were to be closed, and several thousand miners were to be put out of work. The closure plans unveiled by the Coal Board chairman, an American industrialist, were in line with the Conservative government's larger plan for a new, slimmer, more efficient and cost-effective Britain. These were received by the miners and their leaders with rage and fear.

Arthur Scargill, the president of the National Union of Mineworkers, saw the plans as part of "a concerted attack by the ruling class," not just on the miners but on manual workers everywhere in Britain. We were living under "the most ruthless government seen in our lifetime," which was heartlessly bent on turning "our people" into "industrial gypsies, wandering from coalfield to coalfield, pit to pit, searching for work." "We are involved in a class war," Scargill said:

> and any attempt to deny that flies in the face of reality. Confronted by our enemy's mobilisation, we are entitled, indeed obliged, to call upon *our* class for massive support.

Miners arrested by the police on the picket lines were labeled as "political prisoners," and Scargill claimed "the battles of Orgreave, Ravenscraig and Llanwern" as heroic feats ' of class warfare, to be set beside Mrs. Thatcher's famous victories at Goose Green, Teal Inlet and Port Stanley.

In her turn, Mrs. Thatcher used her triumph in the Falklands as a metaphor for the struggle between the government and the striking miners. Again Britain was faced by an impertinent invasion, this time of foreign ideas. The miners' leaders, speaking in the language of European Marxism, were hardly less alien to us than Galtieri and his Junta. They would be defeated, as Galtieri had been defeated, by patient resolution, by another tot of Falklands Spirit.

As the pitched battles were fought out in the sunshine on television, the most curious aspect of the whole affair was the intense family resemblance between Arthur Scargill and Margaret Thatcher. Both had the same upstanding quiff of wiry fair hair and looked as if they were attended by the same coiffeuse. Both had their roots in pious working-class Methodism, Scargill in Yorkshire, Thatcher in the adjoining county of Lincolnshire. When interviewed, their air of truculent intransigence was exactly the same. Neither would give away a rhetorical inch, or admit, at least in public, that any argument, other than their own narrowly ideological one, was worth even listening to. Both were admired by their supporters for their toughness and firmness, that English heart-of-oak quality which so often looked to outsiders like mere pigheadedness. And their supporters themselves were very nearly the same people. Thatcher was loved by the sturdy, chapel-bred English working class, who respected her for being a plain speaker in their own mold. She wasn't toffee-nosed, wasn't a havering, on-the-one-hand-but-on-the-other Conservative aristocrat, she didn't own land; she talked in the language of the corner shop, and made you see England simply, as an enlarged version of Roberts the Grocer, the shop in Grantham (next door but one to the Primitive Methodist Chapel, 1886) where she had grown up.

This was Scargill's constituency too—the constituency of the chapel, of self-help, of prickly independence and forthright blunt talk. The miners saw themselves as the proud elite of the northern working class; had they been born a

few miles south, away from their hereditary loyalty to the
Pit and The Union, they would have been exactly the sort
of untraditional Conservative voters who had brought Mrs.
Thatcher and her untraditional Tory government to power
in 1979.

For nearly ten months I watched the televised war from
an incredulous distance. The violent scenes were taking
place in The North, more than a hundred and twenty miles
away, and therefore beyond the imaginative range of anyone from southern England. Like the bombs and assassina-
tions of Ulster, the miners' strike was foreign rather than
domestic news. When, late in the day, I arranged to join a
"flying picket," friends in London regarded me much as if
I'd said that I was packing my bags for El Salvador.

The arrangements had to be made in secret, as for a real
war. Miners and police both had intelligence services
spying on each other's plans and movements, and there
were Fifth Columnists on each side. I was checked out,
vouched for, and passed on the telephone from "Nottinghamshire George" to "Yorkshire George," who gave me a
number I could call at eleven o'clock at night for details of
the pickets' rendezvous in the small hours of the next morning.

Early in December 1984, I arrived in Sheffield, two hours
up the motorway from London, another world. The city
was full of signs of the strike. In the concrete shopping
precinct in the town center, frozen miners in parkas and
donkey jackets stood by clothes-drying racks to which
they'd clipped sheets of colored Christmas wrapping paper
for sale at 25 pence each. Others were selling Strike greet-
ing cards—linocuts of Davey lamps and winding gear saying "Merry Christmas, Peace and Solidarity, Keep the Lamp
Lights Burning."

In the middle-class suburbs, there were men up ladders
everywhere. For the teaching and lecturing classes, the
Miners' Strike had brought an unexpected bonus: you could
support the cause by getting your house redecorated by a
striking miner at the windfall labor rate of £2 an hour. In
the house where I stayed, a miner was wallpapering the hall

and stairwell between spells on the picket line; next door, a miner was repointing the brickwork and putting up new guttering.

"You have to have a miner working for you here, otherwise your neighbors start putting it about that you're a closet Thatcherite." I had heard all sorts of funny claims made by people trying to argue the case for having servants, but this one was new to me.

At eleven o'clock I made my call and was told to report at 0230 at a pithead between Sheffield and Doncaster.

"Is that where we'll be picketing?"

"No."

Awakened after an hour's sleep, I drove off into the icy dark, along empty ring roads rimmed with rags of dirty snow. There were untimely lights on in the windows of the squat pit villages—a party-time air, confirmed by the firelit scene on the square of snowy mud outside the colliery at Kilnhurst. Forty-five men were gathered round the oil-drum brazier, and, as I raked the group with my car headlights, I was puzzled by the fact that half of them were in fancy dress. One wore a guacamole-green cloak with silver buttons and a tyrolean hat; another had on a pair of baggy trousers, far too long for him, in an outrageous, Evelyn Waugh check. There were huge multicolored scarves, fun-fur overcoats and a few bright red ski suits. The general impression was not of a band of determined men with revolutionary designs on the social fabric of England; the pickets looked like a stranded circus. Two clowns, one short, one tall, in ludicrously ill-fitting get-ups, were playing at being Flanagan and Allen. They had linked arms and were singing "Underneath the Arches."

My contact, Yorkshire George, was a little embarrassed about the appearance of his men. The previous day, a truckload of clothes donated by the Italian miners' union had been distributed by the local Women's Support Group.

"Very generous of the Italians," Yorkshire George said, "but it's not quite what our lads were looking forward to. Still, they're nice and warm, and it's that bitter, they'll wear anything they can get."

He had the latest reports from the miners' intelligence organization. At 0327, six "contractors," members of the Amalgamated Union of Engineering Workers, were to be bused into one pit; at 0430, eight "working miners" were to be smuggled through the gates of another. And so on. The forty-five men around the brazier were assigned to separate cars and a tight schedule of pithead pickets, each lasting just five or six minutes, as the "scabs" were swept to work behind the police lines.

The phrase "flying picket" was a romantic misnomer. We did not fly, we trundled in overloaded Ford Cortinas, sagging on their springs, through the dark and slippery lanes from one pithead to the next. Each time we stopped, we had just time to leave the car, join the shadowy crowd at the gates of another colliery where policemen stood four deep in line backed up against the wall of their blue vans, and shout "Scabby bastards! Scabby bastards!" as the speeding bus went past in the foggy distance.

By six in the morning, I'd lost count of the number of picket lines that I'd manned. It was cold, dark, anticlimactic work. The police defenses were so solid that one rarely saw the hated buses, and never the face of a working miner. At each pit it was the same: the resentful crowd, packed into a narrow brick gully, the policemen, pale under the arc lights, with, waiting behind them, the dog handlers and their animals, the emerging shapes of lift cages and winding gear in the slow and sunless dawn.

"This isn't a picket," said Bob, the driver of the Cortina in which I was riding. "We're nobbut spectators now. This is our pit—and the police won't let us inside of a hundred yards of our own bloody gates."

At one pit, somewhere in a suburb of Doncaster, I came within a whisker of getting our picket into serious trouble. The cars had been parked in a crescent of council houses a quarter of a mile from the pithead. After twenty seconds of shouting at an invisible bus, we were walking back to the car in the half-light. In our grandfatherly group of five, I was the youngest man by a year or two; everyone was in his forties or fifties. As we turned the corner into the crescent I saw we were being followed in by a street-wide line of very young policemen. They were wearing capes and carried truncheons. With their bulging Adam's apples, their sprays of acne and half-formed adolescent faces, they looked like the school bullies on the rampage. They were smacking their truncheons against their palms.

"Get a move on," Bob said.

"But this isn't the pithead—it's just a council estate," I said.

"No matter. Better get on back to the car, quick as you can."

A milk cart was parked on the grass verge. Women in dressing gowns stood curiously at half-open front doors.

The police were so close behind us now that they were treading on our heels. Bob, still walking, still looking ahead, said: "Where you lads from then, the Met?" No answer. Just the crunch of marching feet, within inches of our own.

I turned round, to face a teenager with a face as blank as a scoop of lard. "This is a public street," I said. "No one's demonstrating here. No conceivable offense is being committed. We're just walking to our—"

"He's new here," Bob said to the police; then, to me: "Come on, lad, don't *argy* with them."

As we piled into the car, eight policemen stood round, batons at the ready. They made a slow, menacing show of investigating the license plates, the tax disk, the tires, the windows. A gang of kids, they looked as if they were getting their morning ration of fun out of intimidating a few old farts.

"Let's get out of here," Bob signaled, and backed with exaggerated deliberation, doing everything by the book.

"Christ," I said.

"That were *nothing*."

"That were just the Met," said a voice in the back.

"Or the Army."

"They certainly weren't local lads."

"Did any of the buggers have numbers on them?"

"No. Not a number to their name."

It was part of the basic folklore of the miners' strike that many of the "policemen" who were defending the pits were really soldiers in unmarked police uniforms. Men on picket duty claimed that they had recognized on the police lines their brothers, cousins, nephews, sons, even—men who were supposed to be serving in Ulster with the Army. None of these stories was conclusively proved, but they vividly dramatized the strikers' sense of having been betrayed by their class, of having found enemies inside their own families. They felt that they'd been left in the lurch by other unions, by the working miners of Nottinghamshire and Derbyshire, and by the Labour Party. The essential idea behind the rumors was that the men with the dogs and riot shields *ought* to have been the pickets' brothers. The quisling policemen served as convenient symbols in a story that required several million Judases to account for the miners' predicament now.

"Don't you think you'd have got more support if you'd held a national ballot at the beginning?" I said. It was a dusty question, but it still seemed to need an answer.

"Look," Bob said. "When Margaret Thatcher went to the Falklands, did she need a national ballot? She had a *mandate to govern*. Same as Scargill. He's got a mandate from us. He was democratically elected, just like Thatcher. Why is a mandate so good and democratic when it comes to the Government and so 'undemocratic' when it comes to the miners?

"If we'd had a ballot back in March, it would have been a clear sign of weakness. It would have been giving in to the demands of the Tory Party right at the start."

"But with a binding majority—" I said.

"We got our binding majority. When we elected Scargill and the rest of the executive."

Briefly back to base at Kilnhurst, waiting for our next assignment, I stood at the brazier with Yorkshire George. "There's no question about not winning," he said. "We *have* to win this struggle, even if we're still standing here next year. If we were to lose, they'd close this pit tomorrow, and hundreds like it. You know what that would mean? If this pit were to close? This whole valley—everything you can see—it would be dead, completely *dead*."

I looked down at the territory we were defending. The hillside below us was gray with snow and slurry. A few figures were moving diagonally along it, carrying brightly colored plastic fertilizer bags. They were searching for scraps of loose coal to feed to their domestic fires. At the end of the valley there was a huddle of low, sooty block-houses. Watching the people trudging past with their iron-ically gay plastic bags, I realized that until Yorkshire George had told me otherwise, I'd been looking at a land-scape which I thought had died already.

On our next picket, we were walking away from the shouting when we were joined by a man from another pit. He and Bob were talking about moving on to Rossington, where contractors were due to go into the colliery in half an hour.

"How far's Rossington?" I said.

The man separated from Bob and stood square in front of me, staring. Without a flicker of expression, his eyes went from my hat down to my boots. He turned back to Bob.

"What you doing with *that*?" he said. "*Sleeping* with it?"

Feeling sudden bars of steel in my cheeks, I said, "No, he wouldn't have me."

"Leave him be," Bob said. "He's all right. He's only writ-ing a book."

The man spat a gob of pearly mucus on the ground. "I wouldn't *touch* a fookin' thing like that," he said.

It was the extraordinary speed of it that was so English. It wasn't my clothes—the Italian truckload of winter fashion wear had guaranteed that I couldn't possibly look conspic-uous on a picket line. It was accent, and nothing but accent. *How far's Rossington* was enough to open the chasm of all the dirty and invidious distinctions of the English class setup. It was like the boy scout trick of starting a fire with two sticks. In three words, you could spark off the whole miserable, loggerheaded confrontation between state and private schools, owner-occupiers and council tenants, The North and The South, Chapel and Church, Labour and Tory, those with jobs and those without. It was no good pretending to be a coaster here; you don't coast in Doncaster, you sail with your class colors firmly nailed to the mast. And I was wearing a blue ensign defaced with crowns and anchors and the lord knows what.

It was a small, bitter, inconclusive skirmish in what Arthur Scargill himself had labeled a class war. It was probably the most revealing incident in my short career as a trespasser on the picket lines.

"Come on, lad," Bob said. "That's a daft bugger, any road. He just got out of bed the wrong side this morning."

Kind as Bob was trying to be, there was a lot more to it than that.

The long strike achieved nothing. When, on March 3, 1985, nine days short of a year after the beginning of the strike, the miners gave up and went back to work, pickets outside Congress House in London wept when they heard the news. The strike did not seem to soften the heart of the National Coal Board when it came to closing down pits that were failing to show a substantial profit. As I write (in February 1986), the people of Blyth are still pleading with the Coal Board to give Bates's Colliery a temporary, two-year reprieve. But the regional director of the board has described the pit as "a cancer on the face of the Northumbrian coast," and Blyth is hoping against hope for something not far short of a miracle. I shall be surprised if this footnote* turns out to be a happy one.

I left Blyth with the chutes still pouring coal into the waiting coasters, and I am afraid of what will happen between the writing of this sentence and the reading of it. As *Gosfield Maid* slipped out of the curious gray climate which Blyth had created round itself, and emerged into the sun, I found myself already missing the town and trying to remember the tune of "Oh, Geordie's lost his plinker." The pit,

* March 15: It is not. The N.C.B. has closed Bates's Colliery despite recommendation of the independent review body that they maintain it.

the rickety straithes, the hugger-mugger dark terraces, were
not cancerous; they were a small, proud, embattled bit of
serious life in the blue and empty hills of Northumberland.
Yet it is the tourist handbook which has become the arbiter
on questions like this in modern England, and in the tourist
handbook, Blyth doesn't stand a chance. The *Geographia
Guide to Northumbria* passes a death sentence on the town:

> The coast from Blyth to Newbiggin by the Sea has
> little to offer the visitor, it is partly industrialised.

I sailed on deeper into the same chapter of that book,
where the language turns fruity and rhapsodic, north
through the Farne Islands to Lindisfarne, where the anchor
dropped into water as clear as a block of Lucite. Long
puckered fronds of brown kelp waved sleepily thirty feet
down, and fleets of blue and gold cuckoo wrasse swam in
the shadow of the boat. On a nearby rock, three seals were
basking like gray sausages, their lumpy heads breaking clear
of their skins. Surrounded by stories of St. Cuthbert and
piles of old religious stones, *Gosfield Maid* might have sat
nicely in the foreground of a colored postcard. Paddling
ashore, raising a twinkling blaze of phosphorescence with
every stroke under a three-quarter moon, I thought I'd never
been in any anchorage so beautiful. But it was a cold, too
famous beauty; a beauty to be admired, not lived with; a
beauty of the kind to whom photographers say "the camera
loves you," meaning that he thinks you're a spoiled and
frozen bitch. In the morning I walked round Holy Island,
nodding respectfully at everything I saw, and taking pictures, and thinking *beautiful, beautiful*, and wanting to move
on.

For I was bound now for a mythical city. The ruins of
Troy, Byzantium, Samarkand were much like the ruins of
Lindisfarne. But to the north there was still a living city
whose amazing Renaissance was talked of in places as far
away even as London. People spoke of its lordly wealth as
if it were the imaginary Dallas of the television serial. Its
jeweled inhabitants walked ten feet tall. In the decaying

industrial fabric of Britain, the city was a marvel, a promise of the good life to come.

I had been to Aberdeen when I was sixteen. I remembered it for its gray, stony weight; a town of gloomy and genteel arcades, where I waited to catch the Shetland packet from a drizzly quay. It was like spending the day inside a gaunt cathedral, where everyone spoke in the sepulchral voices of church vergers.

Not now, though. Since the discovery of North Sea Oil, Aberdeen had become a boom town. In Hull and Blyth, I had amused myself by imagining Aberdeen as an astounding counterworld to Hull and Blyth. There'd be . . . there'd be . . . There'd be all-day, all-night saloons, their granite walls drumming with the amplified sound of Dolly Parton and Johnny Cash. You'd be able to buy Manhattans and Tequila Sunrises in dollars and cents. The deep, ravine-like streets would be solid with low-slung Cougars and Chevys, their chrome faces cast in the contemptuous grin that goes with big bucks. Stetsons . . . there'd definitely be Stetsons. And girls. In a city of roustabouts and troubleshooters, the girls would drip with diamanté. Even the corner shops would sell Wheaties and Jell-O and the "English muffins" that you can't buy in England. There'd be rib shacks . . . hot tamales . . . burgers-to-go; poker games in basement clubs and doormen in tuxedos packing .38s.

Such a place would also help to balance the plot. After touching on so many failures and disappointments, the story needed a crock of gold somewhere. A few happy-go-lucky riggers in studded leather jackets, snorting lines of coke and putting back six-packs of Budweiser and Michelob, might go some way to dispelling the narrative gloom.

I reached Stonehaven, twelve miles short of Aberdeen. Its single-story gray stone terraces, its solitary Chinese take-away, its air of having been closed for the duration sharpened my appetite for the city. In Stonehaven harbor I was tied up next to a fishing boat whose owner asked me where I was sailing to.

"Just Aberdeen tomorrow."

"Aberdeen? You'll be needing to hang on to your watch

when you're in Aberdeen. And not only your watch, either, "
he added, in the cheerful Scottish way that takes an excessive pleasure at the prospect of misfortunes to come.

This seemed to fit nicely too. Aberdeen was not merely
the Byzantium of eastern Scotland, it had become its Sodom
and its Gomorrah.

I left Stonehaven soon after 0800 on August 5. The wind
was coming in feeble dog-breaths off the land, and the sea
outside the harbor was riddled with curlicues of morning
mist. I set a course of 040° to clear Girdle Ness and waited
for the sun to show out of a sky that was evenly luminous
from horizon to horizon. It was a pity there wasn't a mile
or two more of visibility; from out here I could so nearly
see Aberdeen that several times I thought I spotted its
bawdy and licentious outline on the film of mist which hid
the hills.

By 0900, with only seven more miles to go, I realized
that the boat was swaddled in thick fog. It had happened
invisibly, the damp air slowly turning white as if it were
aging round me. It was impossible to tell how deep the fog
was. Sometimes it seemed to stand like a bright cliff, a mile
away across the still water, sometimes the bow of the boat
appeared to be gouging a hole for itself in the swirling wall
of fog.

Peering, or trying to peer, ahead, I saw the boat's head
slowly swivel round against the lumps and ridges of the
fogbank. We were turning in a wide circle. I pulled the
wheel round to make the boat point straight again, but then
found that the compass was reading 105°—on a heading to
somewhere in the Friesian Islands. I brought it back to 040°,
and again saw the boat's bow begin to spin against the fog,
while the compass card remained as if glued in its bowl.

In fog, you have to trust your instruments.

I went through the routine that I'd been taught by Commander King. I put on a life jacket. Every two minutes I
stepped out into the cockpit and let off a long blurt from
the compressed-air horn. I watched the needle on the
depth-sounder jittering around the thirty-five-fathom mark.
I checked the chart. So long as the needle didn't start to

back round the gauge, the boat would stay at a distance of two to three miles from the shore. So long as I maintained a strict course of 040°, we were on target.

Out in the cockpit, I listened for ships' engines. Once, a long fold of breaking sea came muscling up on the starboard beam—somebody's wake, but I couldn't hear whose, nor could I securely guess in which direction the ship must be traveling. Every time I worked it out, it was going somewhere else.

I had hoped that the first sound of Aberdeen would be the voice of Dolly Parton. It was the faint, but still horrible, moan of the siren on Girdle Ness, followed by the triple bell on Aberdeen North Pier. I prayed that the radar reflector, a boxy polygonal contraption which was rigged to the top of the mizzenmast, was making a fine splash on somebody's screen, and continued on course into the fog.

I did not dare turn and head for the harbor. Its mouth was wide enough, about two hundred and fifty yards between the piers, but it was surrounded by rocks, and the pilot book warned of "continuous" oil traffic inside the harbor. I couldn't tell now whether visibility was down to ten yards, or a hundred. At a hundred, I'd be safe enough, but at ten, if it was ten, I would at best be in a state of high panic. It seemed a lot safer to squeeze past Aberdeen, keep a mile or two offshore, and anchor as soon as I could pluck up courage to nose into shallow water without taking the risk of going aground on rock.

Several engines were audible now, and every few minutes the water ahead bulged with the wash of an invisible ship. The pier bell rang definitely just astern of *Gosfield Maid*, and I reckoned that I must have safely crossed the main channel into Aberdeen. From now on, there should be only inshore fishing boats, of *Gosfield Maid*'s own size and speed, to tangle with.

I felt the noise in my spine before I heard it—a hysterical jabbering, like a rioting crowd in a Middle Eastern city. It was a noise to run from, a noise that summoned images of abandoned bodies sprawled in streets, and running people, and the muffled popping of machine-gun fire.

In fog, you have to trust your instruments.

Then I saw what it was. The closed circle of sea round the boat was water no longer—it was a solid mass of skidding, flapping, wriggling birds. Ragged puffins were apparently mating with herring gulls, kittiwakes, guillemots and terns. The birds were beyond counting. There were thousands of them—as many birds as there were citizens of Aberdeen, yawping and screaming in joy as they fought and plunged and beat their rivals off with their wings. I had planned on scenes of pretty wild dissipation, but not on this crazed and deafening orgy.

Gosfield Maid had managed, in thick fog, to locate the city's main sewage outfall. The stuff was bubbling up from the seabed. The few spots of water which the birds had left visible were stained dark with excrement—and the birds were in heaven. Jostling their neighbors, stabbing into the sludge with their beaks, they were behaving exactly like people who've hit a crock of gold. The still air smelled foul. I motored out of the cacophony with a handkerchief pressed against my nose.

But I had missed Aberdeen. A mile or two farther on, groping through the fog, listening, watching the instruments, waiting, heart-in-mouth, for a nasty surprise to loom suddenly on the beam, I thought, at least this feels more like real life than my imaginary boom town, and if a boom town is essential to this story, won't the birds do just as well?

CHAPTER 7

ENVOI:
A PECULIAR PEOPLE

This house is full of noises. The cornstalk rustle of the sea makes itself heard from a mile away across the flat and hedgeless fields. There are mice behind the baseboards, and the oak frames of the house creak like a boat's. The four rooms are as low and small as cabins, the lath-and-plaster walls give off a hollow drumming sound when the wind gets up, and at night the house feels as if it's afloat, pitching gently on its mooring among the owls and foxes.

I've been keeping a close eye on the wind. Three months ago I put up a fine black cast-iron weathercock above the chimney pots, but it buckled in the first gale, and the second gale tore the cockerel clean off its perch at the legs. Now the vane spins free in its greased socket and the broken cockerel is going to rust in the uncut grass.

This is not the weather for casting off: not yet. A stubborn mountain of high pressure is centered over Latvia and a deep Atlantic low is poised just south of Iceland, ready to swing in across the British Isles. There are southeasterly gales in the Channel and the North Sea, and from the bedroom window you can see yellow surf breaking far out on the flats. Last week's snow lies in panes of bubbled ice on the lawn. I've been feeding the sparrows with scraps: puffed-out and bloated with cold, they scratch and bicker in the frozen dirt around the back door. I work at keeping the fires going overnight and leave a spoor of mud, twigs and elm bark on the carpets. There are two of us now, and weatherbound in an anchored house, we fret our time away as ships' crews do, waiting for the rumble of the chain on the winch and the inspiriting busywork of making a departure.

In May 1985 I sailed *Gosfield Maid* across the mouth of the Thames Estuary and into the River Blackwater in Essex. On my first circuit of the islands, three years before, I'd steered clear of this meager and featureless coast as too untrustworthy to do business with. The sea lathered over its maze of offshore sandbars; church towers marked on the chart were lost among trees that looked like lines of crouching mangroves in a swamp; I'd investigated the narrow swatchways leading inshore through the sands, and headed north for the broad, safe channel into Harwich.

It was different now: I could watch the serpentine pattern of the place unfold on a radar screen. Essex had hardly any vertical dimension at all; its character lay in voluptuous horizontals—the looping seawalls, the crescent sandbars, the curving throats of the river mouths. Painted in anfractuous splashes of light on the glass, it formed an abstract composition which kept on reassembling itself around the boat as I moved deeper into the picture.

The outlying shoals had turned the area of sea around the mouth of the Blackwater into a series of calm, marsh-fringed lagoons. Big ships holed up here in temporary retirement—out-of-work oil tankers, Panamanian coasters under Customs arrest, bulk container vessels waiting to pick up a cargo at Tilbury or Felixstowe. Nearly a dozen of them swung to their anchors, deep in farmland, with no one apparently on board, growing rust stains on their plates and weed on their chains. In mercantile-marine circles, the Blackwater was reckoned one of the cheapest places to put a redundant ship out to grass.

I found a mud berth for *Gosfield Maid*. For ten hours out of every twelve, the boat was lodged, shoulder-deep, in soft ooze. At the top of each tide she floated clear with a tremendous peptic exhibition of farts and gurgles. Her library was carted off by dinghy in boxfuls, and she was colonized as rent-free accommodation by the gulls and the cormorants. By June, her decks and wheelhouse were caked in white guano, while the saloon smelled of must and desertion.

I found a mud berth for myself too, taking a cottage in the Dengie Marshes. It had been built to house a farm laborer sometime in the seventeenth century, and its cambered beams had probably been salvaged from a ship wrecked on the sands. In this part of Essex, wreckage was the most freely available of all building materials. Houses had been cobbled together out of bits of old ship, and they were fashioned to look like ships, with clinker-built topsides of white weatherboarding and curved mansard roofs.

This architectural absentmindedness about what properly belonged to the sea and what to the land was just one symptom of the general elemental confusion here on this boggy fringe of things, where England petered out into water and water petered out into England. Land and sea were constantly changing places. As the tide shrank away through the culverts between banks of cord grass, it left large islands of shining mud, looking more liquid than the ruffled water round their shores. When the sea came back, flooding in over the salt marshes, drowning the islands and opening sandy footpaths to navigation, it was arrested only by the ancient earthwork of the seawall: at high tide, an arbitrary frontier of piled rubble separated the North Sea from the waist-high corn which stood twenty yards inside the wall. Left to itself, on a spring tide the sea would lap at the cottage door and turn the Tudor farmhouse into an offshore atoll.

There used to be malaria in these marshes. When Defoe visited the area in 1722, he found it settled by a hardy tribe of bog people. The men of Dengie told him that it was customary for them to marry up to fourteen or fifteen wives in a lifetime:

> The reason . . . was this; that [the men] being bred in the marshes themselves and seasoned to the place, did pretty well with it; but that they always went up to the hilly country, or to speak in their own language the uplands for a wife: that when they took the young lasses out of the wholesome and fresh air, they were healthy, fresh and clear, and well; but when they came out of their native air into the marshes among the fogs and damps, there they presently changed their complexion, got an ague or two, and seldom held it above half a year, or a year at most; and then, said he, we go to the uplands again, and fetch another.

The marshes were unhealthy but rich. The Dengie people made a lot of money on a small scale, working from a single boat or a plot of drained swamp, selling salt, butter, cheese, corn, fish and timber to London merchants.

With no great houses and no powerful county families, the marshes lay happily outside the usual class arrangements of rural England. They were cultivated by small farmers who were more like European peasants or American settlers than the general run of cap-doffing English tenants. The flat landscape with its mephitic air was no place for trespassing gentlemen; the nearby sea had no bathing beaches; the marshes were difficult to cross, with narrow lanes twisting round the maze of dikes and drains. The people of Dengie were left largely to their own smelly and profitable devices. When the culture of London spread out far beyond the city, and overran counties like Buckinghamshire, Middlesex and Kent, it kept clear of Dengie. Nor did the Scandinavian name of the place add to its charm: its suggestions of din-

giness and dung made the marshes sound like a very unde-
sirable address.

When I moved in, it was like finding a neglected loop-
hole in the English system. It was wide-open country. The
silence of the place was thick and palpable; the level sweep
of fields under a giant sky made it feel oddly suspended and
provisional, a shimmering trick of the light. I liked its absences. There were no braying gentry voices, no taint of
dry sherry in the air after church on Sunday morning, none
of the squashed and deferential manners which I had
thought inseparable from English village life. I warmed to
the gaunt tabernacle on the village's single street—The
Chapel of the Peculiar People (All Welcome). The sect had
taken their name from the First Epistle General of Saint
Peter: "But you are a chosen generation, a royal priesthood,
an holy nation, a peculiar people . . ."

The Essex dissenters declined to recognize temporal aristocracies, preferring to elect themselves as a spiritual aristocracy in their own right. They were indeed a peculiar
people, living at an oblique angle to the rest of England, so
far out on the country's watery margin that they had almost
run away to sea.

Their architecture and religion were distinctively home-
made. In the Dengie Marshes, people did things for them-
selves without benefit of clergy or the landed ruling class.
The place was a hive of tiny, tax-free private enterprises.
Up every lane there was a brick bungalow with a notice
nailed to a tree, advertising the spare-time products of the
industrious householder: BIRD TABLES FROM £7.50—LACE
BEDSPREADS—KOI CARP—POTTERY—LOGS SAWN TO
ORDER—POND LINERS—HONEY—GOATS MILK—PEDLAR
DOLLS—ROTTED MUSHROOM COMPOST—EGGS LAID
WHILE YOU WAIT—TOMS GLADS AND CUES—REPLACE-
MENT WINDSCREENS—DWARF LOP RABBITS—MAGGOTS—
SWEET CORN—TERRIER MEAL—HORSE PELLETS—KARATE
LESSONS—HAIRCUT, SIR?—GOLDEN LABRADOR PUPPIES
READY SOON—CLAY PIGEONS—CREAM TEAS, WELDING &
RESPRAYS—BABY BUNNIES—PULLETS EGGS BY THE TRAY—
PORK SAUSAGES AND SHOE REPAIRS—CONCRETE TUBS FOR

SALE. In every garden shed, someone was knocking together something salable out of bits of junk. Under every glass cloche, something was ripening in the sun to raise another bob or two. At weekends, the local artists held their exhibitions at roadsides, hawking pictures of Thames barges at sunset to passing art collectors in their cars.

It seemed the right landscape for me. Somewhere between breeding dwarf lop rabbits and the manufacture of bird tables, there had to be a space for my shingle. BOOKS WRITTEN WHILE YOU WAIT. The rosy village postmistress (who also ran a sideline in soft-core videos) asked me, "You do poetry, don't you?," as if trading in literature were a perfectly respectable occupation for an incoming marshlander. Encouraged by all the other bungalow industries in the neighborhood, I settled into the cottage and began to write.

But it was hard to believe that I was now living in the same country that I was trying to describe. The face of England in my typescript had a thin, hurt and sullen look; the face of the England that I could see from the window was fat—a landscape of amazing plenty. The billowing sea waves of growing corn went on for miles. When the combine harvesters moved in, they worked all night, stealing across the marshes in isolated pools of brightness like illuminated trawlers. There was a week of stubble burning when the sky turned inky and the whole peninsula blazed under a low canopy of smoke. Still smoldering, the fields were plowed to take the next crop. Corn, cauliflowers, potatoes, cabbages, oilseed rape—each field was a conjuror's hat from which the farmer produced a stream of harvests in a season. Low-flying aircraft bombed the crops with vitamins and tonics, and the lanes were blocked by the great yellow machines that went growling across country, reaping, threshing, digging, seeding and yanking vegetables up by the roots.

I scratched away at a bare page and added my few hundred words a day to the produce of the marshes, while I could see my neighbor harvesting enough cereal to feed a city. Language seemed a very stony medium compared with his moist chocolate soil. He plowed and reaped, then plowed and reaped again; my pile of manuscript rose by a quarter of an inch, got stuck, and struggled up a further millimeter or two, as if it were rooted in shale.

It kept on being contradicted by the view from the window. Everyone was in work here, the industrial technology was the latest thing from the United States and no one wore that troubled, inward English look which seemed to be passed on from character to character in my typed pages. I prowled through the villages, searching for signs of recession. No luck. Everyone I saw looked irredeemably sunny. It was true that the local butcher had killed himself in the spring, but even this suicide was oddly tinged with the general prosperity of the place. The trouble was, I learned in the pub, he bought himself this catamaran, bloody great thing, a forty-footer, fell behind with the payments and wouldn't get rid of the boat. Plus, there was a bit of the usual how's-your-father with the wife. The story of the boating butcher overreaching himself was one of success-gone-askew; more a Floridian than an English suicide.

It was easy to see what had led the butcher on to his unaffordable yacht. In the tarmac parks of the American-style country clubs of Burnham and Cold Norton, the Jaguars lay nose to nose with the Daimlers and the 300SL Mercedeses. Fleets of scarlet powerboats slashed the Blackwater with their wakes, and the marina at Bradwell was stacked solid with Chris-Crafts and Princesses. People here were fast and flash; they had fun, and they enjoyed letting other people see the color of their money.

We took to going to a restaurant in Burnham where this guiltless style of splashing out had been codified into a ritual order: the table for eight, the steak and champagne, the torpedolike cigars, each with its long warhead of ash, the bold talk of dodges, steals and wheezes. The men talked in rapid Cockney, hurrying over their consonants and economizing on grammar as if they were composing telegrams. *Phoned Friday—all tied up—no problem—bloody giveaway—innit?* This *innit?*, pronounced as a triumphant rhetorical question at the end of every other statement, made its way round the restaurant, going from table to table, a sort of vernacular *Amen*, designed to ratify and strengthen any wish or assertion.

The women at these tables all appeared to be modeling themselves on famous vamps in 1940s movies. They went in for platinum hair, rouge, mascara, monogrammed cigarettes and skirts with slits to the tops of their thighs. While the men talked property and killings, the women dropped brand names like Hong Kong, Antigua, the Seychelles and Pierre Cardin.

All the loudest voices in this part of Essex were Londonbred. On the farms, the accent was still local, but the new people of the marshes were made-good exiles from Bow, West Ham, Hackney and Stratford. The bungalow owners had come out for the fresh air, the bit of garden, the shed to potter in; but they were the poor relations of the East End barons who lived in houses like The Old Rectory, Dogget's Farm and The Cedars. The area, which was blessedly free of the traditional kind of rural aristocracy, was dotted with the country seats of successful London hoods. There were gangsterish cars behind the rhododendrons and Rottweiler dogs behind picket fences. I started to keep a count of the number of times that I spotted the newspaper formula of "Ronnie————(47), company director, of————, Essex," and filled in the blanks with these pink, well-dressed, well-exercised men, riding on horseback or burning up the lanes in their white Mercedeses.

Twice during the summer we were awakened in the small hours by a single-engined plane coming in to land in a nearby field. Standing at the darkened window, we could see someone out there, lighting up a grass track with a pair of torches. As the plane taxied along the strip, the hacking noise of its engine was abruptly cut. There were no further lights or sounds, and in the morning there wasn't a trace of the plane. It was probably only a farming neighbor returning from a joyride, but we enjoyed the illusion, at least, that we'd been secret witnesses to some piece of gangland skullduggery. It neatly fitted the landscape. The Cessna's engine, killed on touchdown, made exactly the right sound for easy money on the move. The second time it happened, I made the mistake of mentioning it in the pub and was told sharply that it was best not to get too nosy about things one saw at night around the Dengie Marshes.

There was something infectious in this general air of license and rich pickings. In the autumn, pheasant and partridge took sanctuary in our garden, which was an isolated spinney in several hundred acres of open fields. Birds are hopeless at holding their drink, and I had to be restrained from baiting the lawn with seed soaked in whisky, an idea so foreign to me in the ordinary way that I blamed it entirely on the landscape.

I went on writing into the winter, at one with the home lacemakers, carpenters, potters and weavers. Soon after the first frost, the pheasants and partridges were shot. I thought it was my typewriter to begin with, but it resolved into the flat echoless popping of gunfire. The plowed ridges of the frozen fields glinted like wires in the sun as the beaters and guns fanned across the marshes. The drifting specks in my vision were dead birds falling out of the sky. The following dogs left jet-trails of white breath behind them as they sprinted to pick up the corpses.

Above this small and brilliant war, there was a tantalizing rim of sea. The masts and deckworks of two coasters showed over the line of the seawall, moving almost imperceptibly from left to right, more slowly, even, than words.

People who live on continents get into the habit of regarding the ocean as journey's end, the full stop at the end of the trek. When North Americans reached the Pacific, there was nothing to do except build the end-of-the-world state of California. For people who live on islands, especially on small islands, the sea is always the beginning. It's the ferry to the mainland, the escape route from the boredom and narrowness of home. It's what you have to cross, even if you do it by plane, whenever you want to strike out and make a break for it. Islanders also know how the sea goes on and on, in a continuous loop of shoreline and life, without a terminus. Knocking about from port to port, you keep on going past the port you originally started out from. In that regard at least, coasting is a lot more lifelike than those epic journeys which reduce the world to a magnificent straight line of conquest; and the coaster's chronic itch, to be moving on only in order to get nearer home, his never-quite-knowing whether he's returning or running away, are more real, in a daily way, than the exotic compulsions of the serious travelers who voyage intrepidly from A to Z.

It is laughable, this business of moving around a small quarter of the world in one's own boat. It is maddeningly slow, frightening, strange, dull, uncomfortable, lovely, inconvenient, revelatory and undignified—all in the right proportions. It teaches you about a world you'd never guessed at when you were on land, and makes you obsessively alert to distinctions invisible to the people you've left behind there. It turns you into a creature of luck and weather. It shortens your horizon and makes you live by the minute and the hour. It grants you a floating detachment (sometimes serene and sometimes appalled) from the land on the beam. But it is the silliest possible way of getting to Brighton, if getting to Brighton was ever the point of the thing.

I had thought that I might well cure this coaster's itch by writing about it, but the condition seems to have worsened, if anything, during the writing. All through this iron winter, I've been steadily adding to the roll of mint Admiralty charts. The sextant, adjusted for index error, is back in its oak case on the boat: we'll need the sextant for this next leg of the voyage.

Gosfield Maid has been repainted, her seams recaulked, her decks sanded down to raw teak, her masts stripped and varnished, her patches of rot replaced by fillets of fresh wood. Afloat again, with books back in the shelves, paraffin in the lamps, charcoal in the stove, the boat's ready to continue, now with two on board. *Die, Dismal Fog.* Very soon now, we'll be able to let go the ropes and submit ourselves to that life of voluntary displacement from the world which answers, more closely than anything I know,

to everyone's infantile dreams of floating. Stepping buoy-
antly off the top stair or from the ledge of the bedroom
window and slowly easing the deadweight of the boat away
from the dockside result in the same magical suspension of
the ordinary rules of reality; and when you do eventually
touch ground again, the world itself has been subtly altered
by your secret flight.

The cottage has been let for the spring and summer, the
lists have been ticked off, the bags more or less packed.
We're waiting for these ferocious weather systems to settle
their differences, for the isobars to drift apart and for the
wind to ease and veer into the west. There was another
dusting of dry snow on the grass this morning, and the
green elm logs spit and jostle in the grate. The chart of the
southern North Sea, pegged out on the floor by a book at
each corner, has a ruled pencil line stretching diagonally
across it from the Sunk to the Noord Hinder light vessels.
It's a fine thing to be able, just occasionally, to cut your
foreseeable future down to a 5B pencil stroke on a piece of
paper. If it weren't for this bitter late easterly wind, we
could be on the start of the line by sunset.

The back door has opened. A corner of the chart is
flapping free of its mooring under Larkin's *Whitsun Weddings*.
The draft is cold enough to make the mice shiver in their
holes. At this rate, we'll be here into next month.

"This cold's *insane*."

"I know, but we can use the extra days."

"How is it going?"

"Slowly." I type *Slowly*. Her coat at my ear is radiating a
winter of its own.

"Where have you got to?"

Not far. Only here where we are now, before we go————

About the Author

Jonathan Raban is the author of *Soft City* (1974), *Arabia* (1979), *Old Glory* (1982), which won the Royal Society of Literature's Heinemann Award and the Thomas Cook Award, and the novel *Foreign Land* (1985).